THE TRIBAL CHALLENGE

PERSPECTIVES ON ISRAEL STUDIES

S. Ilan Troen, Natan Aridan, Donna Divine, David Ellenson, Arieh Saposnik, and Jonathan Sarna, editors

Sponsored by the Ben-Gurion Research Institute for the Study of Israel and Zionism, Ben-Gurion University of the Negev, and the Schusterman Center for Israel Studies, Brandeis University

THE TRIBAL CHALLENGE

ALLIANCES AND CONFRONTATIONS IN THE ISRAELI NEGEV

HAVATZELET YAHEL

INDIANA UNIVERSITY PRESS

Figure fm.1. Member of the Tayaha Bedouin tribal confederation sits erect on his horse while raising the Israeli flag as a gesture of invitation to the IDF convoy that will arrive in his camp, May 2, 1950. *Photo: Fritz Cohen. Source: The Government Press Office.*

This book is a publication of

Indiana University Press
Office of Scholarly Publishing
Herman B Wells Library 350
1320 East 10th Street
Bloomington, Indiana 47405 USA

iupress.org

© 2024 by Havatzelet Yahel

All rights reserved

No part of this book may be reproduced or utilized in any form or by any means, electronic or mechanical, including photocopying and recording, or by any information storage and retrieval system, without permission in writing from the publisher.

First Printing 2024

Cataloging information is available from the Library of Congress.

978-0-253-07079-1 (hdbk)
978-0-253-07080-7 (pbk)
978-0-253-07081-4 (web PDF)

In memory of my loving mother and father,
Sara and Yehuda Liberman,
And my beloved nephew,
Lieutenant Roee Peles, who fell in war
for the defense of the State of Israel

CONTENTS

Acknowledgments ix

A Note on Translation, Transliteration, and Arab Transcription xi

A Note on Maps xiii

Introduction: The Tribal Challenge, Bedouin, Jewish Settlements, and the Mandate 3

PART I

1 Bedouin in the War of Independence, 1947–49 29

2 Creation of the Military Regime: Nominated Sheikhs and Tribal Units, 1949–56 55

PART II

3 Bedouin Exit from the Negev, 1957–60 81

4 The Decline of the Military Administration, 1961–66 99

PART III

5 New Institutions—Old Alliances, 1967–71 125

Conclusion: The Question of Functional Alliances 144

Epilogue 152

Appendix 1: Table of Consonants   155

Appendix 2: Bedouin Groups   157

Appendix 3: Persons (Bedouin)   159

Notes   161

Bibliography   195

Index   211

ACKNOWLEDGMENTS

First and foremost, I would like to express my deep gratitude to my academic home, the Ben-Gurion Institute for the Study of Israel and Zionism at the Ben-Gurion University of the Negev, for providing me a stimulating environment for research. The institute's profound commitment to the advancement of knowledge has been truly inspiring, and I am indebted to all my colleagues there. Our discussions have been invaluable in shaping and fostering my ideas.

I extend my sincere appreciation to Indiana University Press for believing in the importance of this work and for their dedicated efforts in bringing it to fruition.

Special thanks reserved to Professor Ilan Troen, the editor of the Perspectives on Israel Studies series, whose mentorship and guidance have been indispensable in this journey. I also wish to thank Professor Arieh Saposnik, Dr. Natan Aridan, Dr. Uri Mintzker, and Noa Ravinsky Raichel for their helpful comments on the manuscript drafts. To Dr. Emir Galilee, Dr. Tali Tadmor-Shimony, Professor Ruth Kark, Professor Gideon Kressel, Professor Anatoly Khazanov, the late Professor Emanuel Marx, and the members of the Azrieli Center for Israel Studies for your willingness to share your thoughts with me. All of you were critical in shaping the ideas presented in this monography.

I extend my heartfelt appreciation to the reviewers of this book. Their insightful comments and constructive feedback have significantly contributed to the refinement of the content and overall quality of the final work.

I am also thankful to Betsy Rosenberg, Dr. Yafit Marom, Hadas Blum, and Sefi Sinai for their linguistic and graphic contributions, along with their precious advice. To Yephim Maghrill for his resourcefulness in finding materials. Their expertise has greatly enhanced the clarity and contribution of this work.

I want to express my appreciation for the interviewees, who were willing to share their knowledge with me, as well as for the assistance I received in the archives and libraries that I have visited and for all those who have supported me in various ways but may not be mentioned individually. These include my friends and my students, who have enriched my academic journey in countless ways.

I extend my heartfelt thanks to my loving sister, Hagit, for her thoughtful perspectives, unwavering motivation, and exceptional enthusiasm during our long hours of discussions that had a lasting impact on this book. Thanks to her this manuscript was completed efficiently and on time.

To my beloved Eyal, I am eternally grateful for his invaluable insights and wise analyses that have contributed to the development of the ideas presented in this book. His endurance and unwavering confidence in my abilities have been my anchor during challenging time.

Last, but certainly not least, I would like to thank my loving children, Naama, Neta, Omer, and Ido, for bringing so much light, joy, and pride to my life. Each of you alone and the four of you together are the driving force behind my achievements. I am truly blessed to have such a remarkable family.

Thank you.

Omer, July 2023

A NOTE ON TRANSLATION, TRANSLITERATION, AND ARAB TRANSCRIPTION

The names of books and articles in Hebrew and Arabic in the reference list appear in transliterated form followed by a translation in parentheses.

Hebrew words are transliterated according to the guidelines of the Academy of the Hebrew Language.

All non-English quotations were translated by the author, except where there is a reference in the notes to other English sources.

All internet hyperlinks were last accessed in July 2023, unless stated otherwise.

The Arabic names of people, groups, and places are transliterated as they commonly appear in the literature, with certain necessary clarifications:

1. The pharyngeal fricative consonant /ʿ/ (ع) is symbolized by /ʿ/.
2. In Bedouin dialects of the Negev, the reflex of the consonant /q/ (ق) is the velar plosive /g/. Therefore, this is how the names of people, groups, and places containing this consonant are transliterated (e.g., Gderat, Abu Rgayyig).
3. Geminated consonants marked with *shaddah* ([sign of] emphasis) in Arabic are expressed by doubling consonants (e.g., Abu Sittah, Muhammad).
4. The feminine suffix *(tāʾ marbūṭah)* is expressed by /h/ (e.g., Salamah, ʿAzazmah, etc.).

Tables of consonants in Arabic orthography and a list of Bedouin groups and persons that are phonetically transliterated are provided as appendixes. An additional column features their transcription according to Bedouin phonology.

A NOTE ON MAPS

The thirteen maps included in this volume are historical, produced decades ago, and gathered from a variety of sources. Historical maps are by their very nature of significantly lower quality than maps produced today. Every effort was made to improve their quality, and English text and legends have been added.

THE TRIBAL CHALLENGE

INTRODUCTION
The Tribal Challenge, Bedouin, Jewish Settlements, and the Mandate

In January 2022, Bedouin inhabitants of the northeastern region of the Negev clashed with police over Israel's tree planting on disputed land. A year earlier, Sheikh Sliman al-Atrash had petitioned the Be'er Sheva Magistrate's Court for a restraining order against planting on land he claimed to own. When the court refused to grant him the restraining order because he had no proof of landownership, the sheikh decided to drop the case.[1] However, when the planters arrived at the site a year later with the saplings, accompanied by police guards, they faced a large group of protesters who accused Israel of denying Bedouin rights. The situation deteriorated as protesters began throwing stones and burning tires. Gradually, the violence extended to the highway, with more and more stones and even Molotov cocktails hurled at passing vehicles.

In view of the escalating protests, the government ordered the cessation of the planting and sent representatives to restore the peace. Headlines in the Israeli press were divided: Some called for an immediate reinstatement of law and order in the Negev. As stated by Keren Uzan, a prominent journalist and resident of the Negev herself, "[Israel] should enforce the law in every part of the [Bedouin] dispersion."[2] Some agreed that Israel has every right to impose laws in the Negev but questioned the wisdom of doing so in view of the Bedouin protests. As explained by Omer Bar-Lev, public security minister from the left-leaning Labor Party, "The question is: Is it right at this moment after 72 years, in areas that were not planted before, when we're trying to improve relations, to plant—where the Bedouin grow wheat?"[3]

Still others denied Israel's right to impose any laws at all. Prominent Israeli left-wing journalist Gideon Levi argued, "The Negev was Bedouin long before it was Jewish. What's wrong with that?"[4] MK Sami Abu Shade from the Joint List party justified the riots by dint of "the state's insistence on forcing a lifestyle on the Bedouin Arab population of the Negev they do not want."[5]

The three views—that it is necessary and just to impose Israeli law on the Bedouin; that although Israel has a right to implement the law, current circumstances make doing so impracticable, unsuitable, or immoral and the tree planting should therefore be postponed; and that Israel has neither the right nor the imperative to implement its laws—reflect the diversity within Israeli public opinion.

Such controversies in Israel are nothing new. The actions of Israeli authorities in relation to the Bedouin have been punctuated by them since the establishment of the state. These controversies involve not only tactics but also a dilemma: how to establish effective governance of the Bedouin community while maintaining democratic principles vis-à-vis individual citizens within two frameworks—one tribal and collective, governed by traditions and customs shaped over hundreds of years under harsh desert conditions and based on the concepts of honor and blood affiliation, and the other, a newly established democracy with a system of governance based on the separation of powers and written laws that promote civil liberties.

Many Israelis in the Negev who arrived with the intention of establishing Israeli law found themselves puzzled by the complexities of Bedouin life. I myself arrived from Tel Aviv with my family in the late 1990s to work in the southern district attorney's office of the Ministry of Justice, tasked with implementing Israeli law in the region. The differences I encountered in the Negev, where Israeli law is sometimes unheeded and unenforceable, astonished me. When I tried to pursue the methods of implementation I had used at my previous job as a litigator in the Tel Aviv district, I would often encounter weird, offbeat responses like, "Patience. Israeli law is still on the camel to Be'er Sheva," or "Don't be such a stickler. This isn't Tel Aviv." Even more disturbing was the response of a senior manager in my ministry to stop asking questions and not to create extra work with my "noise." Nevertheless, in the ensuing twenty years, I succeeded in doing my job as I understood it, albeit not without raising a few desert storms. A certain amount of inertia was evident from the start in some government offices, but for the most part, those who came in direct contact with the Bedouin community worked with great dedication. I spent much time during my years at the ministry (until 2014), while writing my dissertation in historical geography, and later on in my research at the Ben-Gurion Institute for the Study of Israel and Zionism at Ben-Gurion University of the Negev trying to fathom the disparity between Israeli law and the Bedouin legal ethos. In the process, I met with many Bedouin and administrative officials; explored the Negev by car, on foot, and on camelback; and immersed myself in archival material, including documents, maps, photos, newspapers, dispatches and reports, court rulings—anything at all that might shed light and extend my understanding of Israel's policy toward the Negev Bedouin.

In the current book, I have endeavored to clarify the mystery, blending history, geography, law, and the policies adopted by those who administered Israel's Negev between 1947 and 1971. I hope that the story I am about to relate will help the reader better understand not only the events of the past but current events that are still unfolding in the Negev, where planting trees is much more than just an agricultural activity.

THE STUDY OF NEGEV BEDOUIN

Scholars' interest in the modern Bedouin as a branch of nomadic studies was piqued by the journeys of nineteenth-century researchers like Charles Doughty and Alois Musil to the Middle East and the Arabian Desert.[6] The study of the Negev Bedouin as a separate group was initiated in the 1930s with the publications of two scholars with a profound interest in Bedouin history and culture: the Zionist orientalist Eliahu Epstein (Elath), a member of the Jewish Agency, and 'Aref al-'Aref, an Arab nationalist who served as district officer of Be'er Sheva in Mandatory Palestine.[7]

In the following two decades, the Bedouin topic did not attract much scholarly attention, with two exceptions. In the 1940s, Ya'akov Shimoni, a Zionist who was born in Berlin and moved to Palestine during the British Mandate, published a work on the Arabs of Israel with a section on the Bedouin. He studied Arabic and orientalism at the Hebrew University of Jerusalem, headed the Arab Bureau of the Intelligence Service of the Hagana (the leading prestate paramilitary organization), and later served as deputy director of the State Political Department of the Jewish Agency. During his service, he was involved in decisions regarding the Bedouin.[8] In 1946, Joseph Braslavy (Braslavsky) included a section on the Negev Bedouin in the first edition of his book *HaYad'ata Et HaAretz: Eretz HaNegev* (Know the land: The Negev).[9]

The 1960s gave rise to the first anthropological study of the Negev Bedouin, conducted by Emanuel Marx. Marx had become familiar with the tribes through his earlier work in the Office of the PM Adviser for Arab Affairs and decided to extend his knowledge via academic research.[10] His work discussed Bedouin social structure, economy, and daily life under the military administration.[11] In the 1970s, Gideon Kressel, another prominent anthropologist, focused his research on tribal collectivism in the face of urbanization.[12] Sasson Bar-Zvi, who had come to the Negev in the late 1940s as a member of the Hagana and become fascinated with the Negev Bedouin culture, began collecting and recording Bedouin oral history after his retirement from the military and devoted much of his time to publishing works on

Bedouin customs and traditions. Together with Joseph Ben-David, a historical geographer, he contributed greatly to knowledge of the Bedouin way of life.[13]

The scholarly study of Bedouin oral history continued to develop in the 1980s, with a focus on the Sinai Bedouin, and resulted in an academic controversy over the limits of oral history.[14]

While earlier studies had centered mainly on the culture, nomadic roots, and traditions of the Bedouin, the next stage in research, which began during the 1980s, gave rise to a critical approach to the government policy vis-à-vis the Bedouin, dealing with policy flaws and suggestions for their possible remedy. This line of research was inspired by postmodernism, postcolonialism, post-Zionism, and identity theories. It began with the research of Ghazi Falah, a Bedouin geographer from the Galilee in northern Israel. In 1987, he established the Galilee Center for Social Research in Nazareth, and in 1991 he relocated to North America. In his works, Falah argues that Israel's attempts to settle the Negev Bedouin were immoral and motivated by the Zionists' desire to grab Bedouin and Arab lands elsewhere in Israel.[15] Following the simplistic dichotomy of Arabs and Jews, Falah did not address the distinction between the Bedouin way of life and that of the settled Arabs. They were all put under the umbrella of Arab identity being oppressed by the Jewish state. This path was followed by sociologist Ronen Shamir during the late 1990s. Shamir framed Bedouin-Israeli relations within the broader context of settler colonialism while focusing on the role of the Israeli legal system in what he regards as the deprivation of rights among the indigenous Bedouin.[16] Over the ensuing two decades, although scholars like Emanuel Marx, Gideon Kressel, and Joseph Ben-David and geographers like Avinoam Meir, Shaul Krakover, and later Ze'ev Zivan and Hanina Porat continued to discuss Bedouin issues, their work enjoyed much less academic attention.[17]

From that point onward, the spotlight has been on Israel, with Bedouin relations a salient colonialist phenomenon that lies within the rivalry between Arabs and Jews. This form of discourse, which presents the Bedouin as a passive and submissive society subjected to immoral and unjust government forces, has introduced new spheres and fields of research.[18] Hence, no comparison between Israel and other Arab countries with Bedouin populations has been found relevant. The Israel-Bedouin issue has become the domain of critical scholars, who frame it in terms of the broader Jewish-Arab conflict and settler colonialism. Within this polarized framework, the Bedouin are described as an indigenous ethnic Arab minority on the margins of society, dispossessed through racial bias, and a stronger, imperialist settler state because of their Arab affiliation and Israel's ill intentions.[19] It has become politically incorrect to discuss the challenges Bedouin tribalism poses in Israel through the complex perspective of contradictory values. Tribal fractionation and hierarchies, blood vendettas, and other sensitive issues have been largely ignored.[20] In the twenty-first century, the most popular scholarly writings have focused on the Negev Bedouin through the lens of colonialism, to the total neglect of other factors. A notable example is the 2018 study by Sandy Kedar, Ahmad Amara, and Oren Yiftachel on Bedouin land rights, which omits any reference to Bedouin tribalism and completely isolates the Israeli case from the wider context of the same phenomenon in other Middle Eastern states.[21]

Viewing Bedouin studies as part of the Israeli-Arab conflict and the dominance of the settler colonialist approach in the study of the Negev Bedouin has contributed to their absence in the general discourse concerning Bedouin tribalism in the Middle East. There is no doubt that the Israeli-Arab dispute greatly impacted Israel's policy toward the Bedouin, but does this tell the whole story of the Negev Bedouin situation?

There are numerous Bedouin tribal communities in Middle Eastern states that gained independence around the same time as Israel. In two inspiring works on the Bedouin of the Middle East, the Bedouin of Israel were entirely omitted. One of these, *Tribes and State Formation in the Middle East*, edited by Philip S. Khoury and Joseph Kostiner, probes relations between the Bedouin and the states they inhabit and "the continuing viability of tribal structures and systems in contemporary times, within contemporary nation-states." The contributors to the collection attest to the power held by Bedouin chiefdoms vis-à-vis the state and stress their strong tribal solidarity ('asabiyya). The power of tribal authority in nomadic and formerly nomadic societies may prevail over the territorially based organization of nation-states. The dominance of Bedouin chieftaincies in the states of the Middle East posed a challenge that had to be addressed during the state-building process. Khoury and Kostiner find that Tribalism challenges the process, and while some states have been able to "accommodate" it by empowering the Bedouin and including them in the nation-building process, others have not been able to do so, and in the latter case tribalism plays a destructive role.[22]

Stimulated by the continued viability of tribalism in the course of events, which came to be known as the Arab Spring, Uzi Rabi, an Israeli historian of the Middle East, complied a collection of articles titled *Tribes and States in a Changing Middle East*, which follows the ideas in Khoury and Kostiner's book while focusing on twenty-first-century Bedouin-state relations.[23] The collection examines developments in the states, dictatorships, and monarchies of the region with the understanding that "when considered as ideal types, there seemed to be an incompatibility between tribes and states, particularly nation-states."[24]

Rabi offers examples of strategies developed by various countries to cope with the ongoing challenges of tribalism, ranging from various forms of mutually beneficial alliances that contribute to the stability of the regime to a climate of antagonism and conflict that leads to instability. Rabi's analysis determines that constructive alliances between states and Bedouin tribes are likely to occur when three main conditions are met: the state succeeds in maintaining "a balance of power between tribal families"; the state is willing to incorporate tribal values in its national ethos; and the state allows the tribes a certain measure of political independence to apply their own norms.[25] If the state fails to do so, it loses a mutually beneficial alliance with the Bedouin and is subjected instead to constant antagonism and unrest.

Cases from various other countries in the Middle East instantiate not only the continuum between alliance and antagonism but also the "price" incurred for adopting one or the other and the likely outcome: constant conflict or calm and tranquility. Jordan, Oman, Qatar, the United Arab Emirates, and Saudi Arabia have been able to accommodate alliances with tribalism and achieve relative calm while others such as Yemen, Iraq, Bahrain, and Syria adopted repressive measures that led to constant unrest. Furthermore, even when a state decides to pursue alliances, it must constantly maintain a balance of power between different tribes and between the tribes and the state.[26]

While the insights regarding the Bedouin in the Middle East that Rabi introduced are fresh, the inherent challenges states face from tribal groups are nothing new. A collection edited by the anthropologist Dawn Chatty includes many examples of how tribal-nomadic societies from the Middle East and North Africa contested state authority.[27] There are also numerous non-Arab tribal societies. The array of challenges that such populations pose to modern states has been the focus of anthropologist Philip Carl Salzman, who explored the tribal pastoral shepherds of Sardinia, the Yoruk of southern Turkey, the Bharawad of Gujarat, the Reika of Rajasthan, and more. Most of these societies were forced to settle and subject to assimilation, which completely dismantled their group ties.[28] Another study conducted by anthropologist Anatoly Khazanov indicated that the commitment of tribal members to the tribal-nomadic framework threatens governmental institutions' sovereignty. Khazanov showed that the dominant approach by modern states is to settle the tribal nomads to facilitate control or at least delineate their areas of migration and distance them from the borders. Their way of life was found to be incompatible with the needs of the modern state.[29]

The acknowledgment that tribalism within the state is an ongoing challenge and that no Middle Eastern Arab state can live in peace with its Bedouin communities unless it accommodates the tribal norms and values is a fascinating topic that merits further exploration. How did Israel address this challenge? Which alternatives did the State of Israel choose? What was the influence of its liberal democracy agenda? Was it willing to accommodate tribal norms, and if so, which ones? How has Israel's position vis-à-vis tribalism changed over the years? What figures and institutions were involved in decision-making, and what were their motivations? Finally, what part did the Jewish-Arab dispute play?

Before delving into these questions, there are several factors to explore by way of introduction: the history of the Bedouin and their sociopolitical structures, the pioneering ethos of Jewish settlements in the Negev before statehood, and finally my sources, methodology, limitations, and scheme of periodization.

THE NEGEV BEDOUIN POPULATION

The Bedouin population described in this book, commonly referred to as the *Negev Bedouin*, are mostly descendants of pastoral nomadic Bedouin tribes, also referred to as *genuine Bedouin*.

Pastoral Tribalism and Nomadism

The term *tribe* is hard to define, as there are so many different meanings and contexts in which the term is used. In its basic and somewhat simplified usage, the term relates to a social unit of people ascribed to a common ancestor, real or imagined. Affiliation is determined by birth through male kinship, and blood relations help shape the strong bonds and total devotion to the tribal unit.[30]

Tribalism in general and nomadic tribalism in particular are deeply rooted in human history. Socio-tribal frameworks were formed prior to the establishment of modern states.[31] The tribal framework, developed in the absence of a central government, gave rise to internal systems with a unique code of morality and behavior.[32] As Salzman explains it, "Tribal pastoralists live as members of a political unit that provides protection through collective responsibility, with each individual obliged to support the other. For individual pastoralists, the tribe is the maximal political entity to which he or she has loyalty and within which the rule of law—customary law—applies."[33]

Lacking permanent structures, fortresses, fences, and walls, their only protection against external threats was the protection they could provide for each other. The more warriors a tribe had to call on, the more powerful it became. The tribal system required discipline and unconditional cooperation. All members were duty-bound to participate in raids and bloody disputes. Norms were strictly enforced, with severe sanctions applied in cases of violation.[34]

The linguistic derivatives *tribal* and *tribalism* are used in the current book in their original meaning to describe the Bedouin lifestyle and organizational structure. It is worth noting that some anthropologists have begun to question the use of these highly charged terms, often deemed derogatory.[35] Scholars now use the terms with an overlay of meaning far removed from their original sense, as in various studies of dysfunctional political parties within democratic systems.[36] Nevertheless, the terms continue to be used in academic discourse to describe Bedouin societies in the Middle East.

Bedouin Tribalism

The general term *Bedouin* refers to a Muslim Arab ethnic group of pastoral nomadic herdsmen who wander through the deserts of the Middle East and North Africa and share a local dialect of the Arabic language. Muhammad Yussef Suwaed estimates the Bedouin population at about twenty-five million.[37] Bedouin society is described as a society of honor with its own unique codes.[38] Bedouin rules, customs, and traditions are largely shared by all tribes and predate the advent of Islam.[39] Although they accepted Muslim beliefs and principles, they did not follow all its religious practices, such as praying in a mosque or studying the Qur'an.[40]

Bedouin economy was based mainly on herding domesticated camels, sheep, and goats, supplemented by a certain amount of dryland farming, protection money collected from caravans, and raids conducted on other tribes and settled communities[41] (see fig. Intro.1). The tribes developed their own customary law for the settling of disputes and a system for the enforcement of legal decisions.[42]

Socially and politically, the Bedouin are organized in confederations (*al-Qabilah*), subconfederations, and tribal units (*al-'Ashirah*).[43] Confederations and subconfederations are political alliances between different tribes formed for the purpose of controlling resources, mainly water and land.

The tribal unit includes a group of families in a paternal blood relationship with a real or mythical common ancestor. Although not necessarily closely related by blood, all members of the tribe bear the same last name. The tribal structure is actually tiered according to kinship ties, from the nuclear family unit consisting of spouses and their children to the extended family, which includes at least one primary nuclear family and other families closely related by blood.

Figure Intro. 1. A Bedouin camp in the Negev. *Source: Israeli Government Press Office.*

One of the main affiliations within the tribal framework is the "blood money group," a union of extended families, usually up to five generations, with a paternal blood relationship (*Khams*). Members of the Khams share responsibility for the actions of every other member. If a ransom is demanded, the amount to be paid is divided among them. If a murder occurs, the duty to seek revenge lies with every member of the victim's Khams and can be taken on by anyone belonging to the Khams of the murderer.[44]

Such solidarity, or "balanced opposition" and "complementary solidarity," as it is sometimes called, is evinced in the old Arab Bedouin saying "I against my brother; I and my brother against my cousin; I and my brother and my cousin against the world."[45]

Within the patriarchal framework of the tribe, Bedouin women are owned by men, by their fathers before marriage and by their husbands thereafter, and are restricted to a private area of the dwelling. They are excluded from any involvement in political decisions, which is why they rarely appear in archival documentation.[46] Since power is correlated to the number of male warriors in the tribe, many offspring are an advantage, and this contributes to the phenomenon of extensive polygamy.[47]

Nomadic tribes may also take in families seeking refuge from blood feuds, conflicts, or other threats, and such families may then form subtribal units. In the Negev, most of the subtribal units are descendants of peasant families (hereafter *fellahin-Bedouin*) from the Nile region. Their arrival was part of a larger phenomenon of immigration to Eretz Israel, mainly during the nineteenth century, in the wake of economic distress and political

Figure Intro. 2. Bedouin of the al-Huzayyil plowing with a camel. April 10, 1951. *Photo: Eldad Davis. Source: The Government Press Office.*

pressures in their countries of origin, and the promise of a growing demand for skilled workers and the availability of arable land in Ottoman-ruled Eretz Israel.[48] The fellahin-Bedouin adopted the Bedouin way of life but were perceived as having a lower status than the genuine Bedouin who controlled the land and invested much effort in maintaining their position.[49] Bedouin relations with fellahin-Bedouin were based on patronage. Granting plots of land to the fellahin-Bedouin and receiving a percentage of the crop in return, the genuine Bedouin were able to carry on with their pastoral way of life[50] (see fig. Intro.2). Another subtribal unit was formed by descendants of slaves (Afro-Bedouin) who had been bought by the genuine Bedouin.

After the establishment of the state, Israel became involved in the effort to reconstruct tribal units that had been split into smaller divisions as a consequence of altered borders, as will be explained in chapter 2. In this context, the term *tribe* is used to denote an amalgam of Bedouin families, ancestral or constituted by the authorities, that form a functioning unit under the leadership of a sheikh and appear under his name in official documents.

The word *sheikh* carries several meanings in Arabic: tribal leader, elder, notable, religious devotee, an honorific, and so forth. In this book, it is used in its primary meaning as someone who functions as a tribal leader. The specific tasks of the sheikh differed little from tribe to tribe and included

Figure Intro. 3. Bedouin sheikhs in Be'er Sheva with 'Aref al-'Aref, the district officer. The photo was taken between 1934 and 1939. *Source: Library of Congress.*

administrative, representational, and political functions.[51] Apart from bearing responsibility for the well-being, security, and economic conditions of the tribe, the sheikh also played a key role in the preservation of the tribal ethos. The sheikh's success depended on the support and cooperation of tribal dignitaries including heads of large families. To a great extent, the power of the sheikh derived from his personal abilities and intra-tribal traditions. The position was usually passed down dynastically, with priority given to the son of the sheikh. In the absence of an external source of authority, the sheikh was required to achieve a consensus by means of persuasion, since he could not expect to impose his opinions on the elders. However, when external forces like governments became involved, the tribal leader gained an added source of power, first from the Ottomans, then from the British, and later from the Israelis[52] (see fig. Intro.3).

Many of the Bedouin living in the Negev today are the descendants of nomadic Arab tribes who migrated in several waves over different periods, particularly in the past two hundred years, from Saudi Arabia, Egypt, the Sinai Peninsula, and Jordan.[53] Eretz Israel, which had been administered by the Ottoman regime (1517–1917), became Palestine after the British defeat of the Ottoman forces (1917–48).[54]

Nomadism continued in the Negev until the beginning of the twentieth century, when a transition to seminomadic life began.[55] This was due mainly to the arrival of the fellahin-Bedouin. Near the end of the Ottoman period, the regime had attempted to gain control over the Bedouin tribes by legal means, by incentivizing them to settle, or through military suppression of their tribal wars. The regime established Be'er Sheva as its seat of government and encouraged the Bedouin to settle in the area by allocating free plots of land and establishing a school, a mill, and a market there.[56] The British who replaced them did not encourage Bedouin settlement. They did, however, formulate other means of control and supervision, deploying a network of police stations in the Negev and developing strategies to address the unique challenges posed by tribal groups in the areas they controlled.[57] Legislation like the Bedouin Control Ordinance of 1942 afforded them special powers, and the district commissioner was authorized to direct the Bedouin "to go or not to go, or to remain in a specified area."[58] Another example is the Collective Punishment Ordinance from 1926, which took into account the collective character of tribal societies and the Bedouin methods of solving disputes through customary law, for which tribal courts were established.[59]

Robert S. G. Fletcher's study of the tribal question in different parts of the world under the British shows that their tribal policies were transferred from one region to another, and that issues of Bedouin tribal life had to be addressed separately from those of settled communities.[60]

The location and extent of tribal and confederation territories (*Dirah*) had been determined through a series of wars in the nineteenth century that ended with Ottoman attempts to subdue the region.[61] There are numerous maps that represent the borders of Bedouin confederations.[62] Map Intro.1 shows Bedouin tribal borders in 1947, as presented in an IDF booklet and based on a map sketched by Al-'Aref during his tenure as mandate district officer in Be'er Sheva.[63]

During the British period, the Negev Bedouin were organized in seven confederations comprising ninety-five tribes. Their numbers were merely estimates, as it was difficult to obtain their cooperation for the census. Demographer Helmut Muhsam and others number their population at approximately sixty-five thousand.[64] Table 0.1 shows that the largest confederation was that of the Tarabin in the western Negev, followed in size by the Tiyaha in the northern Negev, smaller by 20 percent, and the 'Azazmah in the southern Negev, half the size of the Tarabin.

Neither the Ottoman Empire, which ruled the region for four hundred years, nor the British Mandate, which succeeded it and lasted for thirty years,

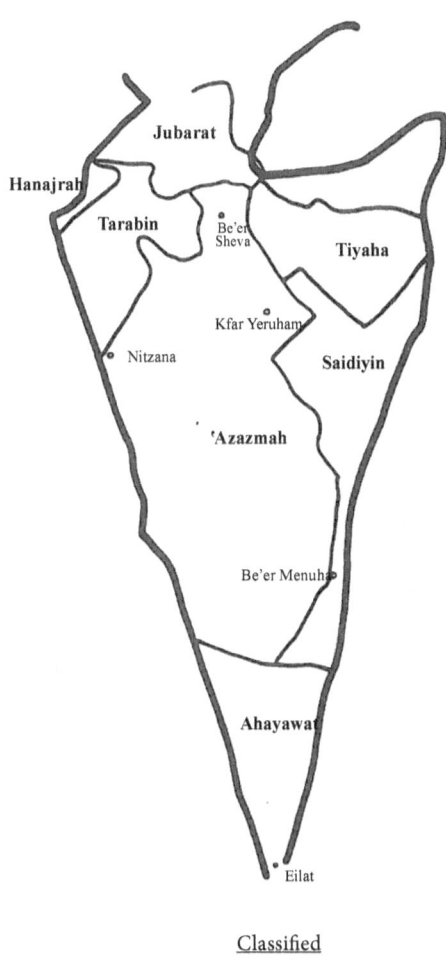

Map Intro. 1. Bedouin tribal borders in 1947. *Source: A booklet on the southern Bedouin, 1959, Appendix D. Source: file 457–72/1970, Israel Defense Forces and Defense Establishment Archives [originally in Hebrew].*

Table 1.1. Distribution of Bedouin population by confederations. Based on data from Muhsam, *Bedouin of the Negev* and Marx, *Bedouin of the Negev*.

Tribal Confederation	Location	Population
Tarabin	Southwest	22,100
Tiyaha	Northwest and northeast	18,850
'Azazmah	South of Be'er Sheva	11,700
Jubarat	Northwest	5,850
Hanajrah	Southwest, near Gaza	5,200
Ahaywat	The most southern confederation	650
Sa'idiyyin	In the east, Arava area	650
Total		65,000

were able to resolve the legal land rights claims of the Bedouin. Much of the land legislation in the country was first enacted by the Ottoman Empire, followed by the mandate government and later by Israel. The two principal laws applicable to the subject were the Ottoman Land Law of 1858 and the Mandate Land (Settlement of Title) Ordinance of 1928. These two pieces of legislation are still relevant today.[65]

Ottoman Land Law classifies five types of land use: *Waqf, Mulk, Matruka, Miri,* and *Mewat*. Waqf is endowed land set aside for a specific purpose; Mulk is land with immovable structures, granted in full to specific people; Matruka is land owned by the regime and granted to a particular group or the general public, with public areas such as roads, creeks, woodland, granaries, and the like for common use.[66]

The remaining two types are Miri and Mewat. Miri is sovereign land granted to individuals for certain uses. In order to prove one's right to these lands, the claimant was obliged to show that it had been assigned to him by the regime and that he had obtained a formal document (*Kushan*) for it. In addition, under sections 20 and 78 of the Ottoman Land Law, the claimant had to prove a series of cumulative terms, including the intensive cultivation of the land in a continuous manner.[67] As opposed to Miri land, Mewat, literally dead land, belonged to the sovereign, and an individual could not acquire rights to it unless he could prove that it had been "revived" (i.e., that the nature of the soil had undergone a complete and permanent change).[68]

According to section 103 of Ottoman Land Law, Mewat is defined as dead land that has not been allocated for public use, while section 6 indicates that such lands "are so remote from any village that a loud voice cannot be heard at the point nearest an inhabited place, (interpreted as a mile and a half, or about half an hour's distance)."[69] The terms *village* and *inhabited place*, used in the law, refer to a permanent settlement dating back to ancient times, not to an encampment of movable tents. Under Ottoman Land Law, Mewat could be revived through cultivation, but the British Mewat Land Ordinance of 1921 ruled out such a possibility and granted a limited period to reclaim lands that had been revived.[70] During both the Ottoman and the British Mandate periods, the Bedouin refrained from registering lands. Al-'Aref explained that when called upon to cooperate in the government process of registration, "they pointed to their swords and rifles and said: 'Here are our titles.'"[71] Other reasons enumerated were the long-standing Bedouin tradition of noncooperation with governments in general, an unwillingness to pay taxes or fees involved in the registration process, a fear of being drafted into the army, inexperience with registration mechanisms, and lack of ownership evidence.[72]

The Mandate Settlement Ordinance was intended to reorganize the Ottoman registration records and introduce a new system of survey claims and cadastral mapping.[73] In one case that reached the mandatory court, the judge expressed his disapproval of the Bedouin's resistance to registering lands and made them pay the consequences.[74] The Jewish community cooperated with the registration procedures, but the Arabs typically did not, hence the mandate government registered no more than a quarter of the lands.[75]

Jewish Settlement in the Negev before Statehood

Relations between the Bedouin and Jewish communities have been difficult and complex ever since the Zionist movement first evinced an interest in the Negev.[76] In the early twentieth century, a number of Jewish families established a community in Be'er Sheva, the city of Abraham they knew so well from the Bible. They built a synagogue and ran a commercial flour mill (consistent with a saying in the *Ethics of the Fathers*: "Without *flour*, there is no *Torah*; without *Torah*, there is no *flour*" [3:21]).[77] Jewish-Bedouin cooperation developed in the region through commercial transactions, which later included land sold by Bedouin sheikhs to Jewish agencies, including the Jewish National Fund (JNF). By then the Jewish community had reached about a hundred members.[78] Nevertheless, hostilities soon erupted, especially during the tenure of al-'Aref as mandatory district officer (1929–38). In 1932, during a visit of the Mufti Hajj Amin al-Husseini to Wadi a-Shari'ah, north of Be'er Sheva, Bedouin sheikhs determined that the blood of any Bedouin guilty of selling land or involvement in the sale of Arab lands to Jews "will be duly spilled."[79]

During the Arab riots that broke out in 1936, known as the Great Arab Revolt, the remaining members of the Jewish community of Be'er Sheva were evicted from their homes and did not resettle in the city until it was captured by Israel in 1948.[80] In the early 1940s, there were only a few kibbutzim in the southern coastal plane and the northwestern Negev. The first three settlements south of Be'er Sheva were established in 1943: Revivim, Gvulot, and Beit Eshel. The Jewish presence there became more significant in October 1946, when eleven Jewish settlements were established in response to the Morrison Grady Plan for the division of the territory under the mandate. The plan reflected an understanding between Britain and the United States regarding the establishment of a Negev District that would include the southern and western Negev and would be administered by a British central government.[81] All Jewish settlements in the Negev were established on lands previously purchased from the Bedouin.[82] The settlements found it necessary to employ local Bedouin to guard the fields.[83] Between February and November 1947, six more settlement were established, most of them south of Be'er Sheva.[84]

The situation in most of the settlements was extremely precarious. They were remote and scattered in the northwestern Negev and around Be'er Sheva. Revivim was the southernmost point, and the easternmost was Nevatim (apart from housing built for laborers at the Dead Sea Works in Sdom). The settlements, most of them with no more than twenty or thirty members, depended on external supplies and the assistance of Jewish institutions. By September 1947, the total number of Jewish settlers was about three thousand.[85]

Rooted in the Ottoman administrative reform of the nineteenth century, the mandate adopted the *mukhtar* system and officially nominated and paid a member of the local community to perform duties and shoulder responsibilities of community leadership. This included, among other things, recording demographic data, issuing needed identification and certificates, and representing the local community before the authorities.[86] The word *mukhtar*, meaning "chosen" in Arabic (or *muhtar* in Ottoman Turkish), refers to the fact that mukhtars were selected by a process that sometimes involved election. Mukhtars were not restricted to the Muslim population and were also nominated for Jews, usually identified as *Jewish mukhtars*. There were mukhtars for neighborhoods in urban towns, villages in rural areas, and tribes in nomadic populations, where they were also identified as "nominated sheikhs."

In the Jewish settlements in the Negev, the mukhtar's official role was to supervise the community and to serve as a mediator between the different settlements and the mandate. They also acted as liaisons with neighboring Bedouin and guards of the settlement fields, which enabled them to provide

Figure Intro. 4. Bedouin affiliated with the al-Huzayyil tribe and Jews of the kibbutz, posing for a picture outside Kibbutz Shoval, November 1, 1947. *Photo: Zoltan Kluger. Source: The Government Press Office.*

information to the intelligence units of the Hagana. Most of the mukhtars did not speak Arabic as their mother tongue and acquired their knowledge in Arabic and Bedouin culture in diverse ways, some by themselves and some in courses taken during their stay in the Negev[87] (see fig. Intro.4).

Michael Hanegbi of Kibbutz Negba (later the first military governor of the Negev) was nominated as a senior Jewish mukhtar of southern Mandatory Palestine while serving as a commander of the Hagana intelligence unit of the Negev. Hanegbi, who was born in 1911 in Poland as Michael Kopitevsky, followed the Zionist call that Jews should return to their homeland and arrived in Eretz Israel in 1934, where he grouped with others to establish Kibbutz Negba, a socialist collectivist settlement in the northern Negev. Like many other Zionists, he changed his last name to a Hebrew name. The meaning of his name is "man of the Negev."[88]

A key factor in the development of the Jewish settlements of the Negev was the water supply. The Jews developed a water pipeline from the pumping facility at Kibbutz Nir Am to supply the other settlements in the Negev, and the mukhtars, led by Hanegbi, played a significant role in laying the pipeline with Bedouin support. The project was promoted as beneficial for Jews and Bedouin alike, and drinking taps were installed in places where the pipe passed through Bedouin encampments. However, some of the sheikhs sold the free water they received to their tribesmen by the drum. The pipeline was only partially completed before serious hostilities broke out in November 1947.[89]

Despite the anticipated cooperation with the Bedouin, the pipeline became a source of daily sabotage and theft, leading to stoppages in the water supply and a breakdown of security. The process of radicalization among some Bedouin tribes ran parallel to that of the Arabs. As researcher Ze'ev Zivan concluded, based on personal interviews, ties between the Negev Bedouin and the Arabs of Mount Hebron and the influence of 'Aref al-'Aref's anti-Zionist propaganda led most of them to join the campaign against the Jewish community. According to Suwaed, pressure was exerted on the Bedouin by the Arab Higher Committee to take part in sabotage operations and assaults against Jews. The Jewish settlers and their mukhtars were not sufficiently aware of the process Bedouin society was undergoing.[90]

State, Nation-State, and Western Liberal Democracy

Although there is no agreed definition for the phenomenon known as *state*, it is usually considered a large politically sovereign administrative unit that has control over a territory. Max Weber's definition regards the state as a political organization that possesses the exclusive right and ability to use force toward a population within a defined territory. According to Weber, state ruling can be based on tradition, charisma, or legal mechanism. A state can be in a form where the administrative staff is either beneath the ruler or separate from him.

Modern states receive their legitimacy through legislation while usually dividing their coercive power over their population between the police and the courts. Through its laws, the state sets binding rules for behavior and is obligated to care for the people's security, economic needs, education, welfare, health, and more. Nation-states are typically states where the majority of their inhabitants share a common ethnicity. These states also serve as a source of affiliation and identity.[91]

Among the various types of states, Western liberal democracies are a kind that has developed from the idea that a person is bound only by his own actions. This idea may seem trivial to those who were born in liberal democratic societies; however, such states are a relatively new phenomenon. As Mark Weiner explains, "The individualistic focus is fundamental to the law of modern liberal societies. It lies in the core of nations that trace their democratic political heritage to the Enlightenment and their economic roots to the Industrial Revolution—and that hold individual self-fulfillment and personal development as a central moral value."[92]

John Locke's political philosophy as set forth in *Two Treatises of Government* holds that "men being, as has been said, by Nature all free, equal and independent, no one can be put out of this Estate, and subjected to the Political Power of another, without his own Consent."[93] A democratic body is thus based on a social contract between individuals, as opposed to one in which members are bound by group ties and whose rights devolve from their status at birth.[94] Other political philosophers like Karl Popper consider democracies open societies marked by a critical attitude to traditional or closed societies.[95]

A liberal state adopts strong measures to ensure that all individuals, regardless of gender, make their own decisions and are solely responsible for the outcome of their own actions. The democratic system is based on the concept that human intelligence gives individuals the right and the ability to make decisions and control their political destiny. This includes freedom of action in many spheres of social, economic, and political life and free will to enter agreements, whether in business or personal relations like marriage. It also means freedom to take part in the political system, to vote and run in free and fair elections, freedom of speech, and the right to be heard. The whole system is based on the proposition that human beings are created equal, regardless of kinship, religion, or color. One of the most important democratic principles is that of the rule of law, the requirement to obey the laws passed in a democratic way. It also ensures the balance of powers between the executive, legislative, and judicial branches.[96] Democracy includes mechanisms designed to protect the individual rights of the minority.

The role of the democratic state is to ensure the well-being of its citizens, as well as their safety and security. Democracy is based on the assumption that ideological disagreements and conflicts will arise in social and political life, and the way to settle them is through public debate and mutual persuasion, according to the accepted rules of the game. The use of force is permitted only on behalf of the state.

Some regimes of modern Middle East Arab states promote a separate national identity. Others are satisfied, at least most of the time, with their Arab ethnic identity. None of the Arab states are liberal democracies.

Israel is self-declared as a modern nation-state that follows Western liberal democratic rules. Some scholars question Israel's claim of being a democracy and argue that as a Jewish nation, it prevents non-Jews from enjoying equal rights. Indeed, during the period discussed in the book, rights and freedoms were temporarily suspended, for reasons that will be explained. However, even during that time, many core aspects of individual rights, such as freedom of speech, free elections, separation of powers, individual responsibility for one's actions, the rule of law, and other aspects of liberal democracies were kept to a great extent.

Sources, Methods, Limitations, and Periodization Scheme

In summary, the book examines Israel's policy in regard to Negev Bedouin tribalism, using a historical perspective and geographical methodologies. It combines an analysis of a vast amount of archival material with field studies and graphic information derived mainly from maps and photos. This methodology is useful in understanding historical events with a strong spatial component.[97] The book's main contribution lies in the material it uncovers and the light it sheds on the institutional decision-making process. For those who are interested in the social and anthropological aspects of Bedouin life, there are many other studies available.[98]

The spatial domains considered here are the northern and eastern Negev, semiarid areas that were designated for Bedouin encampments during the military administration period. The southern Negev, which is mountainous, is described only briefly, as the limited Bedouin presence there was not formally permitted. The history of relations between the southern Bedouin and Israel forms part of another study and deserves a separate platform.[99]

The issues of the Bedouin of the Galilee in northern Israel are also not part of the current research. Unlike the Negev Bedouin, they lived in a rainy area, in small enclaves surrounded by Arab and Jewish settled communities. These tribes, which were in enmity with the settled Arabs, did not control large plots of land and were willing to move to permanent settlements.

Using mainly institutional documentation has its drawbacks, including an absence of primary sources of the period recorded by the Bedouin themselves. Generally speaking, the Bedouin rarely wrote or maintained written records of events and instead transmitted their history orally, in poems and stories. Oral history is highly important, but it is not systematic and hence cannot be used as a primary source and record of events,[100] nor is it available for research in the archives of Arab states, although some Arab documentation is included in this book. It should be noted that the same difficulty occurs in all studies related to the Negev Bedouin, including those conducted by Arab scholars, and thus the focus here is on the Israeli position toward the Bedouin where much documentation is available, and less on the Bedouin perspective. The large amount of documentation used in the research of this book facilitates cross-checking and verification.

In the course of writing, I was uneasily aware that women are almost entirely absent from these pages. Hardly any women served in decision-making capacities with the main authorities involved in Bedouin issues, neither in the Negev Military Administration nor in the Office of the PM Adviser for Arab Affairs. This is highly unfortunate, as women did hold roles during the period of the Jewish "state in the making," as the *Yishuv* was called. The most prominent woman of the period, Golda Meir, held a ministerial position, but it was as foreign minister. Even after her election as prime minister in 1969, she seldom appears in the documentation.

As for linguistic issues, the book uses transliteration to present titles of articles and books from non-English languages. However, it also provides a full translation of titles in the reference list.

Furthermore, the names of people and places that are translated from Arabic are presented according to the unique Negev Bedouin dialect. The full methodology and format of the exact translation are provided in the book.

Overview

The book is composed of an introduction, three sections, and an epilogue. The introduction provides some essential background on tribalism in general and Bedouin tribalism in particular, as political and social phenomena that challenge the modern state; it likewise sets forth the historical and legal context and the prestate demographic and geographical layout of the Bedouin and Jewish populations of the Negev.

The first section includes two chapters detailing the early years that shaped the relationship between Israel and the Bedouin and Israel's effort to accommodate tribalism in collaboration with the sheikhs.

Chapter 1, titled "Bedouin in the War of Independence, 1947–49" explores the period of November 1947 until the armistice agreement and the involvement of the different tribes in the War of Independence. The political dimension of tribalism was manifested principally through the capacity of each tribe, under its own leadership, to operate as a separate negotiating and decision-making unit. This allowed them a certain autonomy in the forging of tribal alliances with Israel and enabled Israel to differentiate among them, allowing certain tribes to return after the war and denying return to others.

Chapter 2, titled "Creation of the Military Regime: Nominated Sheikhs and Tribal Units, 1949–56," focuses on the first postwar decade when the Bedouin came under the inclusive power of the military administration. During this period, two contradictory approaches to tribalism emerged. The first was motivated by those who aimed to disband tribalism and transform the Bedouin into communities made up of individual farmers (fellahin) and hoped to accomplish this by establishing agricultural villages, similar to the Israeli Moshavim. In these villages, each nuclear Bedouin family was to be granted a plot of arable land, thus freeing it from subordination to the sheikh and his possible exploitation. The contrary approach, which eventually won out, was promoted by the military administration—a policy that used the tribal framework, gave official status to nominated sheikhs, reorganized segmented tribes to forge tribal units, and opened tribal courts. The policy of allying with the sheikhs not only preserved tribalism but reinforced it. It was chosen mainly because it was practical—that is, it enabled the sheikh, with the help of a small number of officers provided by the state, to maintain the peace and achieve control over the Bedouin by using structures that were familiar to them.

The second section includes two chapters dealing with the next stage in Israel's policymaking under the military administration. Although various forces were at work to break down tribal life, especially the hardship of prolonged droughts, the pro-tribal policy won out in the end.

Chapter 3, titled "Bedouin Exit from the Negev, 1957–60," discusses the extreme drought conditions that led to a massive migration of Bedouin from the Negev and eroded their tribal structures. Bedouin encamped in regions beyond the control of the military administration and in proximity to population centers where they became acquainted with the Israeli job market and lifestyle. This chapter sheds light on another less discussed episode, Moshe Dayan's 1960 initiative to modernize the Bedouin by transforming them into a settled urban proletariat in mixed cities like Ramleh in the center of Israel. This initiative was rejected by the Bedouin leadership and was therefore quashed.

Chapter 4, titled "The Decline of the Military Administration, 1961–66," addresses the central government's promotion of an urban settlement plan for the Negev and the military administration's attempt to delay it. The attempts to implement state laws dealing with issues of illegal construction and landownership led to confrontations with Bedouin sheikhs who demanded that the state effectively recognize their land rights. Once again, the state suspended its confrontational approach in favor of achieving peace.

The last section of the chapter deals with the years following the military administration, the incentives for cooperation with tribalism that remained in place, and the possible reasons for this.

Chapter 5, titled "New Institutions—Old Alliances, 1967–71," begins with the abolition of the military administration and explains how its powers and responsibilities as well as its collaborative policy were transferred to other agencies. The latter kept the tribal framework as it was. Once again, the authorities' aspiration for three new settlements in the Negev to become a platform for an altered Bedouin way of life came to naught.

The conclusion, titled "The Question of Functional Alliances," presents and analyzes major themes that emerged from the study and explains why Israel ultimately implemented a policy of alliances rather than confrontations.

The book concludes with an epilogue that connects the past with present events.

PART I

1

BEDOUIN IN THE WAR OF INDEPENDENCE, 1947–49

> They are willing to live in a place that will be allotted to them, will do all they are asked to do, they will pay taxes. Why to object?
>
> *David Ben-Gurion, November 25, 1948*

The events of Israel's War of Independence in the Negev, between November 1947 and April 1949, influenced Negev Bedouin life including tribal deployment, land possession, demography, social structure, and the formation of political alliances, both internal and external.

Although the War of Independence has been the subject of much scholarly writing, the involvement of the Negev Bedouin in the events of the war has attracted far less attention.[1] Among studies focusing on the Bedouin in this respect, the most relevant are the works of Suwaed, albeit his emphasis is on the role of the Galilee Bedouin; Ze'ev Zivan's research on Jewish-Bedouin relations in the 1940s and 1950s; and Hanina Porat's research on the Negev Bedouin during Israel's first years.[2]

For the sake of convenience, I have divided the Negev into four subregions: northwest, southwest, south, all bordering Egypt, and east, bordering Jordan. The Bedouin's involvement in the fighting varied from region to region, each of which was generally inhabited by different tribes. The Jewish presence in each region varied as well. While the majority of Jewish settlements were located in the northwest and southwest, a few of them were in the south, and there were also two isolated settlements in the east.[3] Map 1.1 shows the four areas in the small map, and the main map shows the Jewish settlements and the water pipeline.

The events examined here are arranged chronologically: the first stage, from shortly before the war of 1948 with the UN Partition Plan of November 29, 1947, to the departure of the British from Mandatory Palestine, and the

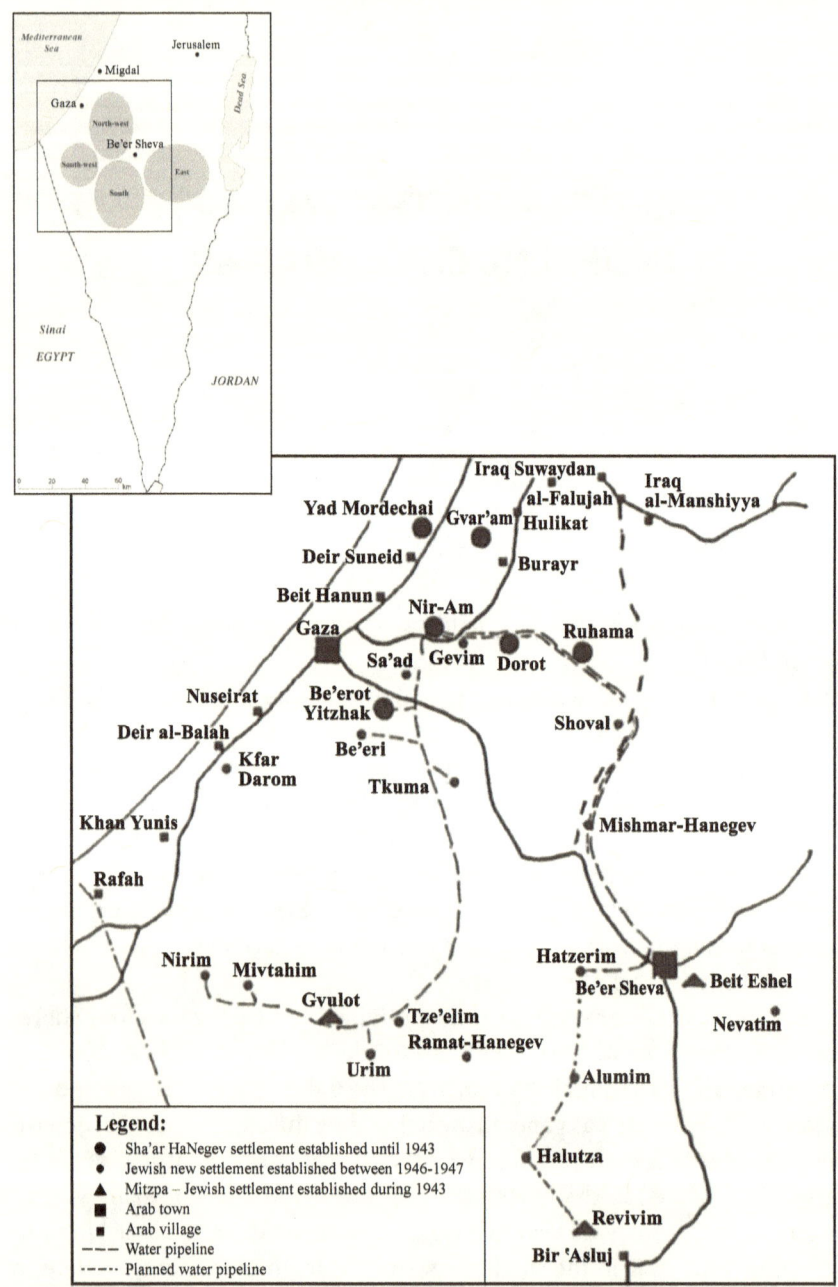

Map 1.1. Top left side shows the four areas. The center shows Jewish settlements and water pipeline. *Source: the author. Based on Amiad Brezner,* HaNegev BeHityashvut VeBeMilhama: HaMa'vaḵ Al HaNegev, 1941–1948. *Tel Aviv: Ministry of Defense, 1994, 346.*

second stage, beginning with the invasion of Arab nations on May 14, 1948, and ending in a series of armistice agreements during 1949.

The war in the Negev was an integral part of a broad military campaign to gain control over the whole of Mandatory Palestine. The inhabitants of the region, as well as the neighboring and distant Middle Eastern countries, foreign governments, and international bodies all became involved in the issue. Our discussion of this, while it has no direct bearing on the Bedouin, casts light on their circumstances.

THE MONTHS PRECEDING THE WAR

The leaders of the Yishuv were ill-prepared to fight in the Negev. In contrast to other areas of Mandatory Palestine where the Hagana was able to gather detailed intelligence about the towns and villages, the influential leaders, and the Arabs' intentions, information on Bedouin tribes in the Negev was sporadically obtainable and included mostly statistical data regarding the tribes and biographies of prominent sheikhs.[4]

The two main forces in the local Arab community at the time were Hajj Amin al-Husseini, the Mufti of Jerusalem and leader of the Arab Higher Committee, and his opponents, the more moderate Nashashibi clan related to the Hashemite family of King Abdullah of Transjordan. The latter aspired to take Mandatory Palestine, the Negev included, under his rule.[5]

Pressure on the Bedouin to join an alliance came mainly from the supporters of the Mufti. Together with the Muslim Brotherhood, he called on the Bedouin tribes and sheikhs to organize themselves in committee-like units and prepare for war and the expulsion of the Zionists from the Negev. The call was answered by a number of sheikhs, mainly from the Tarabin tribes led by Abu Sittah near Gvulot in the southwest region and the Hanajrah confederation in the far northwest region, who encouraged tribesmen to attack Jewish convoys and sabotage the new water pipeline.[6] The Jewish settlements were vulnerable, sparsely populated, and separated by long distances.[7]

Other attempts to recruit Bedouin support for plans to seize the Negev came from the Nashashibi clan and King Abdullah. They had some success in this with tribes from the Tiyaha confederation, mainly those in the northwest region. The al-Huzayyil and their affiliated fellahin-Bedouin, on the other hand, maintained neutrality and forged close relations with neighboring Jewish settlements.[8]

The British, too, tried to recruit Bedouin support for their continued influence and control of the Negev in order to secure a land route to the Mediterranean from Iraq and Jordan, where they were economically and militarily invested.[9]

Archival documentation reflects intertribal support and cooperation between the Bedouin and the Arab Higher Committee but also disagreements among the sheikhs and mutual accusations of disloyalty, corruption, and alliances with rivals.[10]

In 1947, a series of rallies and tribal meetings were held in various areas of the Negev. The sheikhs coordinated their activities and discussed possible assistance to the Arab Higher Committee and the punishment to be meted out for selling land to Jews. The first meeting, on August 15 in Wadi a-Shari'ah in the northwestern Negev, was attended by the sheikhs of that area. A second meeting took place on September 8 in the southwest region under the control of Sheikh a-Sufi of the Tarabin tribes and was attended by dignitaries from the Tiyaha tribes.[11] Participants at another meeting of the Tarabin tribe that month declared their opposition to a Jewish state while expressing resentment against Arab nationalist institutions for their lack of concern for the Bedouin. In mid-October, over a hundred sheikhs met and decided to establish national committees and a national guard under the Arab Higher Committee.[12]

According to an additional intelligence report, in late November 1947, a number of Bedouin sheikhs headed by Ibrahim a-Saneʿ agreed that rather than being subordinate themselves to the Arab forces, they would establish their own independent military division.[13] Although there are different views among historians as to the reasons behind the decision of some tribes to ally with the Jewish side,[14] there is no doubt that efforts were made to obtain it from different directions. Loyalty and cooperation with the Bedouin were always challenging and not always sustainable for a long period. In the course of events, many tribes were attracted to those who were hostile to the Jewish state, allied with them, and participated in activities against the Jews.

Between the UN Partition Plan and the Departure of the British

On November 29, 1947, the UN voted in favor of the Partition Plan for an Arab state side by side with a Jewish state and the city of Jerusalem under international control. The Partition Plan was adopted following the recommendation of the UN Special Committee on Palestine (UNSCOP) in May 1947. Although UNSCOP was set up following Britain's return of the Mandate Letter with requests for clarifications, Britain did not expect UNSCOP to recommend its complete evacuation from the territory.[15]

According to the plan, while the foothills of the Hebron Mountains and Be'er Sheva were granted to the Arab state, most of the Negev area, which

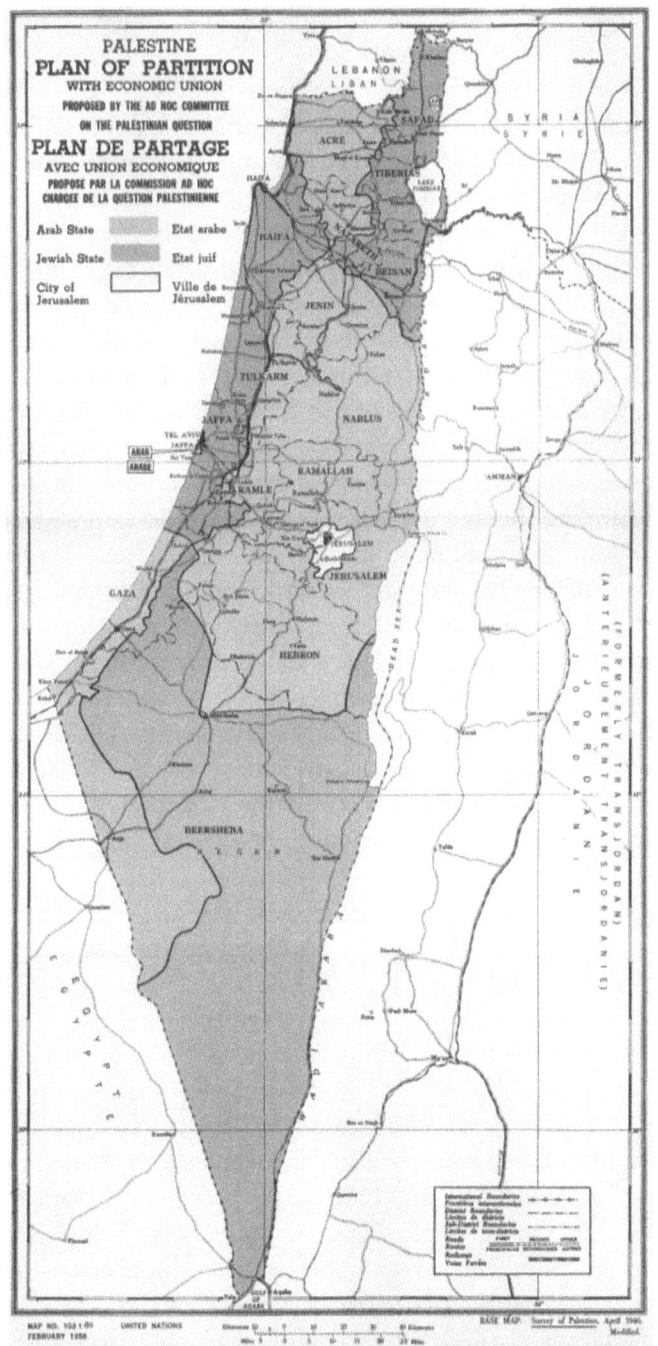

Map 1.2. UN Partition Plan. *Source: UN General Assembly Resolution 181. A/RES/181(II).*

had been under de facto Bedouin control, was granted to the Jewish state.[16] See the UN Partition Plan in map 1.2.

UNSCOP had been impressed by the Jewish settlements in the Negev, especially the new water pipeline that was established for use by both the Jews and the Bedouin. Their opinion was that the Jewish state would be able to further develop the region.[17] While the Jewish community celebrated the Partition Plan, the Arabs launched attacks on the Yishuv to prevent its implementation.[18] Bedouin hostilities escalated during the first weeks of December, starting with small local actions like ambushes and roadside shootings, pipeline sabotage, and nightly harassment of Jewish settlements.[19] These soon extended to large-scale attacks on Jewish squads—for example, on December 11, when members of the ʿAzazmah tribes killed five Jews patrolling the water pipeline and, two days later, another five Jews on patrol in the northwest Negev.[20] The most serious incident occurred on December 17 when two hundred Bedouin attacked the small, isolated Jewish settlement of Nevatim located east of Beʾer Sheva.[21] An airplane bombarding the area finally scared off the invaders, but the attack resulted in several casualties on both sides.[22] In the weeks that followed, there were more Bedouin attacks on Jewish supply convoys, mainly by the Tarabin and the ʿAzazmah tribes, and further acts of sabotage on the water pipeline.[23]

Due to the vulnerability of the Jewish settlements and fear of continuing Bedouin attacks, evacuations were considered.[24] The British, who had their own interests in instituting Arab control of the Negev, acted in support of the Bedouin and sent the Gaza district officer to offer help with the transportation of evacuees.[25]

Jewish leadership, headed by Prime Minister and Minister of Defense David Ben-Gurion, opted to fight for the Negev and to that end established the Negev Committee. Yosef Weitz, the director of the Land Department of the Jewish National Fund (JNF), was appointed chairman of the Negev Committee, and under his leadership, the committee conducted a large-scale operation employing JNF funds to reinforce the Jewish settlements.[26]

In an attempt to halt the escalation, the committee appealed to King Abdullah to restrain the Bedouin and hold meetings with Bedouin sheikhs.[27] Ben-Gurion was concerned and in his diary posed the rhetorical question "Can I find allies?" to which he responded, "Yes, Sheikh Salman al-Huzayyil (near Shoval), Sheikh [Hasan] Abu Jaber (at the northern end of the Fallujah Road)."[28] Leaflets were distributed to the Arabs of the Gaza District and Beʾer Sheva and their sheikhs and dignitaries, calling on them to end hostilities.[29]

In early January 1948, the military policy of the Yishuv was to respond only when fighting erupted but not to initiate hostilities, including ambushes, that might result in casualties.[30] Armored vehicles provided a partial solution to transportation difficulties and served as a deterrence.[31] Likewise, vigorous searches for stolen water pipes were carried out.[32]

In a speech on February 3, Ben-Gurion referred to the dire situation in the Negev while noting that "if we do not send in enough forces, we will be compelled to pull out [of the Negev]."[33] There were also indications that the Bedouin of Sheikh al-Huzayyil in the northwestern Negev "want peace and our rule, at least those who come to negotiate with us."[34]

However, the situation was more violent in the southern and southwestern regions. Nearly all the 'Azazmah, Tarabin, and Hanajrah tribes were hostile and aggressive. Incidents were common, and ambushes persisted.[35] Bedouin sheikhs, like Salamah Ibn Sa'id of the 'Azazmah, who had sold lands to Jewish settlements were among the principal aggressors. This was attributed to their desire to "purge themselves" of shameful past deeds.[36] In February, serious clashes occurred near Khirbat al-Fahr, overlooking an important junction and led by one of the Tarabin tribes.[37] The Jews retaliated by detonating the well from which the mounted Bedouin set forth on their ambush.[38] The sporadic retaliations of the Jews grew more frequent, and they went on the offensive.[39]

At the end of February, in an attempt to prevent other Bedouin from joining the attackers, two Jews were dispatched to the tribal headquarters of the Tarabin near Kibbutz Hatzerim and two others to the 'Azazmah tribe near Kibbutz Tze'elim.[40] According to a British report, "the Jews ask them not to follow the guidance of their leaders."[41] However, all their attempts failed.[42]

The water pipeline continued to be a locus of confrontation. There were many casualties in the areas between Mishmar HaNegev, Hatzerim, and Alumim (Hazale), especially the areas around Be'er Sheva controlled by the 'Azazmah and Tarabin. Certain undefendable points were abandoned. The area that ran through Tarabin territory near the al-'Imarah police station was attacked daily, especially by members of the Abu Sittah and a-Sufi clans.[43] In contrast to them, the area under the sway of the al-Huzayyil and associated tribes between Nir Am and Dorot, Ruhama, Shoval, and Mishmar HaNegev in the northwest suffered far less. Figure 1.1 shows people repairing the water pipeline.

An intelligence report indicates that at a meeting in late February 1948, disputes broke out among the sheikhs of the Tiyaha tribes over their relations with the Jewish settlements. Sheikh Salman al-Huzayyil apparently disagreed with the aggressive line taken by Sheikh Ibrahim a-Sane', who sought the leadership of the Tiyaha and Jubarat tribes.[44] The latter was "an avowed and implacable hater of Israel,"[45] who promoted a general recruitment to the

Figure 1.1. War of Independence. Repairing the water pipeline, September 23, 1948. *Source: The Government Press Office.*

Gaza National Committee.[46] Furthermore, in March, a number of sheikhs, including 'Abadallah Abu Sittah of the Tarabin tribe, equipped themselves with vehicles and arms and called for action.[47] The Tarabin sheikhs held meetings in al-'Imarah, where, according to intelligence reports, three Germans sent by the Mufti instructed them on the use of mines and explosives and organized a training camp.[48] These connections with the Mufti and the allotment of funds created controversies.[49] Tribal divisions and insubordination became a source of major concern. In an effort to coerce those Bedouin who refused to obey, the sheikhs established a youth organization called Jabhat al-Shabab (The Youth Front).[50]

In February 1948, US support for the Partition Plan seemed to fade, and the Israeli leadership feared that the Americans might feel bound to give the Negev to the Arabs.[51] In March, the US formally proposed suspending efforts to implement the Partition Plan and initiated a trusteeship. In February and early March, wide-scale clashes took place throughout Mandatory Palestine. Supply convoys were constantly attacked, the road to Jerusalem was blocked, and the city was under siege. To address this dire situation and better prepare for the upcoming invasion, the Hagana launched what it called Plan D, a strategy for military operations. This entailed going on the offensive and taking permanent control over territories allocated to the Jewish state in the Partition Plan except for the southern Negev. It likewise entailed controlling the invasion routes of the Arab forces and protecting isolated Jewish settlements, including those beyond the boundaries of the Partition Plan.[52] The precise effect of Plan D on the fight for the Negev is difficult to determine, but it clearly entailed an offensive course of action. Reports indicate that fear of Jewish reprisals helped persuade the Bedouin to distance themselves from the vicinity of the water pipeline.[53] Gradually, with more reinforcements coming in, the Jewish settlements felt stronger and more secure.[54] At the end of March 1948, Musa Abu Rashid of the Jubarat Confederation met with members of Kibbutz Dorot and declared that the Bedouin in his area wished for peace.[55] While relative calm continued in the northwestern Negev, severe clashes erupted in the southern regions of the Tarabin and 'Azazmah tribes.[56]

Furthermore, as the British departure approached, the Arab states intensified their involvement. King Abdullah, induced the Bedouin to join his own forces with a promise of salaries.[57] Egyptian and Syrian volunteers arrived in Gaza and attempted to recruit Bedouin to their own units.[58] Kfar Darom near Gaza was a target of attacks, organized and led by Sheikh Mustafa Abu Midyan, the leader of the Hanajrah.[59] On April 5, a group of Bedouin sheikhs met at the home of Musa a-Surani, a representative of the Supreme Muslim Council in Gaza, and agreed to establish three outposts against attacks by the Jews.[60]

While several Tarabin, 'Azazmah, and Hanajrah sheikhs recruited men, Sheikh al-Huzayyil once again refused to join an initiative using the British police station near him as a base for attacking Jews.[61] Moreover, several Tarabin sheikhs met near Kibbutz Hatzerim to discuss peace and the cessation of attacks on the roads and the western water pipeline.[62]

With the success of Jewish military operations, the situation in Mandatory Palestine stabilized. Internal pressures coupled with an understanding that the Soviets were about to recognize the Jewish state persuaded President Harry Truman to forgo the Trusteeship Plan.[63] Although British officers tried to help the Bedouin tribes by transferring control of the police stations to them on the eve of their departure, in the end they abandoned all but the 'Asluj station, which was seized by the followers of Sheikh Salamah Ibn Sa'id.[64]

According to the Palestinian historian and mandatory official 'Aref al-'Aref, when the British announced their retreat from Mandatory Palestine, a garrison force headed by Sheikh Ibrahim Abu Sittah of the Tarabin was created in Be'er Sheva.[65] The garrison was subject to the Arab Higher Committee in Egypt and included sixty Bedouin and permanent residents.[66]

Figure 1.2. 'Awdah Mansur Abu-Mu'ammar receiving a medal from Pinhas Amir. *Source: Pinhas Amir private collection.*

Bedouin, who had maintained good relations with Jews, came under attack from the other faction, which laid land mines near the territory of Sheikh al-Huzayyil in retaliation for his contact with the enemy.[67] The most prominent Jewish ally was 'Awdah Mansur Abu Mu'ammar of the 'Azazmah, who had worked as a guard at Kibbutz Revivim. Although he was a close relative of Sheikh Salamah Ibn Sa'id, 'Awdah Mansur Abu Mu'ammar decided to sever relations with him in favor of his Jewish allies. He later received a medal for his help and continued to be Israel's strongest ally among the Bedouin sheikhs (see fig. 1.2).[68]

Second Part of the War: The Coalition of Arab States

The Eve of the British Departure

In May 1948, information came in about an imminent invasion of Arab armies.[69] Thousands of foreign fighters had reached the Negev. Jordanian legionnaires, funded by the British government, were joined by growing numbers of Egyptians, Sudanese, and Libyans.[70] The Egyptian command seemed confident and declared that "in six days' time it will be seen whether the Jews will harvest their fields and yours or whether you will harvest yours and theirs."[71]

The arrival of Arab troops forced the Bedouin near the fighting zones to take a stand. The sheikhs and their tribes were compelled to decide individually whether to ally with the invading forces and take part in the fighting or to distance themselves from the fighting zones and become known as neutral or friendly toward the Jews.[72] The understanding of Israeli intelligence was that the "neutral, friendly Bedouin had moved far away."[73] It was easy for Bedouin to relocate elsewhere since they were a tent-dwelling seminomadic society.

The tribes of the Jubarat confederation, most prominently the 'Alamat tribe living near what is today Kiryat Gat, joined the Egyptian forces and participated in the bloody battles over Khirbat Mahazz. Upon the defeat of the Egyptians, they moved eastward.[74]

Most of the Tarabin tribes also allied with the Egyptian forces.[75]

Members of the Hanajrah confederation, near Gaza, joined the attacks on Jewish settlements in the area, including Kfar Darom, which was later evacuated.[76] The tribes of the 'Azazmah, south of Be'er Sheva near Revivim and Halutza, were co-opted by the Egyptians and used 'Asluj as a base for their offensives. An exception was 'Awdah Mansur Abu Mu'ammar, who provided information to the Jewish forces about ambushes and anticipated attacks.[77]

The tribes of the Tiyaha confederation who were allied with Sheikh al-Huzayyil, considered an ally of the Jews, distanced themselves from the area. They moved eastward to the foothills of the Hebron Mountains, which at the time were beyond the lines of Jewish control.[78] Other tribes of the Tiyaha confederation, such as the al-'Ugbi tribe, supported the Arab forces.[79] The eastern tribes of the Tiyaha confederation were located at some distance from the fighting zone and did not take a stand after the invasion.[80]

Invasion of the Arab States

On the last day of the British Mandate, May 15, 1948, Israel declared independence. On the heels of the declaration, a massive coalition of Arab armies invaded areas under Jewish control. In the Negev, the most prominent of these was the Egyptian army, reinforced with Saudi and Sudanese volunteers. They progressed by following two ancient routes: the Sea Way, also known as Via Maris, through Gaza and along the coast, and the Hill Way, also known as the Way of the Patriarchs, from Be'er Sheva through the Hebron Mountains and Bethlehem and leading to Jerusalem.[81]

Before the signing of the first truce in June 1948, local Bedouin fought alongside the Egyptians and engaged in fierce battles in the western Negev.[82] The Arab forces split the Negev in two. Kibbutz Yad Mordechai was evacuated, and other Jewish settlements endured long sieges and starvation.[83] The

Jews often took the offensive to ensure the survival of their settlements and movement between them, and they reinforced the hold of the Israel Defense Forces (IDF) on the western Negev by carrying out attacks in imperiled areas. Specifically targeted were the villages of the (non-Bedouin) fellahin and the nearby Arabs, but not the friendly Bedouin living in the region.[84] Members of Israeli intelligence opposed offensive actions like corps destruction, which they claimed might motivate the remaining Arabs to help the Egyptians seize the region.[85]

According to Kamil Isma'il al-Sharif, the Muslim Brotherhood was aided by members of the Bedouin tribes in the Negev who disrupted transportation routes between the Israeli settlements and destroyed their armored vehicles and tanks. In addition, they made their members available to the brotherhood command and provided them with all the weaponry, ammunition, and vehicles at their disposal.[86]

On June 16, 1948, a ceasefire was mediated by Folke Bernadotte, who had been given the task by the UN Security Council. At the end of June, Bernadotte proposed several plans, none of which were accepted, entailing an Arab-Jewish union that would leave all or part of the Negev in Arab hands.[87]

When the fighting was renewed in July, intelligence reports indicated that the Egyptians had co-opted the Bedouin camel corps and paid its salaries.[88] The Israelis attacked tribes that had joined forces with the Egyptians, blew up their wells, and burned the barns of Tarabin camps near Kibbutz Be'eri.[89] The Bedouin of the al-'Ugbi tribe joined Abu Sukut of the Tarabin and "actively engaged in shooting and sabotage throughout the war."[90]

Confrontations over control of the region and its traffic arteries continued in September, especially in the western and southern Negev. When acts of sabotage in the Hatzerim-Tze'elim region increased, IDF intelligence forces tried to recruit members of the Tarabin. Although they were too fearful to join, the Israelis hoped that if they could persuade one of them to agree, others might follow suit.[91] These hopes were soon dashed, however, when the Bedouin blew up a well that was used by Kibbutz Hatzerim and murdered the Jewish mukhtar. In retaliation, the Israelis blew up two Bedouin wells.[92] The intelligence report from September of that year shows that wherever there was no regular army presence, the local Bedouin carried out actions like blowing up the water pipeline, mining roads, and ambushing and attacking Jews.[93] Reports also speak of damage to Israeli vehicles from land mines planted by local Bedouin in the western Negev, near al-'Imarah.[94] Bedouin camps were reportedly used as bases for enemy forces, and an Israeli directive was given to sweep the area, attack the inhabitants, "and expel them." These orders included a directive not to harm "a friendly" tribe.[95]

Figure 1.3. War of Independence. Destruction at Beit Eshel, November 23, 1948. *Source: The Government Press Office.*

When Ben-Gurion was asked on October 6 whether the Bedouin would be expelled from the Negev, he replied in the negative and added that plans were being made to organize the Bedouin and recruit them to the IDF.[96]

In the northern Negev, heavy battles took place during the first half of October, mainly over Khirbat Mahazz, a strategic point. Bedouin from the Jubarat tribes who inhabited the area and participated in these bloody conflicts retreated with the rest of the Arab troops when the IDF ultimately captured the point.[97] In the western and southern regions of the Negev, the Arab coalition, together with the local Bedouin, presented an existential threat to the Jewish settlements. They left Beit Eshel in ruins and nearly destroyed other settlements (see fig. 1.3).

THE TURNING POINT—ISRAELI CONTROL IN THE NEGEV

The Capture of Be'er Sheva

In September 1948, Bernadotte submitted his final proposal whereby the entire Negev would be granted to the Arabs.[98] This was a clear withdrawal from the Partition Plan, and Israel feared that if the Egyptian army were not evacuated from the Negev, the United States might support Bernadotte's proposal. For that reason, and due to the predicament of the Jewish settlements,

Figure 1.4. War of Independence. Battle for Be'er Sheva. IDF Soldiers patrolling the streets. October 22, 1948. *Source: The Government Press Office.*

Ben-Gurion authorized the IDF to carry out a large-scale operation in October 1948, named Operation Yoav.[99] The operation was successfully carried out by the IDF between October 15 and 22. Extensive areas, including the strategic city of Be'er Sheva, were captured.[100] Because both sides understood how pivotal Be'er Sheva was for future control of the Negev, it was highly fortified and guarded by thousands of Egyptians, Jordanians, and other volunteers.[101] The capture of Be'er Sheva was thus symbolic as well. Established by the Ottomans as an administrative center and the critical control point of the region and its Bedouin inhabitants, Be'er Sheva continued to hold this position during the British Mandate.[102] Hence, its capture signaled a change in the military balance of power. See figure 1.4, which depicts IDF soldiers patrolling the streets of Be'er Sheva upon its capture during Operation Yoav.

Soon after the capture of Be'er Sheva, "there were no more than 5,000 [Bedouin] in the area."[103] Sheikhs from different tribes, mainly those of the Tiyaha confederation, sued for peace with the State of Israel and for their return to the Negev. They submitted their request to Michael Hanegbi, who had been nominated as military governor of the Negev after serving as the mukhtar of Kibbutz Negba.[104] In his war diary, Ben-Gurion referred to the appeals by the Tiyaha sheikhs on behalf of three thousand Bedouin, noting that "they are ready to enlist their people, to work, to hand over arms, and to submit to Jewish rule. They number about three thousand people. They are now in the vicinity of Dhahiriyya."[105]

The issue was discussed in the Provisional Government meeting on October 31, 1948. Ben-Gurion was in favor of the peace pact. However, the local inhabitants opposed it, claiming that "so long as Be'er Sheva is in danger and the [Egyptian] army located in the [al-Fallujah] pocket has not yet surrendered, these Bedouin are liable to come to their aid." Ultimately, the Provisional Government decided to wait: "For now," they responded, "it is not worthwhile returning them to their places."[106]

The Delegation of Tribal Sheikhs

On November 2, 1948, Hanegbi held a meeting with a delegation of Bedouin sheikhs of various tribes, including Sheikh al-Huzayyil.[107] Representing Israel were Ya'akov Berdichevsky of the Ministry of Minority Affairs, David Kron and Yitzhak Sokolovsky of the Intelligence Service, and the mukhtars of Kibbutz Ruhama and Kibbutz Dorot.[108]

The sheikhs, who represented thirteen to fifteen thousand Bedouin, "asked the new Hebrew government to recognize them as landowners and Negev residents, and allow them to return to their previous locations—allow them to begin working their lands—to plough and sow for the approaching season—they will accept the authority of the new government about everything concerning taxes and other demands . . ."[109] Hanegbi answered that he would refer their request to the ministers but that "while the war is ongoing we cannot guarantee or take anything into consideration." The sheikhs agreed "not to spread out but to locate themselves in the areas allotted to them and to prevent the penetration of outsiders into the surroundings."[110]

Hanegbi's recommendation was that "it would be worthwhile to maintain contact with a few of the sheikhs, particularly those of the Tiyaha, who are past allies and when the time comes to find an apt solution to their resettlement either in their former regions or other regions, we shall determine it anew."[111] While Berdichevsky recommended "not to treat the Bedouin like the fellahin from our area. . . . A Bedouin will never abandon his land entirely, he will try various tricks to return and settle his land, will always be a disturbing factor—in one way or another [Bedouin] will always cause a lot of troubles.... Now upon receiving their surrender, it is possible to make them useful—and even possible that they will become our border guards in the future [they were known as extraordinarily sharp-eyed trackers] instead of a border army in the vicinity to guard the borders. It should be taken into account and understood that such large tracts of land—are not easily maintainable—and those who know to treat the Bedouin properly—will easily control the entire Negev."[112]

The Eastern Negev under IDF Control

International pressures continued, and on November 4, 1948, the UN Security Council demanded that Israel withdraw from all the areas it had conquered in the course of Operation Yoav, including Be'er Sheva.[113] Israel refused and decided to strengthen and even extend its hold on the eastern Negev region to the Dead Sea with Operation Lot,[114] which took place between November 23 and 25. The IDF achieved its goals. The area was taken without a battle. None of the Bedouin inhabitants resisted or opened fire including several Tiyaha tribes, mainly from the Dhullam subconfederation.[115]

Egypt, backed by the UN, continued to demand Israel's withdrawal from Be'er Sheva and other captured areas.[116] There were indications that Bedouin from the region between Be'er Sheva and Kibbutz Hatzerim were collaborating with the Egyptians, infiltrating Be'er Sheva and laying mines there. Hence, an order was given to keep all Bedouin kilometers away from the city.[117] Nevertheless, during the early days of November 1948, the concentration of Bedouin near Be'er Sheva increased, and both Hanegbi and Berdichevsky urged their superiors to hasten their answer to the appeals of the sheikhs.[118]

In his weekly report of November 9–15, Hanegbi provided further information regarding the Bedouin numbers he had collected and the "possibility of organizing the Bedouin sector within the framework of the military administration during the first phase, in a transitional period to civilian rule." Most of the Bedouin suffer from a shortage of food staples and are prevented from returning to their grain silos, he explained. They infiltrated Be'er Sheva to steal food because they were hungry. Their numbers had grown since the previous meeting, he added, and there was now quite a large number of them, mainly from the Tiyaha and Jarawin tribes. However, he noted, "it is difficult to quote their precise overall number. I estimate it may come to (a maximum of) 8,000–10,000 people."[119]

Hanegbi was in favor of accepting the appeal for a peace pact and noted that "most of the tribal members were neutral during the war and some of them refused the Egyptian demand to enlist to fight the Jews. Some of them actively cooperated with us, and helped us, hence the validity of their demand that we recognize them as a population with subsistence rights."[120] Furthermore, he argued, accepting "such a small population in the vast Negev" would contribute to Israel's foreign image and entail no security risks or jeopardize the development of the Negev. He believed moreover that their acceptance would "complement our conquest of the Negev,"[121] and he noted that another group of Bedouin from the Nevatim area who had been friendly throughout the war and numbered no more than 250 were also asking for help.[122]

The intelligence officers were less favorably inclined. At a meeting held on November 16, they noted there were still hostile Bedouin south of Hatzerim, as well as in the area between Nirim and Mivtahim, and the number of unsupervised Bedouin was growing in the evacuated areas. "Within a short time we will be dealing with 30,000 Bedouin who can argue that they were at least neutral. The Ministry of Foreign Affairs has decided to bring them into our framework."[123]

Israel resolved to publicize the appeal of the sheikhs for political reasons, probably to counteract international pressure regarding the Negev and as "proof to the world that the Negev inhabitants prefer us to Egypt."[124]

The Ceremony of the Sheikhs

On November 18, 1948, a ceremony with wide radio coverage was held for the sixteen sheikhs under the aegis of Israel.[125] Government representatives included Hanegbi and members of the Intelligence and the Ministry of Foreign Affairs. The Israelis requested a written summary of the Bedouin's requests and asked them to select a committee as their representatives.[126]

Five sheikhs of the Tiyaha Confederation signed the written document elaborating their requests.[127] The document contained six main topics. The first addressed their dignity, security, and customs; the second, permission to enter Be'er Sheva in order to procure necessities and mill flour; third, the right to return to their lands in the region; fourth, to bear weapons; fifth, to collect the possessions they had stored in Be'er Sheva; and last, to release tribe members who had been arrested.[128] See sheikhs' appeal in figure 1.5.

The Israelis, for their part, raised certain points at the ceremony that were vexatious for some. First of all, the Ministry of Minorities protested it had been left in the dark.[129] As Weitz noted anxiously in his diary that day,

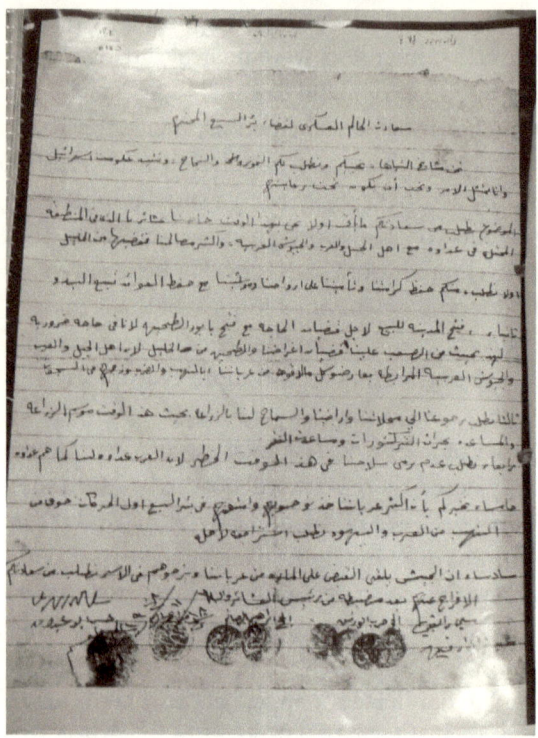

Figure 1.5. Sheikhs' appeal. November 18, 1948. Source: file G-2567/10, Israel State Archives.

"Here, too, there is no policy: is it advisable for us to leave the Bedouin in the Negev?"[130] A day later he wrote, "It [the ceremony] worries me. The presence of Bedouin in the northern Negev is an obstacle on the path of development. I will comment about this to B. G. [Ben-Gurion]."[131]

Ya'akov Shimoni, acting director of the Middle East section in the Political Department of the Ministry of Foreign Affairs, was concerned about the high-profile ceremony and the lack of clarity regarding the Bedouin sites mentioned in the request: "It is clear that part [of the Bedouin] live beyond our borders, part on the border, and the third part within our borders; yet we are still unclear as to the ratio between the parts."[132] Shimoni added that the decision whether to bring fifteen thousand Bedouin into the Negev obliged them first and foremost to clarify policy issues of territory and borders before an additional meeting could take place. Furthermore, he noted, Ben-Gurion was thinking about appointing an Arab, probably a Bedouin, as deputy governor in Be'er Sheva.[133]

Shimoni was angered by the text of the Bedouin sheikhs' request, which differed in many respects from the version suggested by the Ministry of Foreign Affairs. It seemed overly binding to him and propounded their incompatible requests for permission to maintain customs, to enter Be'er Sheva for reasons other than milling flour, to return to their lands, bear weapons, collect possessions stored in Be'er Sheva, and release Bedouin prisoners.[134]

Yet another request, signed by ʿAwdah Mansur Abu Muʿammar of the Mas'udin al-ʿAzazmah tribe on behalf of the 250 Bedouin, asked to join Israel and allow them to use weapons "against Bedouin that collaborates with the Egyptian and invade their lands."[135] They pledged their loyalty, full obedience, and willingness to provide help upon request.

During the second half of November 1948, Bedouin tribes, mostly from the Dhullam subconfederation of the Tiyaha, were located in the northeastern area under Israeli control.[136] The Tiyaha and Jubarat tribes that had previously inhabited the northwestern Negev now pitched their tents in the Dhahiriyya and Khuweilfah regions, which had formerly been under either Jordanian or Egyptian control; remnants of the Tarabin and ʿAzazmah tribes still inhabited the south and southwest, though the Israeli hold in those areas was restricted to the Jewish settlements. International pressure continued, calling for Israel's return to the Partition Plan borders and its withdrawal from areas in the Negev.[137]

On November 25, Nahum Sarig, the commander of the Negev Brigade, issued orders prohibiting aggression toward the Bedouin and their property. In the wake of the sheikhs' request to accept the aegis of Israel, relations with the Bedouin were under deliberation, he explained. The issue had political implications, so the army was not to act in any way that would contravene the political agenda.[138]

The same day, Ben-Gurion conducted a meeting to discuss the sheikhs' request.[139] Among the attendants were Chief of Operations Yigael Yadin; Commander of the Southern Front Yigal Allon; Commander of the Military Administration Elimelech Avner; Adviser on Arab and Middle Eastern Affairs at the Ministry of Foreign Affairs Ezra Danin; Deputy Minister of Defense Shaul Avigur; Ben-Gurion's adviser, Reuven Shiloah;[140] Michael Hanegbi, Yosef Weitz, and Ya'akov Shimoni.[141] Hanegbi presented the issue, noting that nine thousand Bedouin were requesting Israeli citizenship, five thousand from the Tiyaha tribes, three thousand from the Tarabin tribes and one thousand more from the ʿAzazmah tribes.[142] Hangebi supported the request and recommended concentrating the Bedouin "in three places, some of them in the western part of the Negev."[143]

Ben-Gurion was less determined: "They are willing to live in a place that will be allotted to them, they will do all they are asked to do, they will pay taxes. Why to object? Owing to security reasons. Yet, it is possible to fix this by concentrating them in a certain district, for example in Tel Sha'aria [a-Shari'ah]. They are prepared to take upon themselves the defense of the pipeline, the way the Egyptians made the tribes who surrendered to them—sabotage the pipeline."[144] Ben-Gurion dismissed the political argument. "The British Foreign Office might answer that as opposed to the 10,000 Bedouin who want Israeli rule there are 50,000 who do not want." He further noted that 10,000 Bedouin would not be a hindrance to the Jewish settlements once water and irrigation were obtained. The only criteria of importance "[is] the matter of security. Will settling the Bedouin amongst us make things more difficult or easy? There is a danger of war with Egypt."[145] It was the dispersal of the Bedouin that worried Ben-Gurion most, it seems, though he noted that the security risk could be eliminated once they were concentrated in one area.

Yigal Allon was in favor of accepting the request,[146] with the proviso that "only those who have always been with us" should be accepted, since "Bedouin cannot be trusted in remote territories. They might side with the enemy and turn against us."[147]

Weitz persisted in his opposition. He gave several reasons for this, which can be summed up as follows: the issue of demography—the topic would have to be discussed vis-à-vis all the Bedouin, whose numbers he estimated at sixty thousand. And even if the issue were limited to ten thousand, the Jews would end up a minority in the region. Second, the Bedouin might obstruct development. Third, it would be difficult to reach agreements with the Bedouin, and even if they were reached, the Bedouin could not be trusted to follow through on them. They were all adept at dissembling. The fourth reason, the political agenda, was baseless, he declared.[148] Weitz noted in his diary that if the requests were accepted, he wanted to be consulted about Bedouin locations.[149]

Like Weitz, Shimoni remained firmly in opposition. He too had concerns regarding Israel's security, demography, and the reliability of the Bedouin. "If we assume that reducing the number of Arabs [in Israel] is good for us—why [allowing the return of] the Bedouin? The Bedouin are troublemakers even in times of peace. They smuggle to avoid customs and make it difficult to keep order. We will accept them as allies—in their present locales."[150]

In Shimoni's mind, the Bedouin problem was linked to the government's general policy toward Arabs who had vacated areas under Israel's control. This policy held that an Arab return could be discussed only after the war in the framework of peace negotiations.[151] According to Zalman Lif (Lifshitz), the PM's adviser for land issues,[152] and Weitz and Ezra Danin,[153] who had drafted the policy and presented it to Ben-Gurion on October 26, 1948, it would be a great mistake to permit the return of Arab refugees because of their hostility and disloyalty to the state, and because of the limitations they would place on Israel's ability to absorb Jewish refugees and immigrants. But if Israel were forced to allow the Arabs back, it would limit their numbers to two hundred thousand, or no more than 20 percent of the Israeli population. And Israel would then have the right to determine where they would settle on their return.[154]

On November 28, only a few days before the report was submitted, Ben-Gurion spoke of the Bedouin request to the Provisional Government. "Both positive and negative opinions have been expressed, and the Headquarters had been tasked with expressing an opinion: to what extent would the decision influence Israel's security—would it mitigate security, or worsen it, or neither mitigate nor worsen.... To date no conclusion has been reached...."[155] Hence, Ben-Gurion totally dissociated the Bedouin request from the issue of returning Arab refugees and directed the Ministry of Defense to concentrate solely on the security aspects related to the Bedouin request.

The Pact with the Friendly Bedouin

The Committee for Bedouin Affairs, nominated by Ben-Gurion, met on November 30, 1948, at the offices of the Ministry of Defense.[156] Committee members included Weitz, Yadin, Allon, and two others, the deputy commander of the Southern Front for District Affairs and the chief officer for operations at the front.

The Committee for Bedouin Affairs did not conceive of the Bedouin as a homogenous group and varied its decisions in accordance with specific tribes and their actions. Consequently, the Committee for Bedouin Affairs recommended offering pacts only to those Bedouin who were friendly to the Jews.[157] This indicates that the Bedouin were perceived as belonging to a unique category, unlike other Israeli Arabs who were not offered pacts. It also differed from the situation of the Druze and Circassians, whose communities had entered into a pact with the Jews before the war.

Consequently, not only did the friendly Bedouin have to prove that they posed no security threat to the state, but they had to participate in Israel's defense by recruiting "most of the youth"[158] to the IDF within the minorities' unit.

The Committee for Bedouin Affairs referred to the Bedouin tribal structure in its decision regarding future locales. It mentioned two areas for three unspecified tribes with a minimum of ten kilometers between them.[159] From additional documentation, we may assume that the "tribes" were in fact the three confederations, made up of Tarabin, ʿAzazmah, and Tiyaha tribes.[160] The latter included the highest number of Bedouin who had remained in place, mainly east of Beʾer Sheva. The remaining tribes belonged to the Dhullam subconfederation,[161] along with the tribes of al-Asad and al-Aʿsam,[162] and a section of the Abu Rgayyig.[163]

Regarding land issues, the decision indicated that the tribes would be "required to make specific political commitments as well as commitments regarding their lands in accordance with the decisions to be taken by a special committee that will be established for that [purpose]."[164] The committee was to include Weitz and Hanegbi as members. No further documentation has been found regarding the commitments noted in the text. We may assume, therefore, that the Committee for Bedouin Affairs aimed to certify that the Bedouin who were allowed to return would not claim rights over the lands they had left.[165]

According to Weitz, the decisions of the Committee for Bedouin Affairs were subject to Ben-Gurion's approval. Ben-Gurion was waiting for Allon to send him a map of Bedouin sites before he engaged in further discussions on the issue.[166]

Time passed, and Ben-Gurion did not give his approval to the committee's decisions, even though their implementation had in fact already commenced.[167] At the beginning of December, Yadin reported that he had started making arrangements for the minorities' army unit and the assembling of tribes. He also asked the Ministry of Foreign Affairs to send a representative to the special committee mentioned in the Committee for Bedouin Affairs decision.[168]

Furthermore, at a meeting of the Committee Appended to the Military Administration, Elimelech Avner referred to the decision as a done deal: "The Israeli government has agreed to let three Bedouin tribes return to the Beʾer Sheva district. Within the State of Israel they will be allotted special places. To this end a special committee was appointed to deal with the issue."[169] Berdichevsky also seems to have been certain that the decision was approved and wrote to his superior that a census should be taken before establishing the Bedouin military unit.[170]

Between December 5 and 7, the IDF conducted Operation Assaf.[171] The operation diminished the threat posed by the Egyptians and the Tarabin and the fears that Beʾer Sheva would be reconquered.[172] Nevertheless, political pressures on Israel persisted. Ben-Gurion wrote in his diary that he had replied to UN representative Ralph Bunche concerning the Egyptian demand for Israeli withdrawal that "the fate of Be'er Sheva will be decided with the fate of the entire country."[173] Hostilities continued, and between December 9 and 10, armed Bedouin from the 'Azazmah tribes struck south of Nevatim.[174]

By mid-December, the prospective Bedouin locales had still not been decided. IDF intelligence officers were fearful that the number of roaming Bedouin in "our region" would increase. An order was issued to the effect that Bedouin found outside their assigned locales would be arrested and that they would be required to carry proper documents.[175]

As political and military pressure continued, between December 22 of the same year and January 7, 1949, Israel conducted Operation Horev in the southern Negev,[176] an action that was intended to back the Egyptians all the way out of the Negev toward the Sinai Peninsula and force them to begin armistice talks.[177]

Throughout this time, constant pressure was placed on Israel to accept the Gaza–Be'er Sheva–Jericho road as its southernmost border.[178] Britain was intent on maintaining its hold on the land route between the Persian Gulf and the Mediterranean Sea through the Middle East.[179] On December 29, under British pressure, Security Council Resolution 62 called on Israel to retreat to its pre–Operation Yoav lines.[180] Before the ceasefire, the IDF had captured areas in the Sinai Peninsula from which it later withdrew to the international borders.[181] Map 1.3 shows the Israeli lines and the layout of the military districts on January, 1949. It also indicates the lines of the Partition Plan.

Although there is no formal document in the archives with Ben-Gurion's approval of the Committee for Bedouin Affairs' decisions regarding the return of the Bedouin to the Negev, he was no doubt aware of it. In his January 10, 1949 diary entry, Ben-Gurion wrote that Elimelech Avner had reported that we are "returning to the Negev three tribes numbering about 9,000 people. The Tiyaha are on their way, and after them the Tarabin and part of the 'Azazmah."[182] At the January 12, 1949, meeting of the committee appended to the military administration, a decision was made to conduct a census in the Negev.[183]

A week later, Sheikh al-Huzayyil, whose tribe was encamped beyond Israeli lines in the Hebron Mountain slopes, was still waiting to "move to their intended location."[184] The armistice talks in Rhodes between Israel and Egypt, which began in late January, were finalized on February 24 with the signing of the Armistice Agreement outlining the areas of control.[185] The Negev, including Be'er Sheva, remained in Israeli hands. The agreement did not constitute a withdrawal of pending territorial claims. Hence, Egypt

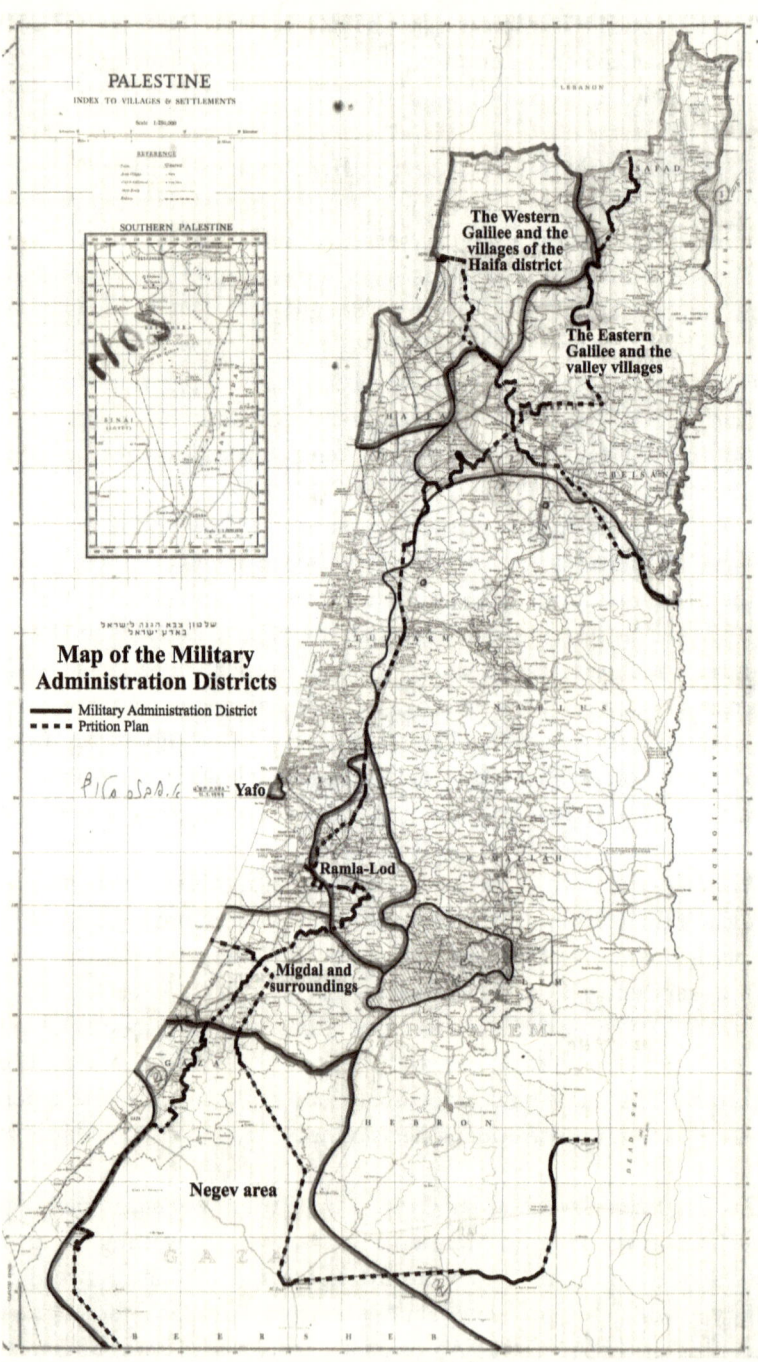

Map 1.3. Military districts and Israeli lines, as of January 11, 1949. *Source: Israel Defense Forces and Defense Establishment Archives [originally in Hebrew].*

maintained its claim to rights on the Negev including Be'er Sheva. In March, as part of Operation Uvda (meaning "fact on the ground"), Israel captured the southern Negev as far as Eilat as well as the southern slopes of Mount Hebron where many of the Bedouin had moved (and which today includes the Bedouin towns of Lagiyyah, Hurah, Makhul, and Drijat).[186]

The number of Bedouin remaining in their prewar locales was not entirely clear but amounted to approximately 4,000.[187] Some 9,500 Bedouin were allowed to return in the first wave, "their status regularized by the issue of identity cards and ration cards."[188] The flow of requests from the tribes to receive Israeli aegis continued during the first months of 1949.[189] A second wave of 3,000 Bedouin was allowed to return "in this way."[190]

According to a report of the Ministry of Minorities, from March to June 1949, "in the vicinity of Be'er Sheva, east and south-west of it, there are Bedouin tribes numbering 13–15 thousand people, who want Israeli rule. ... They have pledged not to disperse and are willing to guard the current Negev borders against invaders."[191]

In a Ministry of Foreign Affairs letter dated October 6, 1950, it was reported that after the Armistice Agreement with Egypt the total number of legal "Israeli Bedouin" had reached 17,500.[192] Those Bedouin who had cooperated with the Egyptians, mainly from the 'Azazmah and the Tarabin tribes, were considered enemies and were not granted Israeli aegis.[193]

Discussion and Conclusions

The alliances chosen by the Bedouin largely determined their postwar situations. A wide divergence existed in their relations with the Israeli side of the conflict, from a spirit of cooperation to fierce hostility. There were tribes who maintained good relations with the Jews of the Negev throughout the fighting while others attacked the Jewish settlements and participated in the assaults of the Arab armies. Bedouin leaders took a stand as independent negotiators and decision-making units. Israel drew distinctions between different Bedouin tribes and between Bedouin tribes and other Arab groups. These findings contradict 'Aref al-'Aref's account of Bedouin unity and his claim that "though there may have been a few individual outliers, there is no truth to statements about the Bedouin having spied for the Jews."[194]

At the end of the war, there were voices for and against the Bedouin tribes on the Israeli side. Weitz, for one, was of the view that they should be treated like the rest of the Arabs. Shimoni acknowledged the diversity of the tribes but preferred to exclude them while the treaties were still under negotiation. However, Ben-Gurion's dominant view at the state level and Hanegbi's at the local level was that a pact with the Bedouin tribes was not only morally just but also beneficial for Israel. The two main reasons for this involved Israel's security needs and its political agenda. The Bedouin were seen as able to contribute to Israel's security through their enlistment in a special Bedouin unit to fight enemy forces, including hostile Bedouin tribes. The second reason was the main one as far as Hanegbi was concerned, even though Ben-Gurion had explicitly invalidated it.[195] Forming such an alliance with the Bedouin would show the world that the inhabitants of the Negev preferred the Israeli aegis and would reinforce Israel's position vis-à-vis international demands, mainly from the Egyptians and the British, for Israel's withdrawal. Such an alliance was possible due to the character of Bedouin tribalism and the powers of the sheikhs. All tribes and their leaders were regarded as independent units in terms of decision-making and negotiations. They were free to form their own alliances according to their individual perceptions, relative strengths, and agreements with other tribes and their assessments of the outcome of the war, although some of them switched alliances.

Another factor that affected them further was the tendency to communicate with sheikhs on behalf of their tribe. This pattern continued and would bedevil the relations between Jews and Bedouin once becoming individual citizens.

For those tribes that chose to ally themselves with Israel and were considered friendly, the war resulted in a mutually beneficial alliance. In the context of the events of the war, *beneficial alliances* should be viewed as a relative term. The situation of the returnee tribes was conditioned on and included restrictions, yet they fared much better than the majority of tribes that had allied themselves with Israel's enemies. It was a deviation from Israel's general policy to avoid discussing the return of the Arab refugees until peace agreements could be reached.

The allied Bedouin tribes under the military administration were compelled to live in designated areas. In the following chapter, we shall focus on the deliberations over Bedouin locales that began with the end of the fighting.

2

CREATION OF THE MILITARY REGIME
Nominated Sheikhs and Tribal Units, 1949–56

> Moving them [the Bedouin] to a mountainous area, without water and connection would mean leaving them in their current state without a systematic solution.
>
> *Michael Hanegbi, Committee for Refugee Affairs, September 1, 1949*

Israel's Declaration of Independence, accepted on May 15, 1948, guarantees complete equality of rights and freedoms for all citizens of Israel. Even so, those rights were not granted to the Arabs when the war ended, and the new state faced challenges after the war proved overwhelming. First and foremost, Israeli leadership feared that the local Arab minority would join forces with the enemy in future rounds initiated by neighboring countries to annihilate the Jewish state. The two poles—Israel's view of the Arabs within its borders as a security risk as opposed to its democratic ethos—played a central role in the country's political deliberations. During the first eighteen years of the state, security considerations took precedence over liberal policies, and a military administration was imposed on the Arab population of Israel, which suspended many of their political and civil rights.[1]

Although the military administration has been the subject of a great deal of scholarly writing, the specific characteristics of its policies toward the Bedouin have attracted much less attention.[2] Many studies have viewed its policies in terms of the Jewish-Arab conflict and as a means of negating Arab rights.[3] This perspective is too narrow. The policy of the military administration toward the Negev Bedouin was tailored to specific features of Bedouin life in the region, as perceived by the authorities. In many respects, it followed the policies of its mandatory predecessor, which were also tailor-made.[4] Studies have also drawn attention to the partisan politics in the military administration, such as the recruitment of Arab votes for the ruling party of the day, Mapai (the Workers' Party of Eretz Israel).[5] This factor was less applicable to the Negev region, at least during the early years when the military governor was a member of a kibbutz affiliated with the left-wing opposition party, Mapam (United Workers Party).[6]

The Aftermath of the Arab-Israeli War and the Formation of the Military Administration

The Arab-Israeli war ended in victory for Israel, but the fledgling state could not rest on its laurels. Having suffered thousands of casualties and massive destruction, Israel was in dire need of investments. With the heavy influx of Holocaust survivors, including those released from the British camps in Cyprus, and a multitude of Jewish refugees who fled from Arab lands and usually arrived without resources, the state was compelled to adopt food rationing and other austerity measures (see fig. 2.1).

The state needed every piece of arable land from which food could be produced in the western Negev. To provide waves of immigrants with accommodations, it had to build numerous absorption centers or transit camps (*ma'abarot*) to shelter the Jewish immigrants (*olim*). Conditions were extremely harsh, and it was years before the olim could be moved from their tents or tin huts and the ma'abarot could at last be dismantled.[7]

Meanwhile, Israel continued to face security challenges due to the reluctance of the Arabs to concede Israel's victory. Along the Israeli frontier and border regions, life was under constant threat from *fedayeen* and other infiltrators.[8]

For the local Arabs, the outcome was even worse. Their leadership had fled, and they too had suffered many casualties and extensive destruction to their settlements. Most of the Bedouin became refugees, prohibited from returning to their former homes, unlike the friendly Bedouin tribes who were allowed back. Arabs who had never left or had been allowed to return were placed under the jurisdiction of the military administration declared by the Provisional Government in 1948. The military administration was based on the British Defense (Emergency) Regulations of 1945, which were incorporated into Israeli legislation.[9]

These regulations granted extensive powers to restrict freedom of movement and other rights such as due process. Its stated rationale was that Arabs in Israel who did not accept the sovereignty of the new state or participate in its society were liable to engage in fifth-column activities. Another security issue was the infiltration of Arab refugees and fedayeen.[10] In 1950, the military administration formed a system of supervision and control over three main areas inhabited by Arabs and Bedouin tribes: the Galilee in the north,

Figure 2.1. Bedouin collecting food rations in Be'er Sheva, June 1, 1949. *Source: The Government Press Office.*

the Middle in the easternmost boundaries of the central district, and the Negev in the south, each headed by a military governor. Map 2.1 shows the military administration zones as of February 28, 1951.

Although the governors operated under the same formal framework and received their instructions from headquarters, they were granted broad discretion in determining their own policies (see fig. 2.2).[11]

In addition to security concerns, the military administration was responsible for the everyday life of the inhabitants of the restricted zones under its jurisdiction.[12] Although many of the needed resources were provided by other ministries, they were supervised and coordinated by the military administration. Education and health services and even food supplies were dispensed in proximity to military administration agencies.[13] In addition, the military administration controlled the permits in and out of its zones and was empowered to approve or reject work permits, formally the task of the labor office.[14] While acting within the same official framework, the precise nature and effect of the military administration on individuals subordinated to it were largely determined by the governor of each zone.

Among other authorities involved in the lives of the Arabs, the most active ones with regard to the Negev Bedouin during the period under discussion were the IDF Southern Command, the intelligence units of the Israeli

Creation of the Military Regime 57

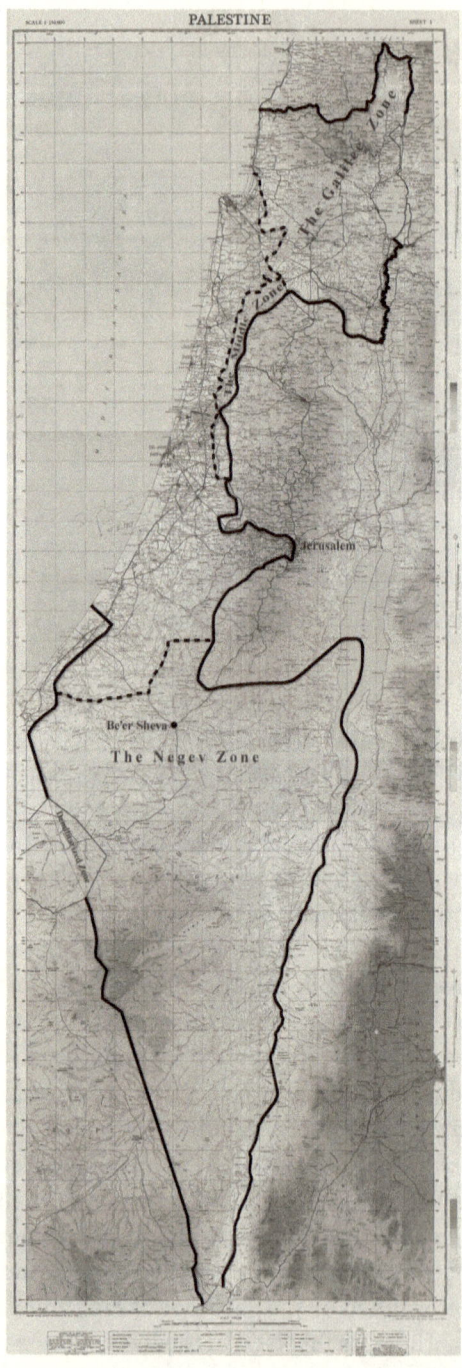

Map 2.1. Military administration zones as of February 28, 1951. *Source: Israel Defense Forces and Defense Establishment Archives [originally in Hebrew].*

Figure 2.2. Bedouin and a military policeman, February 2, 1950. *Photo: Cohen Fritz. Source: The Government Press Office.*

Security Agency, the prime minister's adviser for Arab affairs, the Ministry of Agriculture, and, as of 1950, the Development Authority.[15]

THE BEDOUIN AS INDIVIDUAL FARMERS ON MOSHAVIM

As for the standing of the Negev, Israel was successful in its military control of the region and even extended its borders beyond the Partition Plan, notwithstanding several disturbing issues. Egypt, hoping to regain a hold in the Negev, encouraged the constant looting, smuggling, and infiltration of an ever-growing number of fedayeen.[16] The Jewish population of the Negev was in dire social and economic straits after months of intense attacks and battles with hostile forces. Some of the Jewish settlements were completely destroyed, and several, including Beit Eshel, Alumim, and Ramat Negev, were permanently abandoned.[17]

The situation of the Negev Bedouin tribes was also extremely difficult. The time had come to discuss a settlement policy for the several thousand Bedouin who remained in place and those that Israel allowed to return.[18]

In late January 1949, Yigal Allon, operational commander of the Southern Command; Asa'el Zuckerman, military governor of Migdal Gad;[19] Michael Hanegbi, military governor of the Negev; and other officers together with Weitz, who was highly involved in settlement issues, arrived at an understanding that it would be prudent to move the Bedouin eastward.[20] Although reasons for this decision were not given, we may surmise that it was intended to distance the Bedouin from the borders with Egypt and Gaza, which were a source of unrest. The Egyptians continued to lay territorial claim to the Negev while soliciting Bedouin tribes to provide them with intelligence on IDF movements. Moreover, the Bedouin hid infiltrators and fedayeen in their encampments. In addition, certain lands used inefficiently by the Bedouin, particularly in the western areas, were suitable for intensive cultivation and sorely needed for food production. Land was also necessary for development and for the settlement of olim so as to ensure Israeli rule in the Negev.[21]

According to available documentation, the first comprehensive deliberations over the future of Bedouin settlement were conducted within the Committee for Refugee Affairs. This state-level committee was launched after the war at Weitz's initiative to address Arab refugee issues. He was joined in this task by Zalman Lif, adviser on land issues at the Prime Minister's Office, and Ezra Danin, adviser on Arab affairs at the Ministry of Foreign Affairs, who submitted several joint reports to Ben-Gurion on abandoned properties and their legal status and proposed the establishment of a development authority to administrate them. In September and October 1949, the committee held three meetings with several invited officials including Hanegbi in attendance, to discuss Negev Bedouin concerns.

The two main proposals brought forth by Hanegbi and Weitz concerned the future of the Negev Bedouin after the war and in times to come. Both proposals included privileges resembling those granted to the Israeli agricultural cooperatives, the *moshavim*, with individually owned farms, each with a plot of land of fixed size. According to data provided by Hanegbi, the Bedouin numbered about 3,500 families, 16,000 to 18,000 people in all, temporarily settled within three confederations—the Tarabin in the western Negev between two kibbutzim, Hatzerim and Tze'elim; the 'Azazmah, south of Be'er Sheva between Halutza and Alumim; and the Tiyahas, spread over an area of half a million dunams in the northeastern Negev around Khuweilfah, Shoval, and Nevatim. Hanegbi explained that some of these Bedouin were infiltrators, that their locations were temporary, and that they had already been moved several times.[22]

During the discussion, Hanegbi and Weitz presented two basically similar options for their declared aims: settling Bedouin communities in different locations as agricultural villages. Hanegbi suggested establishing twelve to fifteen of these with some 230 to 300 villagers in each, all in the western Negev, near the water pipeline and surrounded by Jewish settlements. According to this plan, each family would be allotted a farm unit, which would include a house, arable land, equipment, and water rights for irrigating crops. The size of each unit would not exceed three hundred dunams, in accordance with its soil quality and specific location.[23]

Underlying Hanegbi's proposal was the notion that the Bedouin had no ownership rights to the land, as evident from his statement that "among the Bedouin there is no sooner or later in terms of rights as in the Galilee and plans can be carried out in stages."[24] According to the prevailing land laws, it was possible, in time and under certain conditions, for possessors to gain ownership rights of Miri lands, as was the case in the Galilee region. Hanegbi was of the opinion that the lands in the Negev were not Miri lands and therefore could not be subject to these rules.[25]

The other proposal, made by Weitz, was that an estimated 500 Bedouin families would refuse to live in permanent villages and hence would leave Israel. Ten villages would be located east of Be'er Sheva, in an area covering 600,000 dunams of arable land, each village accommodating 250 families. Out of these families, 200 would be involved in cultivation and receive about 300 dunams each, and the remaining 50 would work in services. In addition, four or five smaller villages would be developed in the western Negev, each accommodating about a hundred families who would all receive five dunams of irrigated land.[26]

Weitz justified the proposed location by arguing that the eastern Negev is mountainous and therefore difficult to irrigate and unsuitable for the "self-indulgent Jews" who had so deeply disappointed him by abandoning their Negev settlements. Three months earlier, in a discussion with Allon, the latter noted the necessity to establish new Jewish settlements in the Negev, and Weitz commented, "Salt you sow on my wounds! And where are the people? Where are the soldiers who willingly agree to settle in the Negev?"[27]

It should also be noted that the eastern Negev was the area in which most of the Bedouin had remained during the war and where the majority of them lived at the time.

Both proposals aimed to transform the Bedouin from pastoral nomads into members of settled communities of nuclear families working in agriculture. Hanegbi envisioned their full transition to a livelihood that would be based, like that of the fellahin, solely on irrigated crops. Weitz adhered in principle to Hanegbi's proposal but for practical reasons consented to allow them some measure of pasturing. This displeased Hanegbi, who feared it would jeopardize the desired social and economic changes and noted that "moving them [the Bedouin] to a mountainous area, without water and connection would mean leaving them in their current state without a systematic solution."[28] Nevertheless, he added, "It would be impossible just to order the Bedouin to live in settlements."[29] In his view, a policy that involved confrontations with the Bedouin was simply unfeasible.

The abovementioned meeting was the last documented occasion in which Hanegbi argued in favor of individualization and permanent settlements for the Bedouin. From then on, and throughout most of his term as military governor, he promoted a policy of tribal frameworks for the Bedouin as opposed to their reorganization as village fellahin.

The committee met again a few times and determined a process of land allocation to the Bedouin through the submission of individual forms, which followed the previous understanding that lands would not be distributed in the western Negev.[30] While the second part of this decision was later implemented, the first part was not.[31] The idea of individual applications was utterly new to the Bedouin, to whom land had always been granted collectively via their sheikhs. Individual Bedouin who had never been in direct contact with the authorities as well as their sheikhs were not pleased with the idea either.[32] Such allocations were supposed to be carried out jointly by the Negev Military Administration and local representatives of the Ministry of Agriculture. However, the locals found reasons to postpone the full implementation of individual allocations by raising technical obstacles. Whether these reasons were genuine or not, the outcome was that the bulk of the landholdings continued to be allocated via the sheikhs.[33]

Another issue that was formally determined at a state level was landownership. Lif, a committee member, when asked by the custodian of absentee property why he had not been included in the process of allocating Negev lands, answered that the government's position on the Bedouin did not comprehend their ownership rights:

> The government sees the entirety of all the Negev land as state land for which no one—including Bedouin who lived there—has or had the right of possession to the land....
>
> The Mandate Government as well did not recognize this possession as ascribing to the holder's ownership of the type of 'Miri'....
>
> There is no support for the notion that the land was granted to them by the Ottoman regime according to law and therefore they did not and do not belong to them. Even if here and there facts of possession were created, they are not sufficient to detract from ownership by the government to which and only to which belongs the land in this region.[34]

In an inquiry conducted by Hanegbi, the Bedouin sheikhs had claimed ownership of about half a million dunams of land, 40 percent of them in areas they were not allowed to cultivate. Hanegbi added his opinion that such claims were exaggerated and surely included absentee property.[35] Lif's position, like Hanegbi's earlier statement, contradicted the Bedouin perception of landownership. However, there is no indication that Hanegbi took active measures to enforce state ownership rights in the years that followed.

THE MILITARY ADMINISTRATION IN THE NEGEV

As we have seen, local and state-level decision-makers agreed in 1949 that the Bedouin would be settled as cultivators of state lands and rejected their claims to private ownership. No subsequent state-level discussions were held, however, and no resources of any kind were allocated to promote the implementation of this policy. The only prominent nonmilitary figure who expressed interest in Bedouin settlements was Weitz of the JNF. Although highly influential, Weitz was not a member of the government, and his efforts were unproductive. As he noted in his diary, discussions about the Bedouin "go on and on and lead nowhere."[36] By the end of 1949, no government guidance had been given to frame a comprehensive Bedouin policy. It was left to Hanegbi to determine an appropriate way of administering the Bedouin. For this mission, he received only a few officers and very limited resources.[37]

In January 1950, at a coordinating meeting, Hanegbi shared his view that the temporality and lack of a clear aim with regard to the Bedouin was "a difficult problem in terms of the stabilization of rule in the region."[38]

The Negev Military Administration held agencies in several locations: Tel Malhata (Tall al-Malih) for the tribes of the east, mainly the Dhullam subconfederation; one in Umm Batin for nearby tribes, including Abu Rgayyig; one near Shoval, mainly for the al-Huzayyils; and a southern one for the ʿAzazmah and Tarabin tribes.[39] Map 2.2 presents the agencies of the Negev Military Administration and indicates the locations of tribal centers, where the tents of the sheikhs were located.

Hanegbi framed his policy according to three main dimensions: the territorial dimension—that is, the creation of a territory restricted to Bedouin tribes; the social dimension, through the formation of eighteen so-called "tribal units," each headed by an authorized sheikh; and the legal dimension, using tribal courts to settle disputes and minor offenses according to Bedouin norms. I shall discuss these gradually developed dimensions in a chronological context.

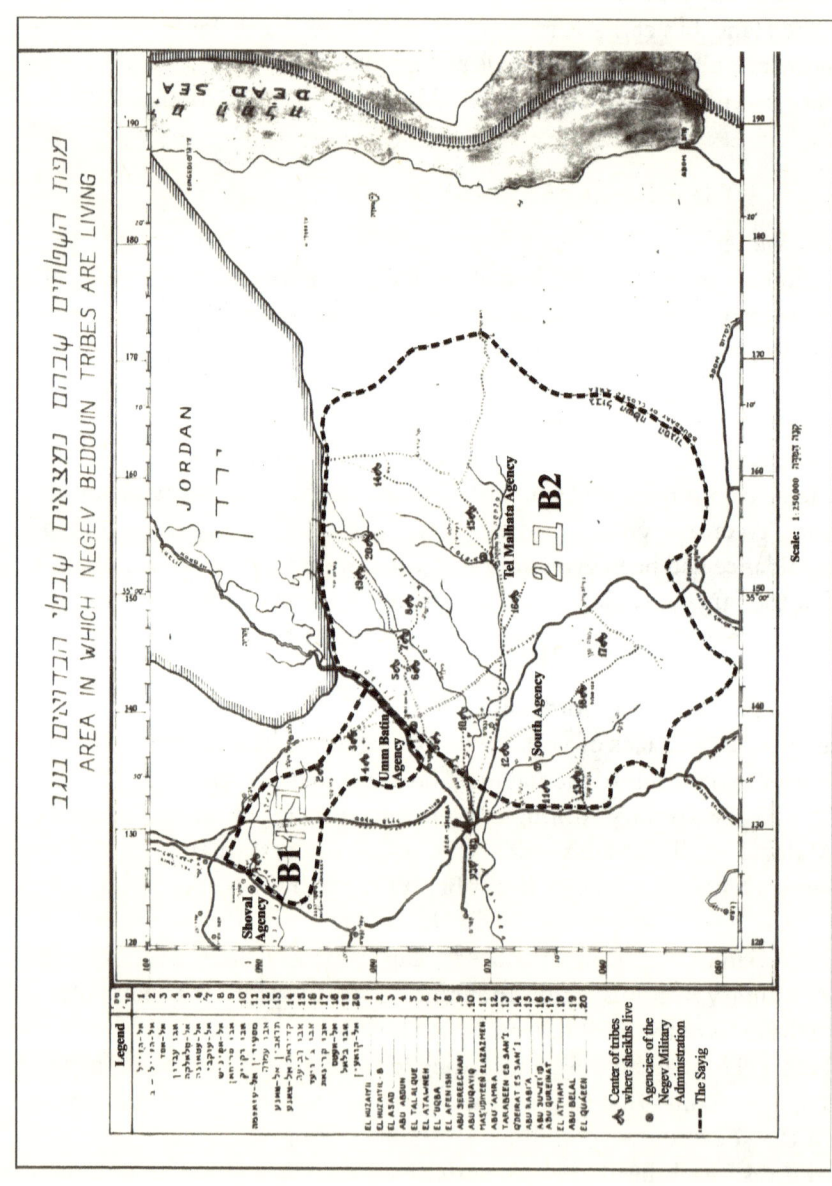

Map 2.2. Agencies of the Negev Military Administration and locations of tribal centers. Ben Assa Archive [legend was extended].

The Creation of Restricted Bedouin Territory

As explained, after the war, most of the Bedouin encampments were in the northern and eastern Negev while the tribes of the Tarabin and the ʿAzazmah confederations were located east and south of Be'er Sheva. In May 1950, a meeting and a tour of the areas were held to address Bedouin issues. Weitz repeated his proposal for settling the Bedouin in the eastern Negev and made a note in his diary to schedule a meeting with Ben-Gurion, probably to ask for his approval.[40] Although there is no indication that such a meeting ever took place, the Negev Military Administration invested great efforts in the following months to move the Bedouin eastward to a designated area, ten to fifteen kilometers from Be'er Sheva.[41] This area of approximately 1.1 million dunams (271,816 acres) would be later known as the Sayig, meaning "fence" in Hebrew. The Sayig was divided into two sections: B1, the smaller area, located west of the Be'er Sheva-Hebron Road, and B2, the larger, where the majority of the Bedouin population lived, east of the Be'er Sheva-Hebron Road (see B1 and B2 in map 2.2). In the Sayig region, each tribe received a specific site for its encampment and land to use for grazing or cultivation. However, no measures of any sort were taken to establish a permanent settlement.

During this relocation process, many Bedouin were assigned territory previously used by other tribes. Both those who moved in and those who had remained but were now called upon to absorb others into an area formerly under their control felt uneasy in the new situation. This seemed to be token unrest; no fighting ensued.

According to the available documentation, the move eastward involved lengthy negotiations between the Negev Military Administration and the Bedouin sheikhs. Mapam queried the Knesset on the forced evacuation of the Bedouin, and Ben-Gurion replied that on October 17 the sheikhs of three tribes had signed an agreement to move eastward in return for financial compensation. He noted further that the sheikhs had chosen their new locations, and that the government had plowed their lands and filled the cisterns with water. He also explained that the move had been necessary because the three tribes previously inhabited lands at the juncture of the smuggling routes between Gaza and Hebron.[42] Hanegbi's report of November 1951 elaborated on his negotiations with the sheikhs of three tribes numbering over a thousand people, who were promised large sums of money and lands in return for their move to the east.[43] It is unclear whether the sheikhs ever distributed this money among members of their tribe.

Not all the Bedouin accepted the new terms. A substantial number of them chose to emigrate from Israel for various reasons: a reluctance to move east, Israel's restrictions on wandering, or a desire to reunite with kinfolk in Jordan and to benefit from the UN distribution of free food there. They departed with all their belongings, herds, and provisions and the funds they had received from Israel. Between March and April 1951, Hanegbi reported that about one thousand Bedouin had immigrated to Jordan and that the Jordanians had welcomed them. Overall, between 1950 and 1951, some eight thousand Bedouin left the Negev.[44]

In 1952, Sheikh Ibrahim a-Sane' publicly refused to relocate eastward to the Arad Valley and made it known that he preferred to emigrate to Jordan with his tribe.[45] The Jordanians had welcomed newcomers informally but shrank from the publicity that might imply collaboration with Israel. Once the issue became public, Jordan submitted an international protest to the UN. The sheikh and his tribe waited at the Israeli-Jordanian border but were forced to return to Israel, where they received the allocated territory near Arad.[46]

In 1954, the Negev Military Administration was ordered to change the boundaries of the Sayig, eliminate B1, and relocate all the Bedouin who lived in the vicinity to B2, particularly the al-Huzayyil tribe, with whom members of Kibbutz Shoval had a special relationship. Mapam strongly opposed this action, and as a result of their parliamentary question, the idea was shelved.[47]

The Formation of Tribal Units and Their Leadership

The war had left some tribes as functioning entities and others with a very small base of people. Though tribalism was alien to the Israeli system, the Negev Military Administration found it expedient either to organize all the remaining Bedouin as multi-tribal units or to annex them to other tribes. Archival documents attest that some Bedouin clans asked to become affiliated with specific tribes or to change their affiliation.[48]

For these groups, the term *tribe* was artificial and somewhat misleading, since they were not related by blood or intrinsic affiliation. However, the definition had become a procedural component of the Negev Military Administration, and they were referred to as such in all documentation. The term *tribe* was used as the main designation in all Bedouin documents including identity cards and formal addresses. In 1951, the authorities recognized the existence of eighteen such tribes in this manner.[49]

Each tribal unit, whether original or not, was headed by a sheikh, generally one who had remained in the country during the war; if a former sheikh had departed, a new, lower-ranking sheikh was appointed in his place.[50] A sheikh had to be approved by the Negev Military Administration, from whom he derived his authority.

According to the sociologist and anthropologist Emanuel Marx, the Negev Military Administration easily adapted to the traditional tribal framework and refrained from interfering in the Bedouin's choice of a new sheikh in the belief that tribal dynamics would lead to the selection of the most acceptable person.[51] Hence, in cases when a sheikh died, the Negev Military Administration preferred to go along with the choice of the tribe. Marx explained further that the Bedouin found this a useful, less restrictive arrangement since they could leave it to their sheikhs to negotiate with the Negev Military Administration and carry out their oral instructions to the best of their understanding.[52] Sometimes a tribe would request a different choice, as when the al-'Ugbi tribe asked the military governor to replace their sheikh, who was known to be involved in unlawful activities.[53]

On May 2, 1950, an important event took place at the encampment of Sheikh al-Huzayyil, attended by Chief of Staff Yigael Yadin along with Commander of the Southern Command Moshe Dayan and others, and several sheikhs from the Tiyaha confederation. The sheikhs welcomed them all with great ceremony and declared their loyalty and willingness to protect Israel against the surrounding Arab states (see photos from the events in figs. 2.3 and 2.4). The sheikhs then petitioned for the right to maintain their tribal traditions, referring to the rights they had received under the mandate and requesting a fixed salary according to the number of their respective tribe members,[54] thus joining the appeal twelve Bedouin sheikhs had submitted a few days earlier.[55]

Indeed, the sheikhs were gradually given extensive powers and privileges as well as duties and responsibilities for all tribal members and territories deployed by the tribe. The sheikhs were charged with the distribution of allocated lands, food rationing in times of austerity and drought, franchising tribal markets, registering birth and death records, granting documents necessary for the acquisition of entry and exit permits, and handling employment lists. They were the sole address for their tribesmen's mail and were likewise charged with maintaining the peace, reporting crimes, and surrendering suspects.[56] An example of these duties was a call issued by the Negev Military Administration on October 11, 1951 to the sheikhs of the Dhullam subconfederation "to order all those in their tribes without IDs to leave the country within a week," otherwise "they would be personally considered responsible for accommodating infiltrators."[57] The sheikhs were issued formal seals and were permitted to bear arms (see fig. 2.5).

The position of the sheikhs with the Negev Military Administration, as historical geographer Joseph Ben-David explains, was mutually beneficial to the Bedouin, who needed help in mediating interactions with the authorities. Most Bedouin did not speak Hebrew and had no experience with Israeli bureaucracy. Some were also illiterate. The sheikhs became

Figure 2.3. al-Huzayyil's reception ceremony for Moshe Dayan and Yigael Yadin. May 5, 1950. *Source: The Government Press Office.*

Figure 2.4. Sheikh Salman al-Huzayyil, Moshe Dayan, and Yigael Yadin. May 5, 1950. *Source: The Government Press Office.*

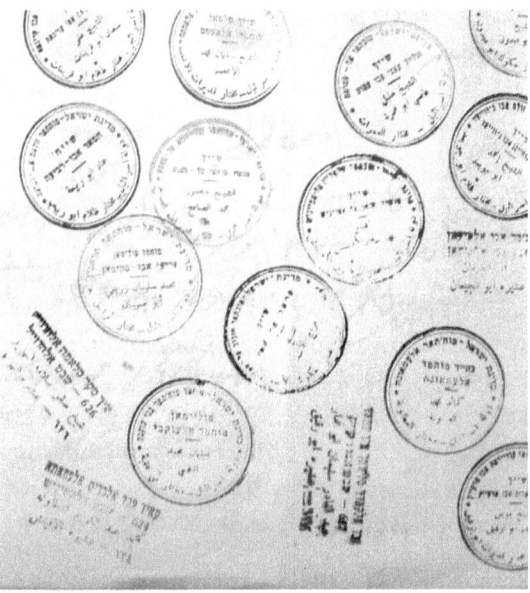

Figure 2.5. Sheikhs' formal stamps. *Source: file 17006/13, Israel State Archives.*

advocates with the power to obtain relief and assistance from the military administration.[58]

Tribal Court

Another mechanism officially authorized by the Negev Military Administration was the Bedouin Court, referred to generally as tribal court. Bedouin tribal courts had gained authorization under the British Mandate to settle disputes and implement tribal norms.[59] The Negev Military Administration saw fit to continue the work of tribal courts under the auspices of the military governor. In 1951, several tribal courts in the region were operational, but Negev Military Administration officers decided to limit them to a single tribal court at the Umm Batin agency. The rotational bench of Bedouin judges was established with the approval of the governor and one Negev Military Administration representative.[60] Tribal court powers were limited. They could impose fines and up to three months of imprisonment. Because there were no prisons in the area, most sentencing ended with fines and conciliations. Hanegbi reported that "the Bedouin fears and respects more the Bedouin court [tribal court] than the Magistrate court."[61]

However, the tribal courts lacked true legal jurisdiction.[62] It was not until 1955 that the Ministry of Justice formally approved their existence, and this

Creation of the Military Regime 69

was only as a result of mounting pressure. This reluctance was due to the fact that even though the tribal court was limited in scope, it implemented tribal norms as a binding system, not only in civil matters but also in cases of minor criminal offenses, without due process and with no clear appeal jurisdiction. Such a system contradicted the basis of the liberal democratic state.[63]

When it served the Negev Military Administration's purposes, other aspects of tribal relations came into play, such as the use of local tribes as a barrier against hostile tribes that infiltrated mainly near the Israeli-Egypt border, and to a lesser extent the Sayig region of the eastern Negev.[64]

In March 1954, a terrorist group led by a Bedouin of the ʿAzazmah who infiltrated from Jordan attacked a bus in Maʾale Akrabim in the Negev, killing eleven passengers and injuring five more. The Bedouin were prevented from free entry to the Beʾer Sheva market for several months after the attack. An appeal to the UN for sanctions against Jordan was rejected. The attack was linked to a group called the Black Hand, dominated by Bedouin from the ʿAzazmah and Tarabin tribes near the Israeli-Egypt border, mainly in the Auja demilitarized zone, who engaged in hostilities against Israelis and Bedouin and other Arabs suspected of being Israeli informants.[65]

Visionary Agrarian Reform

Although the Negev Military Administration accommodated tribalism at the local level, bureaucrats at the state level declared the opposite in the press and in Knesset committees. An article from June 1953, published in the Mapai-related newspaper *Davar*, called for a change in the organizational framework of the Bedouin and the curtailment of the power of the sheikhs in order to "free the tribes from feudal control."[66] The article also claimed that once the Bedouin were settled and received a fixed allotment of land for each family unit, they would become free and independent farmers working in irrigated agriculture.[67] It further alleged that while the sheikhs shouted that the Bedouin were "dying of hunger," they amassed vast quantities of seed in their warehouses, which found their way to the black market.[68] Another article in *Davar* some months later was titled "Sheikh Exploits His Tribe."[69] The sense of exploitation is evident in this verse recorded from an oral Bedouin poem:

> The goatherd's future is surrender / You spend your nights without sleep.
> Much trouble in your search for grazing / Woe unto you if you do not find water today.
> On Saturday the sheikh will come to you / And you will have to slip him some cash right away.[70]

In June 1954, during a Knesset committee discussion about absentee property, Reuven Aloni, head of the Land Department in the Ministry of Agriculture, called for the abolition of the tribal system within a comprehensive agrarian reform, with the following rationale:

> In the Negev, unfortunately, persisting [among the Bedouin] the system of the sheikhs, who get a specific percentage of the crops. We are going to change that system and stop their Bedouin [way of life], and in this way protect the rights of the Bedouin farmer. If we will succeed in allotting land [directly?] to the Bedouin, and the Ministry of Agriculture helps them with the distribution of seed etc., by that the Bedouin will be released from his dependence on the sheikh. I hope that this problem will be resolved. It is clear that this cannot be achieved immediately, as the recognition of their rights is a very difficult problem.[71]

Furthermore, Mordechai Shatner, the custodian of absentee property and director of the Development Authority, gave a speech in 1954 pointing out the advantages of the newly passed Land Acquisition Law (Validation of Acts and Compensation 5713–1953).[72] He noted that this legislation would promote agrarian reform for the thirteen thousand Bedouin of the Negev and enable their settlement in new villages with sufficient land and water for their livelihood.[73]

The Intelligence Division of the IDF, which probably received its information from local officers in the Negev Military Administration, did not consider these statements applicable. An Intelligence booklet issued in 1954 explained that the Bedouin had no special desire for permanent settlement, quoting an illustrative Bedouin proverb: "Allah be praised for fellahin who become Bedouin but not for Bedouin who become fellahin."[74]

The differences between the Negev Military Administration and those who associated with state-level officials grew even more pronounced when Yoav Zuckerman became involved in Bedouin issues. Zuckerman, a land expert, had previous dealings with the Bedouin in the course of his work as a JNF agent in the Negev. He was appointed by Shatner to a subcommittee of three to help finalize Bedouin land issues within the Land Acquisition Law.[75] The other two members were Svardalov from the Ministry of Agriculture and Joshua Verbin, who had been appointed military governor of the Negev in 1953. The subcommittee's role was broad: to offer advice on land rights, compensation, permanent settlement of the Bedouin, housing, and water "if the tribes themselves wish it."[76] Zuckerman started to conduct a survey and collect claims from Bedouin all over the Negev, not merely in the areas expropriated in the Land Acquisition Law.[77] Disagreements and confrontations soon arose between Verbin and Zuckerman. Zuckerman understood the subcommittee's mandate as a means of linking the solution of landownership with a permanent settlement. Verbin was displeased with Zuckerman's interpretation.

Their first major clash occurred when Verbin demanded the limitation of Bedouin land grants to the B2 area. Zuckerman objected. Their relations further deteriorated during the months that followed. Verbin claimed that Zuckerman's activities interfered with the work of the Negev Military Administration and wrote a formal letter criticizing Zuckerman for his failure to coordinate, thus "creating obstacles."[78] Another clash occurred in November 1954, when Zuckerman convened a meeting to discuss the planning of a model Bedouin village. As far as he was concerned, planning of this kind was an integral part of their mandate. However, Verbin completely opposed the initiative and argued that Zuckerman had no authorization to deal with the matter.[79]

The need to decide on land policy was brought to the tables of Shatner and Aloni. At a meeting with the subcommittee in January 1955, Zuckerman complained that without clear instructions he could not promote negotiations with the Bedouin. Aloni and Shatner backed him in this and the linkage between landownership claims and permanent Bedouin settlements. Aloni said that during five years of regression, "each tribe has taken over and possessed certain areas. Even within the tribes there is no just distribution." Shatner explained that in terms of Bedouin settlement issues they would be willing to revise and reduce the proof required according to the Acquisition Law.[80] It was decided to let Zuckerman continue with his collection of Bedouin claims.

And indeed, Zuckerman continued his work, and at the next meeting with Shatner and Aloni he provided full details of all the Bedouin claims he had collected. This included 558 claims to an area of some 300,000 dunams.[81] He repeated his request to determine the terms of compensation for each Bedouin family, without which he could not promote the negotiations.[82] Shatner backed his request and stressed the importance of determining "the right of every individual and not just the tribe as a whole."[83] Aloni also backed him and suggested a compensation formula.[84] Nevertheless, the matter of Bedouin claims was not finalized.

Although the subcommittee continued to meet in 1955, according to Verbin, their work lacked "any practical content" and did not operate along "right and effective lines."[85] Soon after, Zuckerman quit the subcommittee and never returned to work on the matter.[86]

SHEIKHS BECOMING A SOURCE OF CONCERN

In the fall of 1956, the 1950 decision to lease land directly to the tribesmen had not been fully implemented, and lands were still allocated via the sheikhs, who were allowed to sign contracts on behalf of their tribesmen.[87] After Zukerman's withdrawal, the Negev Military Administration continued to operate via the sheikhs with minimal interference from civilian bureaucrats.

The new subcommittee members were less antagonistic toward the Negev Military Administration and agreed they should restrict their work to the expropriated lands according to the Acquisition Law.[88] However, two circumstances were causes of concern for the pro-tribal policy of the Negev Military Administration: the Ratner Committee and the security crises that preceded the Sinai Campaign.

By the end of 1955, the future of the military administration in Israel was in doubt. Left-wing parties argued in the press and at the Knesset that the military administration should be terminated for practical as well as moral reasons: it promoted hatred and detachment from the state among the Arabs, and it went against Israeli commitments and values as a liberal and democratic state.[89] These claims were not new, but due to political coalition considerations, Ben-Gurion now agreed to nominate a committee of civilians to evaluate the legitimacy of maintaining the military administration.[90] The committee was headed by Yohanan Ratner, a professor of architecture at the Technion and previously a high-profile member of the Hagana and the retired head of the planning department at the IDF General Staff. The Ratner Committee heard testimonies from some ninety Bedouin, military administration employees, and members of the public.

Verbin was among those who testified. He stressed the crucial need to maintain the military administration and detailed the security risks to the Negev from infiltration, espionage, and collaboration with the enemy. Only the military administration, he argued, had the capacity to provide the kind of coordination needed to handle these issues. He calculated the amount of manpower that would be required for this, laid out the complexities involved, and discussed the characteristics of "Bedouin mentality."[91] The Bedouin had no wish to change their way of life, he explained, and traditionally held centralized governments in contempt. Meir Amit, deputy head of the military administration, also testified. When asked about regulating the power of the sheikhs, Amit agreed that notwithstanding socialist considerations and the justness of allotting land directly to cultivators rather than via sheikhs, the existing system allowed for more control and supervision of the tribes.[92]

The Ratner committee meeting took place at a time when the security situation in the Negev was going from bad to worse. Secret talks between Egypt and Israel had recently failed, and Egypt still opposed Israeli control of the Negev and, in 1955, gained the support of the United States and Great Britain.[93] During the second half of 1955, the Egyptians initiated a growing number of border incidents and sent fedayeen into the country on sabotage and asset recruiting missions. To combat more fedayeen attacks, Israel established Unit 101, headed by Ariel Sharon, tasked with "reprisal operations."[94] The reprisal policy, however, did not prove helpful in halting the deterioration in the security situation.

Some of the Bedouin allied themselves with Egypt, and a report from December 1955 indicated that enemy spies, terrorists, and foreign intelligence personnel were assisted by tribesmen who provided them with training, guidance, information, supplies, and shelter.[95] Another report from January 1956 indicated that the "Bedouin have very close contact with the enemy"[96] and that the phenomenon of "contact with the enemy for espionage purposes is very worrying because of its wide-ranging dimensions. Many members of the tribe assist the spies both in carrying out their work and in providing information of various sorts and protecting them from the patrols of [Israeli] security forces." The report noted several instances of Bedouin convicted of espionage in 1955 and referred to the problem of blood ties, as in the case of the two nephews of Sheikh Salman a-Shteywi Abu Blal of the Abu Blal tribe, who both were involved in sabotage missions for the Egyptians.[97]

In February 1956, the Ratner committee confirmed the need to maintain the military administration for reasons of state security, although it acknowledged that in certain cases the military administration had proved injurious and discriminatory.[98] The Ratner report says nothing about the Bedouin per se but approved the continuance of the Negev Military Administration policy.

Early in 1956, Pinhas Amir replaced Verbin as military governor of the Negev. Soon after his appointment, the sheikhs raised their call for ownership rights and, in May 1956, addressed the public through the press and in the Knesset, blaming the government for not granting them landownership rights.[99] One cause of the tension was a dispute between the Development Authority and Sheikh Salamah Sager al-Huzayyil over a vast amount of land he had presumably cultivated without permission.[100]

In October, Sverdalov of the Ministry of Agriculture, who was put in charge of land leases, announced that "all lands in the Negev over which there is no proof of ownership, shall be considered state land," and until the Bedouin proved ownership, they would have to lease the lands.[101] In response, Sheikh Salman al-Huzayyil announced that the Bedouin refused to lease land they owned themselves and demanded that the government implement a process through which they would be able to prove their ownership.[102] The ongoing landownership issue created discord between the Negev Military Administration and the sheikhs. The issue was under the jurisdiction of different governmental agencies, so the military administration could not make it disappear entirely, but it did play a role in postponing an inevitable confrontation.

As the security situation worsened, the actions of the sheikhs were further scrutinized. Marx described a "new class of sheikhs" who "socialize together and share their interest."[103] The growing power of the sheikhs made its way to the press. In July and August, a series of articles on the Bedouin appeared under the caption "The Bedouin—A Rich Minority in Israel." One of the articles included an interview with Sheikh 'Ali [Salman] Abu Grenat, who declared that the Bedouin were reluctant to accept state plans that would force them to live a settled life like Jews and Arab fellahin.[104]

The troubling activities of the sheikhs were most clearly described by Sasson Bar-Zvi, then a high-ranking officer in the Negev Military Administration who later became its governor: "The sheikhs by virtue of their powers have managed to concentrate within their hands most of the key positions in the area."[105] Theirs were the "safest, richest and largest smuggling and infiltration centers in the Negev" through which all major smuggling routes had to pass. In addition, they had become well-known "professional collaborators" with both Israeli and enemy intelligence. They had learned not to overtly assist Israel or to provide valuable information. They controlled the economy and trade as well as contact with the authorities. They had unsupervised control over the distribution of land and food rations. And last, they managed to circumvent almost all competitors and opponents.

Bar-Zvi did not suggest abolishing the tribal system, only using it more wisely, in a way that would diminish the power of the sheikhs while expanding the supervision and control of the Negev Military Administration. Years later, Bar-Zvi explained in an interview that the Bedouin could not "be controlled in any conceivable way without acting through the traditional tribal structure, namely, the head of the tribe and the heads of the factions."[106] His practical suggestion was to promote the growing desire within Bedouin subtribes and groups to seek independence from traditional tribal leadership, a desire he linked to the influence of the surrounding Jewish population. Hence, the Negev Military Administration should grant heads of groups within the larger tribal structures an independent status. Indeed, this method of creating splits within the larger tribes to achieve desired goals was later used several times.[107]

By the end of 1956, the Negev Military Administration retained Bar-Zvi's co-tribal policy as far as possible. The security issues in the Negev were resolved only through the Sinai Campaign (October 29–November 5, 1956), during which Israel took over the Sinai Peninsula; several months later, Israel withdrew under US pressure.[108]

Discussion and Conclusions

During the early years of the state, two contradictory approaches to tribalism were followed. One was motivated by social democratic principles and modern liberal agendas that aimed to transform the Bedouin into a community of individual fellahin in order to free them from the constraints of tribalism, including their subordination to sheikhs who tended to exploit them. The other approach favored a kind of indirect rule, a policy that sidestepped Bedouin individualism and cooperated with tribalism while embracing alliance with the sheikhs.

Initially the vision of the Bedouin becoming fellahin seemed a matter of consensus. Though Hanegbi had advocated for this together with Weitz, once he found himself face to face with reality, his views inclined toward pro-tribalism. The need to control a region and its population lacking in resources, with only a small number of officers and no clear-cut policy vis-à-vis Bedouin settlement, made pro-tribalism crucial.

As governor, Hanegbi acted to implement in full the advantages the tribal social system had to offer. First, he made it operational again, after the turbulence of the war. This included a restructuring of tribal units and leadership since some of the Bedouin tribes had split up. Then he gave formal standing to tribal norms and adopted the Tribal Court as an operational legal system.

Although the decision to assemble the Bedouin in the Sayig area was dictated to him, Hanegbi was resourceful enough to negotiate the move with the sheikhs rather than with individuals. Formal incentives were granted to the tribes as a unit, but the Negev Military Administration did not supervise the sheikhs. Tribesmen who relocated to new areas became more dependent on their sheikhs.

Once the social reorganization was finalized, the tribal units and their sheikhs functioned sufficiently well as administrative units, each in designated tribal territory. The system enabled the Negev Military Administration to rule while keeping the region in a relative state of calm, at least for most of the period. Hanegbi's successors carried on the same policy and successfully banned any involvement by civilians and bureaucrats in Bedouin issues.

Cooperation with tribalism became so intrinsic that even as the sheikhs grew in power to such an extent that they posed a threat to the ability of the Negev Military Administration to fulfill its mission and provide security to the region, the idea of abolishing the policy was never discussed. Instead, it was decided to use the tribal system in another way.

Thus, largely due to national prioritization, the military administration evaded the program to delimit tribalism and counteract the interests of the sheikhs by freeing the Bedouin from subjugation, settling them as individual fellahin, and instituting a formal land policy. Because Israel faced challenges in areas far more critical to decision-makers at the time, Bedouin issues were low on the agenda and tribal norms were reinforced at the expense of human rights like individual freedom and equality. Democratic values had been put on hold for all Israeli Arabs, and the fact that a relatively small group of Bedouin in the distant Negev were continuing their traditional way of life did not seem to require urgent intervention.

As we shall see in the following chapter, changes in the dominant policy were imposed on the Negev Military Administration as a result of external events, especially the harsh drought that drove the Bedouin in large numbers to the center of Israel.

PART II

3

BEDOUIN EXIT FROM THE NEGEV, 1957–60

> Drought years are frequent in the area.... This situation requires a fundamental solution for Bedouin settlement based on alternative income sources, and in particular to turning the Bedouin from nomads into permanent inhabitants ...
>
> *Reuven Aloni, director of the land division in Israel Land Authority, February 2, 1960*

The outcome of the Sinai Campaign in the fall of 1956 advanced Israel's understanding that it was still strong enough to defeat Arab enemies who might wish to pursue a "second round," and therefore it was time to address the problems of the Arab population in Israel.[1] During that period, issues concerning the Bedouin continued to be addressed mainly separately from the rest of the Arabs.[2] This period can be identified by the influx of proposals and initiatives by those who understood the urgency of providing swift solutions to the issues of land and settlement of the Bedouin of the Negev. However, all these human initiatives were overshadowed by a force of nature: the drought, which began in 1957 and continued for six years. The dependence of nomadic cultures on their natural environment made this a critical period with a transformative effect on the Negev Bedouin.[3]

Our period starts in 1957, when the military administration played a key role in forming the basis of Jewish-Bedouin relations. However, other institutions increasingly participated, among them the PM Adviser for Arab Affairs (hereafter PM Adviser); the Ministry of Agriculture, largely directed by Moshe Dayan of the Mapai party (1959–64);[4] the Development Ministry under Mordechai Ben-Tov of Mapam (1955–61);[5] and nongovernmental organizations like the Bnei Shimon regional council and the Histadrut.

Following Israel's military success in the Sinai Campaign, and despite Egypt's continuing insistence that Israel relinquish the Negev, the numbers of Egyptian-driven infiltrators and fedayeen in the Sayig region and the northern and western Negev were dramatically reduced, and military calm was restored. At the time, there were Bedouin families encamped in the Sayig region, according to tribal units, though the exact location of each tent changed from season to season.[6]

We ended the previous chapter with the military administration's dismay at the growing power of some sheikhs and the attempt to find a way to curtail it within the tribal framework without instigating major changes in Israel's relations with the Bedouin. But Bedouin issues, mainly concerning land policy, had led to public dispute and great unrest. At first, Bedouin litigants were optimistic that their land claims would be approved by the authorities. In 1956, certain sheikhs signed a declaration calling on the government to continue with the land proceedings and agreed to provide proof of ownership within a year.[7] However, by the beginning of 1957, some sheikhs were having second thoughts. It was now apparent to them that their documentation, which contained unofficial and internal agreements, claims of inheritance, and proofs of possession, would not satisfy the authorities, who demanded primary proof of landownership rights. A letter to the Ministry of Agriculture and the Development Authority signed by six sheikhs, most of them from the tribes that had remained in place during the war, stated that they would rescind their previous declaration but would accept Israel's initiative for land settlement only if the courts accepted their existing documentation. If so, they would cooperate with the authorities and provide every assistance to prevent land fraud. In conclusion, they wrote that they expected "the State of Israel, as a democratic regime, to know to settle the land problem by keeping the private property rights of each and every one."[8]

Meanwhile, Shalom Svardalov and Elyahu Shayek, along with other local representatives of the Ministry of Agriculture and Development Authority, managed to lease about 244,000 dunams annually. Their offices had constantly pushed for individualization and promoted the land settlement process even at the risk of confrontation. But much as they tried to lease to individual families, almost all the leases were handled by the sheikhs. In their report, Svardalov and Shayek pleaded with the authorities "to find a way once and for all to eliminate this problem called Bedouin ownership of Negev lands."[9]

In order to avoid a confrontation with some of the most influential sheikhs, Pinhas Amir, the Negev military governor, suggested acknowledging landownership for tribes that had remained in place during the war, or acknowledging their rights to part of the land they claimed and compensating them monetarily for the rest. In addition, he requested that a water pipe be laid out for them.[10]

Bnei Shimon Proposal

Following the decision of the Ministry of the Interior to extend the boundaries of the Bnei Shimon regional council, some 2,500 Bedouin came within its jurisdiction and hence under its aegis. The Negev Military Administration faced a new intervention when the head of the council, Meir Berger, wrote to the Ministry of the Interior, noting that the Bedouin in his region suffered greatly from neglect in education, health, and financial resources. He provided a plan to redress these issues, which included adequate funding to establish more schools and clinics and to lay a water pipeline, as well as the allocation of more land and the extension of land leases.[11]

Amir totally dismissed Berger's position, which he regarded as an attempt to intervene in Negev Military Administration matters. He called on the military administration to send an unambiguous reply immediately "and make the boundaries of their authority clear in order to prevent misunderstandings that may arise out of overly diligent of council members."[12] Amir's efforts apparently succeeded since the Bnei Shimon Council called off the plan.

Emanuel Marx's Proposal

Another initiative on behalf of the Bedouin was undertaken by Emanuel Marx, who was assistant to the PM Adviser at the time. Marx's plan involved settlement, social decentralization, and placing limits on the power of the sheikhs. In May 1957, Marx sent out a detailed proposal calling for the establishment of centers of economic activity as a first step in the permanent settlement of the Bedouin. It was essential, he explained, to settle the Bedouin and to enhance their relationship with the state; otherwise the Bedouin settlement process may be "accompanied by the development of a national [nationalistic] society and in an increased capacity to cause damage to the security of the State."[13] What was needed was a "social center," Marx explained, to serve as a focus of economic activity.[14]

Once again, Amir tried to stall the discussion and noted that settlement issues, like those mentioned in Marx's plan, would become relevant only once land issues were solved.[15]

The Sheikhs' Demands

The pressing need to find solutions for Bedouin issues, particularly with regard to permanent settlement, intensified in September, when three sheikhs submitted requests for building permits.[16] The requests required immediate attention since it was clear that additional applications would soon follow. This time, the matter was brought to the table of the highly influential Central Committee (also known as the Central Committee for Security Issues).[17] The Central Committee was a small top secret body that, together with Ben-Gurion, was authorized to make the most important operative decisions concerning the Arabs. The committee issued three directives: first, that the military administration should submit a proposal determining the location of the settlements in coordination with the Division for Settlement and Territorial Defense in the IDF, with the Development Authority, and then with the Coordination Committee for Municipal Affairs in the Ministry of the Interior. Second, the process of land settlement was to be dealt with by the Supreme Committee for Land Settlement, which until then had handled it only in the Galilee region. And third, the committee approved the Negev Military Administration's recommendation to continue supporting the tribal structure while empowering heads of family units in cases that required such an action to limit the excessive and undesirable influence of the sheikhs.[18]

When it was later reported that several sheikhs had organized a forum to promote their rights,[19] the military administration saw it as an additional justification to "rein in the sheikhs by encouraging the heads of the sub-tribes (*Ruba*) . . ."[20]

To sum up, 1957 ended with the Negev Military Administration successfully pushing back on the interventions of the regional council and the PM Adviser. It also gained support for its policy on the problematic sheikhs; however, the issues of Bedouin land and permanent settlements had reached a turning point that portended a confrontation.

In keeping with the decision of the Central Committee, the Supreme Committee for Land Settlement in Galilee met in February 1958 to discuss the question of settlement in the Negev. Ya'akov Tartakover, head of the Land Registration and Settlement Department in the Ministry of Justice, began by stating that the process of land settlement in the Negev where there were no villages would be much easier than it was in the Galilee.[21] This statement implied that he did not believe the Bedouin had landownership rights. Mishael Shacham, the military governor, noted that land settlement would not help solve the Bedouin problem and referred to the issue of the burden of proof, meaning that under the standard requirement, the Bedouin would not be acknowledged as landowners. Weitz proposed the appointment of a subcommittee for land settlement in the Negev.[22]

In April 1958, the sheikhs of eleven tribes that had relocated to the Sayig region after 1948 applied to the minister of justice with a request to advance the land settlement process. The sheikhs explained that they were sitting on lands that did not belong to them and feared losing the rights to their own pre-1948 territories. They noted that they had been told their problem was complicated since previous regimes in the Negev had not instituted land settlement, and therefore the documents they had provided were insufficient evidence for the settlement process.[23] They also stressed the fact that it was difficult to cultivate allocated lands since leases to them were temporary.

The letter of the sheikhs was widely circulated. Binyamin Lubotkin at military administration headquarters sent it on to the PM Adviser while demanding practical and expeditious action in the case.[24] Yosef Kukia, the general manager of the Ministry of Justice, asked the Development Authority to provide an answer to the letter, noting that he thought the Bedouin request should be resolved not through land settlement but with sufficient monetary compensation or alternative lands.[25]

Furthermore, Aryeh Efrat, coordinator of the Negev region of the Arab Department of the Histadrut from Kibbutz Dorot, had sent the letter of the sheikhs to the military administration with a note about his own views on the severity of their living conditions in other respects.[26] Amir responded that solutions for their living conditions had been found but that the land issue required "a budget of millions, the creation of an apparatus, and a decision in principle by the government."[27]

The land issue was brought up for deliberation in the Knesset through a parliamentary question submitted by Mapam MK Yusef Khamis regarding the government's position on Bedouin lands. Kadish Luz, the minister of agriculture, replied that a process of landownership through settlement was desirable, but since the Bedouin were only leasing the land meanwhile, his ministry was helping them develop new agriculture methods, and that took time.[28]

The Harsina Proposal

Following the Central Committee's decision to involve the Division for Settlement and Territorial Defense in planning solutions, Lieutenant Colonel Aaron Harsina, head of the division, submitted a plan in July 1958. It was a lengthy proposal that included agrarian reform, land settlement and development, and the establishment of permanent settlements.[29] Harsina called attention to the IDF decision to reduce the area of the Sayig region, which at the time comprised roughly 1.1 million dunams, by eliminating B1 and designating it for future Jewish settlement, thus distancing the Bedouin from major traffic routes and the borders with Jordan and Egypt and preventing Arab territorial continuity and contact along the frontier. His plan included a reallocation of lands since some of the tribes currently had "large tracts of land

Figure 3.1. Bedouin of al-'Atawnah tribe outside their encampment in the Negev. December 10, 1958. *Photo: Moshe Pridan. Source: The Government Press Office.*

while others hold little land in relation to their relative size."[30] The outline of the plan included a swift decision on the issue of land rights, followed by a determination of eight to ten centers that would later be expanded into permanent settlements with a water pipeline, and would accommodate the newly grouped tribes near wadis where floodwaters would contribute to their livelihood. The inhabitants would subsist by dryland agriculture and grazing.[31]

The Subcommittee for Land Settlement in the Negev, 1958 (Tartakover Committee)

The meeting of the subcommittee for land issues tasked with providing proposals to the Land Committee took place on August 18, 1958.[32] Tartakover presided over the meeting of a group comprised of JNF representatives, members of the Survey of Israel and Assets Division, and the military administration. In the meeting, Shacham presented two alternatives for action on land rights: ordinary land settlement in conformity with a compilation of documents and submission of claims. This "requires a long time, even several years."[33] The sheikhs would demand an immediate recognition of ownership based on testimony [rather than documentation], which would inevitably lead to confrontation with the state. The second proposal was a short but radical alternative that involved the enactment of a special law titled the "Settlement Law of the Bedouin," according to which:[34] "by settling the Bedouin in the Negev, and allotting tracts of land in keeping with their required number of units, there would be no ownership, and the state is settling the Bedouin, this is a shortcut, without [the problem of] ownership [and] compensation. The Bedouin [could then] be settled in permanent centers in line with prior planning and according to the [required] number of units."[35]

Although it seems from the discussions of the subcommittee that new legislation would fit the importance and follow the urgency of the matter, a detailed proposal formulated by a secondary committee headed by Tartakover was satisfied with the existing legislation.[36] The proposal divided the Negev into three areas, with a different legal policy for each:

A. *The northwestern Negev* (land west of the Hebron–Be'er Sheva Road, including B1) comprising 2 million dunams, most of which belonged to absentees, and some 200,000 dunams expropriated under the Acquisition Law of 1953. The Bedouin submitted claims for 27,000 dunams of expropriated land, but since there were Bedouin already living there, it was understood that they would have to settle in B2. They would then be granted compensation through an accelerated process by a special committee.

B. *The northeastern Negev* (land east of the Hebron–Be'er Sheva road, mainly B2), an area of some 700,000 dunams that would serve in part as a permanent Bedouin settlement. On the margins of this area were some 30,000 dunams belonging to Jewish settlements (Nevatim, Beit Eshel). This area, formerly unregistered, would be expropriated according to the Mandate Land Ordinance (Acquisition for Public Purposes) of 1943.[37] It would then be registered to the State, after which it would be allotted to the Bedouin on the basis of either ownership or long-term leasing. The proposal did not prevent anyone who claimed ownership from taking action to prove land rights on the eve of the expropriation. But if a claimant won, he would receive only monetary compensation. The land north of the Be'er Sheva district up to the armistice line, some 585,000 dunams, on the slopes of the Hebron Mountain villages, would be registered in the name of the state and the custodian and used for the purpose of Jewish settlement.

C. *The southern Negev*: the rest of the southern region down to Eilat, roughly 10 million dunams, would be registered in the name of the state as unallocated state land.

In December 1958, Sheikh ʿAwdah Mansur Abu Muʿammar of the ʿAzazmah filed for ownership of over 10,000 dunams. Though the Bedouin had agreed to become settled farmers, he charged, complaints like the uncertainty of having to renew land leases every few years had not been redressed.[38]

The Ministerial Committee Examines the Military Administration (Rosen Committee)

Simultaneous discussions were held by the Rosen Committee appointed by Ben-Gurion following pressure from members of his coalition on March 16, 1958 "to examine the problems of the military administration and its methods of operation and present its conclusions to the government."[39] Pinhas Rosen, the minister of justice, headed this committee of five ministers of the three coalition parties. The committee finished its work in June 1959. Its recommendations were divided, with the majority of the three non-Mapai members calling for the abolition of the military administration and the minority of the two Mapai members recommending its continuation.[40] On August 4, 1959, the government sided with the minority, mainly in light of persistent security risks. However, it was willing to promote some easing, for example, by allowing the Bedouin to enter Beʾer Sheva two days a week instead of the one day formerly accorded by the military administration (see fig. 3.2).

It likewise announced two broader decisions: the relocation of tribes to permanent settlements in the Negev and the enactment of a settlement law for the Bedouin.[41] The task of drafting the Settlement Law of the Bedouin was put in the hands of Tartakover and the attorney general in December 1959 by the Supreme Committee for Land Settlement.[42] By that point, however, the drought had overshadowed all other initiatives.

> The Drought
> This *Dira* brought us much travail, the cost was dear,
> We try but fail to find the funds.
>
> The burden of the drought was heavy upon us, until we
> Were like camels, running on to stay alive.
>
> The fair ones made us pillage enemy camps,
> Because our pockets were empty, the animals wasting away.
>
> God, look upon us, please, we need a little luck.
> What can a poor man do when such a year befalls him?[43]

Figure 3.2. Bedouin in marketplace (souk) in Be'er Sheva. February 1, 1959. *Photo: Cohen Fritz. Source: The Government Press Office.*

Studies indicate that marginalized resource-dependent groups, Bedouin included, are highly vulnerable to the impact of climate change.[44] According to anthropologist Philip Salzman, climatic disasters and the failure of the nomadic economy versus the market economy are the two main reasons that nomads transform their way of life and become sedentary.[45]

The Negev Bedouin lived by herding goats, sheep, and camels in rain-fed pastureland and by dry farming, mainly wheat and barley, since 40 percent of approximately 1.1 million dunams in the Sayig region were arable.[46] The crops were a secondary source of income and were dependent on rainfall.[47] Rain precipitation in the northern Negev is around two hundred mm, with a high variable and droughts that tend to appear in cycles.[48] The droughts, which began in 1957 and continued for six years, struck the Negev regions just as the Bedouin were beginning to increase the size of their herds, meat being in high demand in Israel. Larger herds were beneficial for all the Bedouin but especially for the sheikhs who owned the biggest herds and were in a better position to obtain permits for pasture lands in and out of the Sayig region. The authorities did not regulate the size of the herds, and in 1958 the number owned by the Bedouin exceeded 120,000 head.[49]

In order to survive the drought, several options had to be considered. If the Bedouin were confined to their present locations in the Negev, the authorities had to provide them with water and food and help them obtain fodder for their livestock. They could also initiate public works projects in Bedouin areas.[50] Another option involved Bedouin relocation by opening pastureland outside the Negev, mainly in the Mediterranean region, which suffered less from drought, and including nature reserves and fields of stubble unproductively cultivated by Jewish farmers.[51] Outside the Sayig region, they could also find employment as working hands, which was much needed. Each of these solutions had short- and long-term implications for Bedouin relations with the authorities whose policies changed over the drought years. It was then that the Bedouin primary source of income was transformed from high dependency on livestock breeding and dry farming to wage labor.[52]

When the drought began at the end of the 1957 winter season, its effects were not immediately severe. The Bedouin, like other cultivators, submitted claims for crop compensation, and these were paid.[53] However, when the drought continued the following winter, the water shortage in the Negev brought a further decline in conditions, and the Bedouin cried out for help.[54] By February 1958, in the middle of the second winter of the drought, concern arose that the Bedouin might not be able to maintain their livelihood in the eastern Negev.[55] The drought, in combination with the larger flocks, made pastureland in the Sayig region increasingly sparse. The Bedouin demanded permits to migrate north, either to find enough pasture for their flocks or to seek employment as wage laborers. Amir could not come up with a solution for them in the nearby Sayig and reported that although pasturelands were open to the Bedouin, there was not much productive land in the Jewish settlements, which left even less for the Bedouin herds.[56] A few months later, in July 1958, Bedouin shepherds sabotaged the pipelines in the northwestern Negev because of the water scarcity, and this led to confrontations between the Bedouin and the nearby Jewish communities.[57]

As the drought continued in 1959, with no solution in sight, thousands of Bedouin migrated northward from the Sayig with sixty thousand head of sheep and ten thousand camels.[58] The Bedouin sheikhs asked the Ministry of Agriculture for help with the water supply. They acknowledged the need to diminish their flocks but asked to do so according to quotas.[59] Annual reports show a high mortality rate among livestock and a significant drop in herd size between 1958 and 1961.[60]

The increasing number of wage earners among the Bedouin likewise demonstrates the profound change their economy underwent as a result of the drought.⁶¹ While in 1958 there were fewer than one hundred Bedouin laborers in the country, a report based on a survey of the Bedouin economy submitted to the Ministry of Agriculture three years later, in 1962, indicated that about three thousand out of the four thousand families earned their living as laborers rather than herders and dry farmers.⁶²

The drought had repercussions not only on their economy and place of residence but also on Bedouin social structure and the status of the sheikhs. At the beginning of the drought, the role of the sheikhs as mediators had been extended because tribe members were dependent on their help in obtaining exit permits so they could wander north to graze their herds or work as laborers elsewhere. The sheikhs' position as mediators increased their revenues, but once tribe members left the Sayig and were removed from the immediate supervision of the sheikhs, their tribal framework, and the Negev Military Administration, they attained a certain amount of independence. Wage workers did not need much of a tribal structure anymore, at least not as a life necessity. They could communicate directly with their employers and gradually adapted to the lifestyle of individual settlers.

The drought also influenced the balance of power among different authorities and institutions. The military administration's role diminished, and other agencies' involvement increased. The Ministry of Agriculture became more dominant as it was now in charge of providing solutions for herders outside the Sayig. This ministry controlled the allocation of lands and water in Israel, opened nature reserves for grazing, and effectively promoted the enhancement of pastureland. The ministry also mediated conflicts between herders and farmers. This was no small issue. The presence of Bedouin herders in various areas of the northern Negev and the Mediterranean zone created tensions with the Jewish farmers. In certain areas the Bedouin encroached on cultivated land with their flocks and damaged crops. The farmers requested police protection in the event of violent clashes. These clashes sometimes resulted in casualties, mainly in areas far away from the Sayig.⁶³

The role of the Ministry of Labor also grew as it monitored the employment market and was responsible for granting employment permits. With the dramatic rise in the number of laborers due to the drought, more Bedouin entered the labor force and needed services from the Ministry of Labor. Bedouin were highly needed in the workforce since Israel was enjoying unprecedented economic prosperity at the time.⁶⁴

The Histadrut, too, gradually became involved in Bedouin issues and started to advocate on their behalf. Led by members of Negev kibbutzim like Aryeh Efrat, the Histadrut encouraged the Bedouin who remained in the

Negev to establish agricultural cooperatives that would incorporate families from different tribes. The first such cooperative, al-Salam, led by Sheikh Musa Hasan al-'Atawnah, incorporated eight Bedouin families who aimed for collective cultivation and the establishment of a permanent settlement for their members.[65] The second was the New Negev Cooperative (also called Abu Siyam Cooperative) of twelve families with various tribal affiliations. However, since these initiatives were not endorsed by the Negev Military Administration, they had to appeal for individual land quotas rather than tribal quotas via their sheikhs.[66] MK Yusef Khamis submitted a parliamentary question in the Knesset stating that the authorities were avoiding the cooperatives, a claim the government denied.[67] The emerging cooperatives did not survive the drought and remained marginal.[68]

Map 3.1 presents the locations of tribal centers and the boundaries of B1 and B2 zones as of 1960.

The Settlement of Bedouin in Mixed Cities—the Dayan Plan, 1960

During the three-year drought, winter 1960 was the harshest of all.[69] The hardships of the Bedouin were addressed in numerous parliamentary questions.[70] Their population was estimated by the Ministry of Agriculture at fifteen thousand in three thousand households and eighteen tribes. By winter of that year, between five hundred and seven hundred Bedouin families had already moved to the central region, where they lived in tents, ruins, or hovels and worked in the orchards around Rehovot, Ness Ziona, Rishon LeZion, Lod, and Ramleh. An additional one hundred to two hundred Bedouin worked in Be'er Sheva. The rest lived in the Negev region, in tents "other than the few dozen families . . . [who] erected tin shacks and huts without building permits" and relied on their crops herds for subsistence.[71]

The ongoing drought prompted the realization that long-term adaptation was inevitable. This was a turning point in the Bedouin settlement policy after years of discussions that had led nowhere.[72]

On December 17, 1959, a new government was formed, and Ben-Gurion appointed his trusted ally and a newly recruited member of Mapai, Moshe Dayan, as minister of agriculture, replacing Luz. This was Dayan's first ministerial post after ending a long career in the IDF as chief of staff. He was well-acquainted with the Bedouin of the Galilee from his days in Nahalal and had served on the general staff of the Hagana as an expert in Arab affairs and also with the Negev Bedouin in his IDF service as commander of the Southern Command. Dayan took an active stand vis-à-vis the Arabs, trusting power over compromise, and had opposed the IDF's withdrawal from the Sinai Peninsula at the end of the Sinai Campaign.[73]

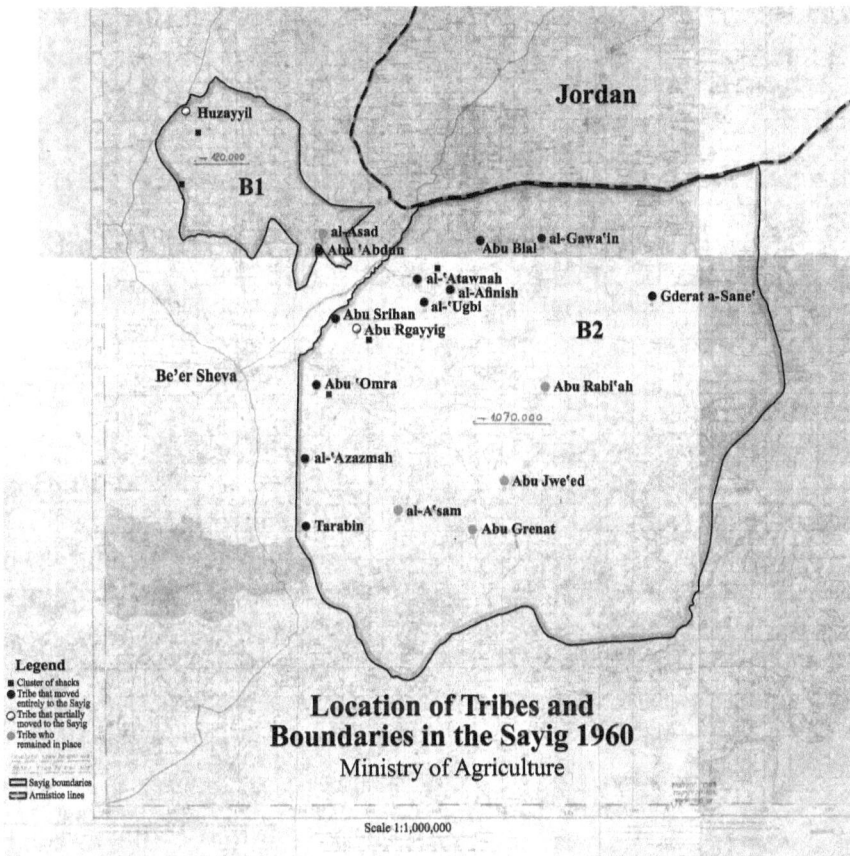

Map 3.1. Ministry of Agriculture. Location of tribes and Sayig boundaries, 1960. *Source: file 19703/2, Israel State Archives [originally in Hebrew].*

One of the first things Dayan did after his appointment as minister of agriculture was to task Reuven Aloni, director of the land division in his ministry, with putting together a proposal for the settlement of the Bedouin. Aloni handed his recommendations over to him in February 1960: "Drought years are frequent in the area under discussion and do not allow for agricultural planning and development and fair survival from agriculture. This situation requires a fundamental solution for Bedouin settlement based on alternative income sources, and in particular to turning the Bedouin from nomads into permanent inhabitants in regions where labor is available for salary employees in orchards or in development projects." Aloni suggested housing a thousand families on half-dunam plots in the Lod-Ramleh area. There they could find employment either as hands in the surrounding orchards or in industry and construction; another thousand families could be settled in the

Be'er Sheva region, where they could work in the phosphates industry. The rest could remain "in their current places of residence and earn a living from herding and dry farming." The success of the plan would be assessed three years later.[74]

On March 20, 1960, the government authorized the Ministry of Agriculture to coordinate the interministerial handling of all damage inflicted by drought conditions on the Negev Bedouin tribes.[75] Notably, the decision made no mention whatsoever of the military administration.

Dayan utilized only certain parts of Aloni's proposals and created a more far-reaching plan. Convinced that conditions in the Negev could not accommodate a livelihood based on agriculture, herding, or cultivation, he envisioned a transformation of the Bedouin in terms of both their place of residence and their employment. In the plan he submitted to the PM in May 1960, he explained that its aim was to achieve a long-term solution in which "the government will encourage the relocation of the Negev Bedouin in mixed cities and help create sources of employment for them (mainly in agriculture) with housing arrangements in locations that will be determined in cooperation with the security bodies."[76] The plan also included the allocation of funds and government authorization empowering him to act in all respects upon consultation with other ministries as to their relevancy.[77]

This initiative, if accepted, would have resulted in a profound transformation, bringing to an end the Bedouin way of life and risking a serious confrontation with the Bedouin whose sheikhs were already organizing a task force to promote their ownership claims. While Dayan himself did not think twice about confronting the Bedouin if the need arose, others, including members of his office, evinced a less belligerent approach. The PM Adviser was uneasy about Dayan's initiative and demanded that he amend it in the following way: first, relocation and settlement would be voluntary, and second, limiting discretionary power so that the Ministry of Agriculture would have to consult the other relevant ministries.

Dayan had to amend his proposal to address the PM Adviser's objections before submitting it to the government. The final version was that "the government will encourage the relocation of Negev Bedouin who wish to move to mixed-cities. The government will help those citizens create sources of employment (mainly in agriculture) and housing arrangements in locations that will be determined in cooperation with security bodies."[78]

However, the government was unwilling to adopt Dayan's proposal, notwithstanding his oratory, and also was unwilling to grant him the authority to do as he pleased. On May 29, 1960, it chose to transfer the discussion of the issue to the Ministerial Committee for Economic Affairs.[79]

The Ministerial Committee for Economic Affairs, which met to discuss the issue on June 12, 1960, decided to follow Dayan's proposal to a limited extent and tasked him with drawing up a plan for the settlement of a few hundred Bedouin families in the center of the country.[80] Since no objection was raised, the committee's decision automatically became a government decision two weeks later. The following month, Dayan submitted a corrected proposal, similar to Aloni's earlier proposal, according to which the government would promote the settlement of five hundred families in the cities of Ramleh and Jaffa. Five hundred housing units would be built for them, each on a one dunam plot, enough to set up a secondary farm. The Bedouin would enter the labor market and work mainly in agriculture near their homes and would receive financial support. The move was planned for April 1, 1962.[81]

When Amir discovered the plan, he was furious. The government's decision went against his better judgment. He noted that the government's intention to relocate the Bedouin to mixed cities was irresponsible and had "caused a great deal of unrest which will undoubtedly cost the state a lot of money."[82] He also claimed that the scheme was harmful and unrealistic, as the Bedouin would never agree to move. He questioned the wisdom behind it and declared that "the prominent line in all the solution proposals succeeds in completely ignoring the basic problems."

Furthermore, he argued, the Bedouin who move to cities will have to travel around the country and create a security risk.[83] Moreover, claimants to landownership will consider the decision an attempt to deprive them of their rights in the Negev, and "they will build stone structures in order to create unassailable facts on the ground which would prevent their transfer."[84] Amir expressed willingness to play an active role in settling the Bedouin in the Negev. In his view, the Sayig provided the most satisfactory solution for the Bedouin of the Negev.

Amir's objections were not supported, not even by the IDF, which favored Dayan's plan. On July 5, 1960, Dayan sent his proposal to the Ministerial Committee for Economic Affairs, indicating that he had the approval the of the IDF and the Ministry of Labor to relocate five hundred Bedouin families to Ramleh and Jaffa, half the number of families now employed outside the Sayig.[85] To implement the plan, Aloni needed cooperation from the Negev Military Administration officers, and he specifically requested the assistance of Major Sasson Bar-Zvi, Amir's deputy, and a list of Bedouin who wished to move.[86]

Although the plan had not yet been concluded, by July and August, scores of families had applied for relocation to the center.[87]

On August 14, 1960, the Ministerial Committee for Economic Affairs decided to approve the relocation of one hundred Bedouin families to mixed cities that would be determined by the Ministries of Labor and Agriculture. Funding was to come from both ministries together with the Ministry of Finance.[88] There were still budgetary issues that caused delays.[89] In October, Aloni reported that after consultations with the IDF, Ramleh had been chosen for Bedouin relocation, with some eighty-five families already registered and positioning their tents there.[90] Nevertheless, when December came, Dayan learned that his plan had not received the necessary budget.[91]

Dayan's was not the only plan promoted in 1960 without Negev Military Administration's involvement. Mordechai Bentov, the Mapam party minister of development, initiated a plan to establish an exemplary Bedouin village for the al-'Atawnah tribe in Khirbat Hurah, located between Be'er Sheva and Hebron. Bentov recruited two architects, an Arab and a Jew, to draw up a draft,[92] but he did so without notifying the military administration, the Ministry of Agriculture, or Dayan.[93] Mapai perceived Bentov's plan as a political maneuver linked to Sheikh Musa Hasan al-'Atawnah's support for Mapam and an attempt to win over Bedouin votes.[94] Bentov tried to convince Dayan that both their plans might stand, but in practice, his plan was eliminated.[95]

As Amir had anticipated, many of the Bedouin rejected the idea of mixed cities.[96] There was a steep rise in unauthorized buildings in the Sayig. Mapai accused Mapam of inciting the Bedouin against the mixed-cities plan and of encouraging the unauthorized construction.[97] One of the most prominent voices among the Bedouin was that of Sheikh al-'Atawnah, who published an article titled "What Do the Bedouin Want?" in which he explained that only a small minority of Bedouin would willingly move away from the Negev, and those with claims to land would want to settle there. Until their claims were granted, he wrote, the Bedouin would be willing to work as dryland farmers on plots of 250 dunams each, in addition to shared pasture lands.[98]

Throughout the 1960s, only a few dozen families relocated permanently to the center of the country, mainly in the neighborhoods of Ramleh.[99]

Although the Bedouin tribes were scattered now, they were still under the aegis of the Negev Military Administration and treated differently from other Arabs in many respects. They were formally registered according to tribal units, regardless of their location.[100] They did not enjoy the same ease of movement as other Arabs. When asked in a parliamentary question about the level of military administration involvement in Bedouin issues, Shimon Peres, deputy minister of defense at the time, replied that the Negev region with its nomadic population required "more rigorous security oversight."[101]

While the main attempt of the Ministry of Agriculture was to settle the Bedouin as laborers, it also continued its long-standing and unsuccessful efforts to implement a reform of allocating land individually. For example, in June 1960 the Ministry of Agriculture proudly announced that it had revised the necessary papers so that drought damage compensation could be claimed individually, and allocations would no longer have to be mediated by the sheikhs as they had been in the past. This new method, as the Ministry of Agriculture explained, would help prevent discrimination against families who disobeyed the sheikh.[102] However, the paperwork did not do much to change the way things were done in the Negev.[103]

Discussion and Conclusions

During the three years after the start of the drought, the Negev Military Administration lost its position as the driving force in Israel-Bedouin policy. At the beginning of the drought, it seemed to succeed in calming tempers amid interventions that might have stirred unrest and diminished the military administration's capacity to carry out its tribal policy. These interventions came from different directions: from Bedouin sheikhs and claimants supported by Knesset members who demanded recognition of their land rights and the granting of building permits to them; local public figures like Meir Berger of Bnei Shimon or Aryeh Efrat of the Histadrut, who demanded change; government officials like Svardalov, Shayek, Marx, and Harsina, all of whom had initiatives and views of their own; and the two highly influential committees, led by Tartakover and Rosen, that stepped in with a recommendation that, if promoted, might have made a difference.

However, the forces of nature brought a vast transformation in Bedouin life over which the Negev Military Administration had little control. Many of the Bedouin ceased herding, their occupation from ancient times and the mainstay not only of their livelihood but also of their tribal structure, culture, and tradition. A large number of Bedouin entered the labor market. Those Bedouin were primarily self-driven and motivated by drought conditions, not by any deliberate governmental plan. Among those who retained their flocks, many moved away from the Negev. Though they needed the sheikhs and the Negev Military Administration to obtain exit permits, once they left the Negev, they were less constrained.

For Bedouin workers, labor offices became primary, while for herders, the Ministry of Agriculture was the dominant agency. The latter was responsible for providing compensation and solutions during the drought. The dominance of the Ministry of Agriculture gave Moshe Dayan government authority to set off a policy for the Bedouin.

The Dayan plan presents an episode in trying to change the Bedouin way of life and overturn the existing tribal order. This was not the first time the Ministry of Agriculture had advanced a policy to overturn the existing tribal order. Even before Dayan's appointment as minister, the Ministry of Agriculture had called for individual farming and an end to land claims. However, this time it was carried out by the ministry—not as a result of political or other needs but as a response to changes in the ecology and natural conditions under which the Bedouin lived.

The moves to mixed cities had not been negotiated with the Negev Military Administration or with the Bedouin themselves, although they were clearly controversial and entailed a total deviation from the previous policy. The Bedouin responded to Dayan's plan with distress and erected hundreds of dwellings in an effort to put facts on the ground. But even though Dayan's policy was controversial, in reality a considerable number of Negev Bedouin were now living in the center of Israel in close contact with the general population, and this created new challenges.

This and the growing number of unauthorized Bedouin houses persuaded the Negev Military Administration to amend its tribal policy and advocate Bedouin settlement as inevitable and necessary. But it may also have helped push back initiatives like the Dayan plan.

To conclude, the drought undermined Israeli-Bedouin relations and gave rise to new forces and policies that led to confrontations that will be discussed in the following chapter.

4

THE DECLINE OF THE MILITARY ADMINISTRATION, 1961–66

> Arab countries like Syria and Iraq have not stayed away from enacting special laws for the concentration and settlement of the Bedouin. Why is this action appreciated when it is done in a neighboring Arab country but does not receive the same treatment when it is done in Israel?!
>
> *Aharon Layish, deputy PM adviser for Arab affairs, December 20, 1964*

By 1960, as the drought wore on, hundreds of Bedouin moved to the center of the country, where they grazed their herds or worked as laborers, far from their tribes and the Negev Military Administration. Dayan's failed initiative to urbanize them in mixed cities backfired, and they held on to the Negev lands for fear of being dispossessed. Meanwhile, plans for the Arad region, where many Bedouin families were encamped, had been set in motion. Arad was considered an area with potential gas and oil wells, as well as a possible basecamp for workers at the Dead Sea mineral production plants. The development of the region included paving a new road from Be'er Sheva to Arad and from there to the Dead Sea, and the construction of the city of Arad itself.[1] Once the plans were put into operation, building materials became available and easily accessible for Bedouin use.

Development of the Arad Region

In early March 1961, with the issue of landownership at a stalemate and fearing relocation, several sheikhs, led by Musa Hasan al-'Atawnah, were inspired by Jews to organize a task force for land issues. The task force demanded permission to return to the lands they had previously inhabited or else to receive alternate lands for permanent use. Military Governor of the Negev Pinhas Amir was troubled by this initiative.[2] He was also uneasy about the need to

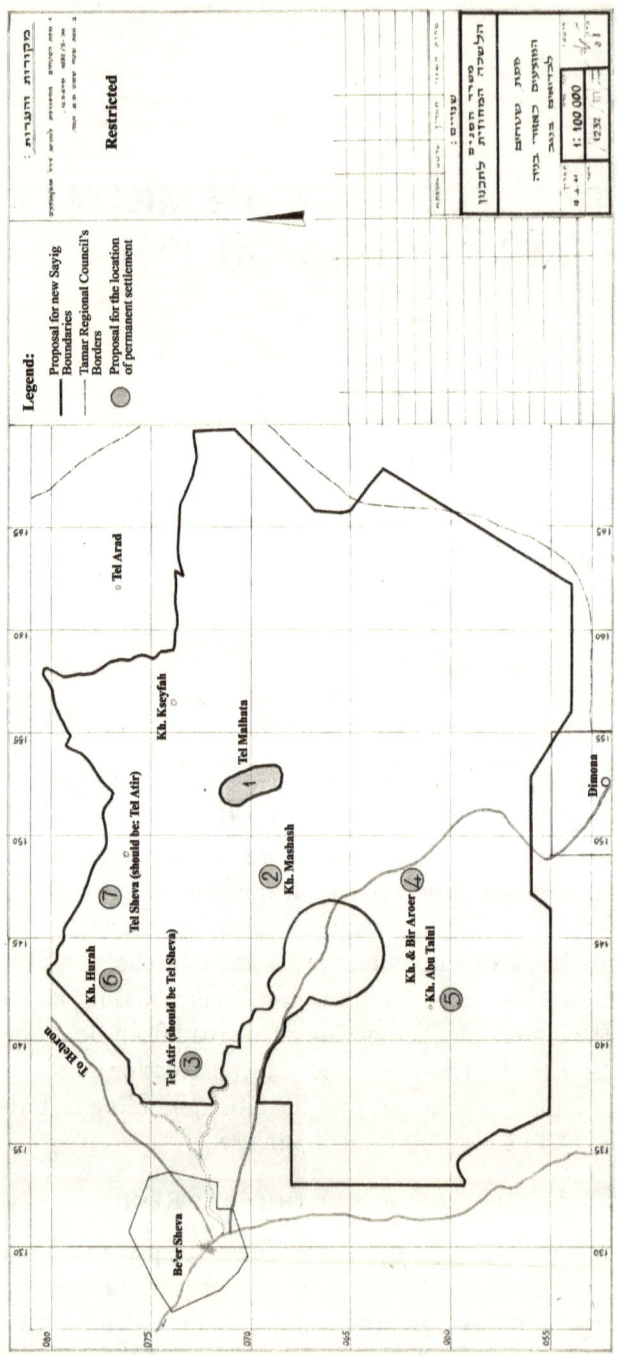

Map 4.1. Plan submitted to the head of the Southern District Planning Bureau by the head of the Department for Settlement and Territorial Defense in the IDF, March 16, 1961. *Source: file G-2746/3, Israel State Archives [originally in Hebrew].*

relocate some of the Bedouin in the wake of regional developments and to distance them from the Bedouin across the Jordanian border. The relocation affected mainly the Abu Blal and the a-Sane' tribes. The latter had previously been relocated to the region after their failed attempt to move to Jordan in 1952 and the UN involvement in the ensuing crises.[3]

On March 16, Aharon Harsina submitted an outline map on behalf of the IDF to the Southern District Planning Bureau in the Ministry of the Interior for Bedouin relocation to permanent settlements (see map 4.1).[4]

The plan showed seven locations, all east of the Be'er Sheva-Hebron Road and numbered according to priority; the first was the Tel Malhata site, where the tribes of the Dhullam subconfederation encamped. Also outlined were new boundaries for the restricted Sayig area, excluding B1, and adjustments along the Jordanian border and Arad.

Later that month, a meeting with high-ranking officials was convened at the office of the Negev Military Administration to discuss alternative sites for the relocated Bedouin.[5] Participants included Weitz, director of the newly established Israel Land Administration; Reuven Aloni, head of the land use division of Israel Land Administration;[6] Uri Lubrani, adviser to the PM on Arab Affairs; Yosef Pressman, the newly appointed military administration governor; Binyamin Lubotkin of the military administration; and Aharon Harsina, Pinhas Amir, his deputy Sasson Bar-Zvi, and several others. Although the meeting had initially been convened to discuss Arad's development issues, participants elaborated on the problematic reality where no coherent policy had been agreed upon in the government and not enough was being done to apply the state's rights and laws.

Aloni began by stating that the government had not formally declared ownership rights over lands that were necessary for the security of settlements on the Hebron slopes near Arad, but he was not optimistic that it would in fact do so. He proposed relocating the a-Sane' from the border area near Arad to Khirbat al-Lagiyyah in B1 or to the a-Sirr lands, located east of Be'er Sheva, where they would be provided with one hundred houses with two dunams each, a water supply, and the chance of employment in nearby Be'er Sheva. Aloni also spoke of opening employment bureaus for the Negev Bedouin.

Lubrani argued that although a comprehensive solution should be sought, the urgency of the Arad issue required the immediate evacuation of some fifty thousand dunams. Nevertheless, he opposed returning the a-Sane' to B1, presumably because of the IDF outline plan to exclude B1 from the Sayig. Harsina backed him and noted that there are other locations for Bedouin settlement, such as Tel Malhata. Yosef Pressman put forward Dayan's recommendation to focus on urgent issues for the present, rather than those of the region as a whole, implying that Dayan still believed in his mixed cities plan. Yosef Weitz criticized Dayan explicitly: "If the policy is that of the current agriculture minister, then the matter [will be] closed for [the next] 15–20 years."[7] According to Weitz, the Bedouin way of life, as well as their mentality and psychology, had to be taken into account. He called for a decision on the locations of their permanent settlements and on granting them building permits and all the support they might require.

Amir was uncomfortable with this line of reasoning. "Temporary measures will do no good," he said. "Any attempt to find temporary measures will be firmly resisted by the Bedouin."[8] Such solutions, Amir argued, would only complicate matters. He called for the formation of a committee to decide all land issues: ownership, location, quotas per family, etc. Bar-Zvi backed him up on this. Some Bedouin sheikhs, he said, had asked for clarification of future plans and whether the move to B1 would be temporary or permanent.[9]

The protocol of this meeting does not include any comprehensive decisions, though it does note Weitz's proposal to open employment bureaus (without specifying where) and indicates that the relocations would first have to be approved by the Ministry of the Interior.[10] In practice, the a-Saneʿ tribe was relocated from the encampment near Arad to Khirbat Hurah in B1, a location that became their permanent residence.

According to the national census of May 1961, the Bedouin population of the Negev was composed of 18 tribal units, 3,544 families, and 17,774 individuals. In order of size, the largest tribe, Abu Rgayyig, included over 3,000 members, followed by the Abu Rabiʿah tribe with slightly over 2,500 and the al-Huzayyil tribe with fewer than 2,500. The smallest tribe was Abu ʿOmrah with fewer than 100 members (see the full list in table 4.1).[11]

Plans to relocate the Bedouin to permanent sites in the Negev were gaining momentum, notwithstanding Moshe Dayan's position. When these plans were submitted to Yitzhak Vardimon, southern district officer at the Ministry of the Interior, he completely disregarded them and declared that the IDF plan to cut B1 was "not realistic" because it ignored "the existence of three relatively large encampments."[12] When asked to comment, Amir, who was bound by his IDF position, suggested only a few minor changes in the location of the main site.[13]

A great deal of confusion and embarrassment among the authorities ensued in October 1961, when *Al Hamishmar* reported that Mapam-affiliated Sheikh al-ʿAtawnah's request for a building permit was approved by the Ministry of the Interior. The newspaper noted that many Bedouin were bound to follow suit and replace their tents with concrete houses.[14]

Table 4.1. The Bedouin tribes in the Negev, May 25, 1961.

Tribe	No. of Families	No. of People
Tarabin	80	382
al-Gawaʻin	47	242
Gderat a-Sane'	253	1,210
al-Ugbi	90	504
al-ʻAtawnah (inc. Talalga)	74	464
Masʻudin al-ʻAzazmah	375	1,657
al-Huzayyil	436	2,430
al-Afinish	69	335
al-Aʻsam	221	1,072
al-Asad	61	304
Abu Rgayyig	618	3,060
Abu Rabiʻah	484	2,516
Abu Grenat	314	1,583
Abu ʻOmrah	22	93
Abu ʻAbdun	39	218
Abu Srihan	27	154
Abu Jwe'ed	269	1,210
Abu Blal	65	310
Total	3,544	17,774

Source: Central Bureau of Statistics. Minority Statistics Unit

Vardimon was blamed for granting the permit and asked to submit his explanation. In his explanation he elaborated that the approval was not for a new house but rather for the enlargement of an existing house; al-ʻAtawnah's father had already been granted a permit in 1945, though he had moved to Jordan meanwhile.[15]

Yigal Allon Takes the Lead

On November 2, 1961, a new government was formed, with Ben-Gurion remaining as PM. Yigal Allon from the Ahdut Haavodah–Poalei Zion party was appointed minister of labor while Dayan continued to hold his position as minister of agriculture. One of Allon's first actions was to put the development of the Arad area and the problem of Bedouin encampment there on the government agenda.[16]

By the end of 1961, Bedouin shacks had become commonplace on the new road to Arad as well as in other areas. The *Yedioth Ahronoth* newspaper reported that overnight, members of the al-Huzayyil tribe had erected scores of shacks to replace their tents, encouraged by a "certain party," meaning Mapam, that hoped this would be of political benefit to them.[17] Vardimon asked for help from the Ministry of the Interior's CEO, explaining that illegal construction had "taken on very serious dimensions" and created "a situation gone wild." However, he explained that he found it difficult to enforce the law requiring building permits, since there were no legal alternatives planned for the Bedouin's housing needs.[18]

On January 12, 1962, Harsina circulated a briefing about Bedouin issues that maintained that the surge in illegal construction had been motivated by rumors of displacement. Asked by the planning division to name alternative sites, Harsina suggested ten possibilities, noting, however, that unless the proposals were immediately put into action, the growing trend in illegal construction might block the option of rational planning, and the idea of relocating the Bedouin from B1 to B2 would no longer be viable.[19] A smaller number of localities, he noted, would mean more demolition and supervision.[20]

Twelve days later, Allon submitted a resolution to the government. Titled "The Problem of Bedouin Concentration and Settlement in the Arad Area," the resolution proposed that cooperative measures and state incentives be applied to persuade the Bedouin of the Arad area, approximately half the Bedouin population of the Negev, to settle in two to three large sites and in housing projects in Be'er Sheva (sec. B). He then suggested forming an interministerial committee, chaired by Weitz and comprised of members from the Ministries of Labor, Interior, Commerce and Industry, Social Affairs, Housing, Agriculture, and the Arad Regional Authority, who would discuss planning details (sec. C). The implementation of the plan, as Allon suggested, would be left to the Arad Regional Authority (sec. D). Allon stressed the urgency of promoting the plan, noting that "the more homes that are built and the more the region develops, the harder it will be to persuade the Bedouin to move as a group into the planned sites as needed, on the one hand, and the price and value of the land will rise steeply, on the other hand."[21]

The military administration and the IDF personnel, particularly Harsina, were clearly displeased with the plan, which made the new Arad authority responsible for over half the Bedouin population. In February, Harsina drafted a motion calling for a new government resolution addressing the Negev Bedouin and the proposed establishment of six to seven localities and an interministerial committee with members from the IDF, the Ministry of the Interior, and the Ministry of Justice (sec. 2 and 3). The practical implementation of this plan was to "be fully coordinated with the IDF (Military Administration)" (sec. 4).[22] Amir backed the motion, though he suggested that the interministerial committee should draft a legislative proposal that would include additional members.[23] Years later, when asked about Harsina, Amir was clearly uncomfortable. He commented that although they knew each other they did not engage in dialogue. And Lubotkin, who worked in the military administration at the time, added that "Harsina's proposals were of little consequence." Clearly there was much resentment between the two men and Harsina as a result of past interactions.[24]

The origin of the hesitation to enforce the law on the Bedouin in view of the unchecked spread of illegal construction is presented in a correspondence between the minister of interior from the Mafdal, the National Religious Party, who demanded answers on the matter from Vardimon. Vardimon responded that the law would be easier to enforce if government policy were less ambiguous and had the military administration not delayed its response and submitted alternative plans. At that point, seven indictments had been submitted against violators, and more would follow. He had only one inspector to work with to enforce the law. He added that he held a meeting with the sheikhs on the issue, but to no avail.[25] Some indictments ended with a demolition order and a fine, but their execution was postponed because the lack of available solutions burdened the court.[26]

The Interministerial Committee Plan of Seven Localities

Owing to Allon's persistence, the Bedouin issues were placed on the government's agenda for the March 25, 1962 meeting.[27] The government voted to amend Allon's motion and extend its scope beyond Arad to include all the Negev Bedouin, with the proviso that the building of any structure in the Negev without a permit "shall be strictly prohibited" (sec. A).[28] In keeping with Allon's motion, the government approved the creation of an interministerial committee to review locations for Bedouin settlement in the Negev within two months.[29] Weitz was appointed chair of the committee, and Arad regional director Aryeh (Lova) Eliav was named committee secretary. The motion listed the ministries to be represented (sec. B), and the following month, the list of committee members was finalized and included officials that had previous experience in dealing with Bedouin issues. The list included, along with Weitz and Eliav, Aloni and Vardimon as well as Harsina and Aharon Layish, deputy PM adviser for Arab Affairs in the Prime Minister's Office, who was an orientalist scholar and later become a professor for Islamic law in the Hebrew University of Jerusalem. Although the Ministry of Defense was able to place two representatives on the final list of committee members, neither of them was chosen from the military administration.[30]

The interministerial committee held a series of discussions and consultations and on September 14, 1962, Weitz signed a report that included data and recommendations.[31] The report noted that the Bedouin dwellings, which were dispersed over a large area of about 1.2 million dunams, "may determine facts on the ground in occupying lands and locations that are not suitable for settlement of the Negev from a security and planning perspective."[32] The report attested further that the Bedouin were divided among themselves and that their internal disputes made it impossible to settle them all in a single locality. Hence, it proposed 7 localities indicated on a map of the Negev (see map 4.2) to be populated as follows:[33] 1,600 members of the al-Huzayyil on a plot of 700 dunam at their current site near Kibbutz Shoval (in time Rahat, marked no. 1 on the map); 1,300 members of the al-Asad, the Abu ʿAbdun, and a branch of the al-Huzayyil tribes on 550 dunam (in time Lagiyyah, marked no. 2 on the map); some 2,300 members of the ʿAzazmah, part of Abu Rgayyig, Abu Blal, Abu Srihan, Abu ʿOmrah, and Tarabin tribes, on 1,000 dunam near Beʾer Sheva (in time Tel Sheva, marked no. 3 on the map); some 3,900 members of the al-ʿUgbi, al-ʿAtawnah, al-Afinish, al-Gawaʾin, al-Aʿsam, and Abu Blal tribes and part of the Abu Rgayyig on 1,600 dunam near their current location (marked no. 4 on the map); some 2,400 members of part of the Abu Rabiʿah tribe in their current location and members of a-Saneʿ—which, according to the committee, constituted a security risk—would be relocated to 1,000 dunam (in time, Kseyfah, marked no. 5 on the map); 3,500 members of the Abu Jweʿed, part of Abu Rabiʾah, the Abu Grenat, the a-Saneʿ, and the rest of the Abu Rgayyig tribes on 1,500 dunam (marked no. 6. on the map); and 2,800 members of the al-Aʿsam, Abu Grenat, Tarabin, and ʿAzazmah tribes on 1,250 dunam (marked no. 7 on the map). In each of these localities, a labor office was to be opened.

The selection of these sites, the report noted, had taken into consideration factors of state security, accessibility of water and employment, limiting the proliferation of public services with a reduced number of settlements, relations between families, clans and tribes, and proximity to current locations. The size of each locality was calculated based on the number of families that would populate it, with a quota of "two dunam gross per family, half of the land for [residential] plots a dunam each and half for public services (roads, public buildings, green [grass] etc.) and reserve for extension."[34]

As for the issue of landownership, the report recommended registering it according to legislation in which the district court would decide on rights to cultivated areas.[35] To implement the program, a survey would be carried out by the Israel Land Administration and the Department of Surveys (sec. 2). Upon authorization, the recommended planning and development would be initiated by the Israel Land Administration and the ministries of the interior and labor. Once the planning authorities approve the sites as outlined, court demolition orders regarding structures outside the planned sites would be put into effect (sec. 4). A labor agency would be opened at each site, and a

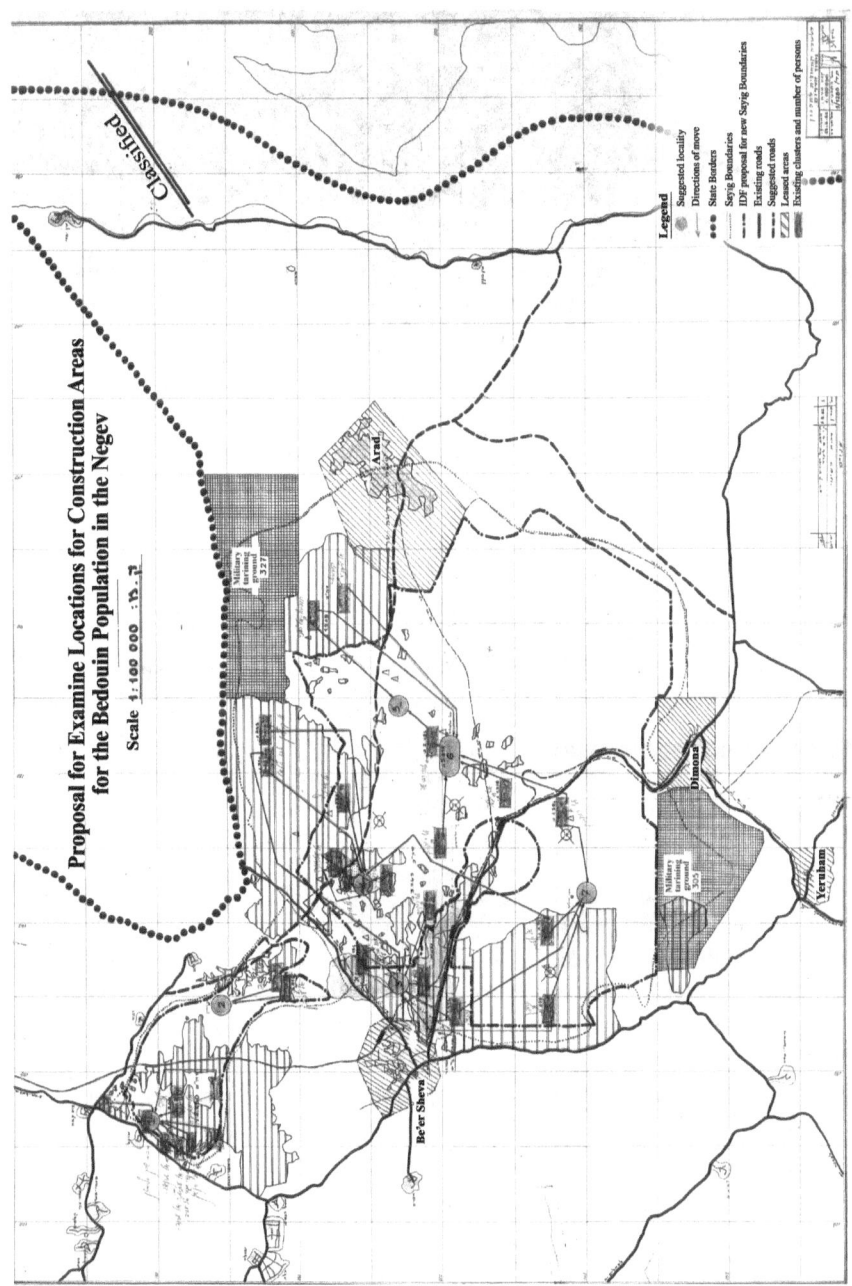

Map 4.2. Proposal for examining locations for construction areas for the Bedouin population in the Negev. *Source: file GL-17092/1, Israel State Archives [originally in Hebrew].*

committee of representatives from the Ministries of Labor and Agriculture and the local authority would encourage employment and provide advice on methods of cultivation.[36]

Although Weitz signed the report on behalf of all the interministerial committee members, a memo by the cabinet secretary indicated that Weitz did not actually take the comments of members into consideration. Hence, the submission of the report to the government was delayed until that issue could be resolved with Weitz. Nevertheless, it became clear in November 1962 that Weitz did not intend to change the report.[37] On December 2, 1962, upon receiving the interministerial committee report, and due to rejections, the government decided to continue discussions in the Ministers Committee for Economic Affairs in conjunction with other ministers interested in the matter.[38] After more delays, and following a parliamentary question on the issue, Levi Eshkol, who had replaced Ben-Gurion as prime minister, determined in July 1963 that the findings of the committee would be brought before the government.[39]

STOPPING THE DROUGHT COMPENSATION

The drought continued as the Bedouin planning issues were gradually being decided on without any input from the Bedouin or the Negev Military Administration. After the easing of restrictions declared by the government in 1962, the Bedouin were equipped with permits that enabled them to move about more freely throughout the country.[40] About a thousand families moved to the center of Israel and found employment there, mainly as laborers. Dayan regarded this high number as confirmation that Bedouin could indeed earn their living as urban dwellers as he had claimed. With that in mind, on June 5, 1962, Dayan appointed a committee to prescribe boundaries for lands cultivated by the Bedouin that entitled them to compensation.[41]

The state compensation policy had begun several years earlier, when the Ministry of Agriculture decided to pay Jews and Bedouin alike for agricultural losses resulting from the drought. In the Bedouin sector, compensation was paid in accordance with the recommendation issued by the tribal committees chaired by the sheikh and accompanied, in the case of the larger tribes, by the heads of clans.[42] When the decision to reconsider the compensation policy was introduced after five consecutive years of drought, the Ministry of Agriculture decided it was unreasonable to encourage the investment of resources for cultivation of crops that were doomed to fail. The change in the policy of compensation for the Bedouin was decided on after the Ministry of Agriculture had already determined changes in the compensation policy for the Jewish sector.[43]

The committee charged with determining compensation for the Bedouin was chaired by Haim Molcho from the Ministry of Agriculture. The committee based its conclusions on updated surveys. Their findings indicated that cultivation was a marginal source of income (after manual labor and herding) and did not yield crops but was used as pasturage. With the advent of agricultural machinery, Bedouin cultivation ceased being a source of employment. Herds were kept as an investment because the drought had so depleted the flocks and lowered prices in Jordan that the Bedouin smuggled herds over the border into Israel, where grazing land was provided by the state. The committee recommended that drought compensation be given in the same areas to Bedouin and Jewish sectors alike, above the "aridity line" that followed minimum amounts of average rainfall—that is, the northwest-east line from Kibbutz Magen to Moshav Patish to Kibbutz Mishmar HaNegev to the Jordanian-Israeli Armistice border. Included was a general recommendation to develop further the study on grazing for the herd and promote experimental farms based on the use of runoff water.[44]

In October, Amir arranged a meeting with the sheikhs and Aloni to explain the issues of land leases and pasture lands. Sheikh al-'Atawnah said he would be willing to accept the recommendations since they applied equally to the Bedouin and Jewish communities. Despite the risks and the policy of noncompensation, he said, the Bedouin would continue to plant their crops. However, he did not agree to the policy requiring Bedouin who had been displaced to pay a land lease fee and asked that they be exempted from such payment. In principle, he was not opposed to developing the land but insisted on finalizing the ownership process that Yoav Zuckerman had initiated years earlier. Aloni declined. The fees were nominal, he explained, and the papers the Bedouin had in their possession showed insufficient proof of landownership. Other sheikhs asked for cultivable land in exchange, but Aloni replied that such land was unavailable. When they brought up their need for pastureland, Aloni argued that they engaged in too many husbandries in the expectation that the government would grant them pasture and that they would be able to find enough employment as laborers.[45]

While the risk of crop failure without compensation brought changes in the use of lands in Jewish settlements below the aridity line, it was less so within the Bedouin settlements, where many kept doing dry cultivation. In December 1962, when the drought affected their crops, they became uneasy about not being compensated. Bedouin sheikhs argued before the president of Israel, government ministers, and Knesset members that the policy discriminated against them by giving drought compensation only to Jewish cultivators but ignoring the fact that compensation was given only to cultivators

Figure 4.1. A Bedouin family and their motor car camping near Lod. August 1, 1963. *Photo: Moshe Pridan. Source: The Government Press Office.*

above the aridity line. Furthermore, they complained that the drought and severe water shortage had decimated half their flocks, and their pleas for more grazing land had gone unanswered. These were urgent issues, they remonstrated, that had to be directly addressed.[46]

At the beginning of 1963, the driest winter in years, grazing land in the Negev was scarce, and conflicts erupted again between Bedouin herders and Jewish farmers.[47] The herds invaded irrigated areas and plantations producing severe damage and loss. When asked for help, the military administration declared that it was willing to interfere only in the case of security risks, not in civil disputes over Bedouin tents and trespassers.[48] As the situation deteriorated further, Bar-Zvi, who had replaced Amir as Negev military governor, convened a meeting of IDF officials, intelligence bodies, and the police to discuss the matter. The outcome was a stern letter of warning about the severity of the situation and the lack of data and supervision of the Bedouin outside the Negev region. It also noted the rising frequency of scrimmages and smuggling activities and the intensification of hostile nationalism unchecked by the governor and the police.[49]

Their concerns proved justified, and in May violent clashes broke out, injuring scores of Bedouin and Jews.[50] Only then did the government intervene. The Ministry of the Interior called on the government to establish an interministerial committee to frame the measures "against the damages caused by the free movement of Negev Bedouin herds."[51] The suggested interministerial committee would include representatives of the Ministry of the Interior, the Ministry of Agriculture, the police, and the military administration. Dayan, who was in favor of moving the Bedouin north, objected to the motion, claiming it was not within his ministry's authority to restrict Bedouin movement. Hence, instead of the interministerial committee, the government decided to create only a consultative forum made up of the Ministries of the Interior and Agriculture, the police, the head of the military administration, and the PM Adviser, who would recommend measures to forestall any damage caused by the free movement of Bedouin herds away from the Negev.[52]

In late July 1963, Dayan gave an interview to *Haaretz* in which he explained that although the Jewish farmers in the northern region were not very happy about it, he was pleased to see Bedouin herders there. He reiterated his view that the Bedouin should settle in towns and cities where they would be able to earn a living as laborers, a state of affairs that was achievable within a few generations, he believed. To his mind, the idea of establishing Bedouin agricultural villages was patently absurd.[53]

On receiving the proposal for a consultative forum, the government convened and decided to address the problem of the herders on a case-by-case basis and not as a comprehensive policy. Accordingly, if a Bedouin herder threatened public safety or caused damage to property, the police had the discretion to notify the Ministry of Agriculture, and the latter had discretion to recommend the cancellation of the herder's free movement permit by the military administration. Likewise, when necessary, the Ministry of Agriculture would increase the water supply to those farms that provided the Bedouin with water.[54] This was far less than the Ministry of the Interior had intended with the motion.

In August 1963, a few weeks after Levi Eshkol became prime minister of Israel, Sheikh al-Huzayyil wrote to him calling for his help to ensure that Bedouin lands would be registered in their name.[55] After that, eleven sheikhs convened a press interview in which they pleaded with the government not to expropriate the lands outside Arad as part of their regional development plan.[56]

In October, after several attempts by the Knesset to bring an end to the military administration, PM Eshkol declared that he did not think the time had come for this. His plan, he said, was to make the military administration "invisible" and minimize its role, which would gradually be transferred to the police.[57] The plan did not entirely succeed, but it brought some relief to

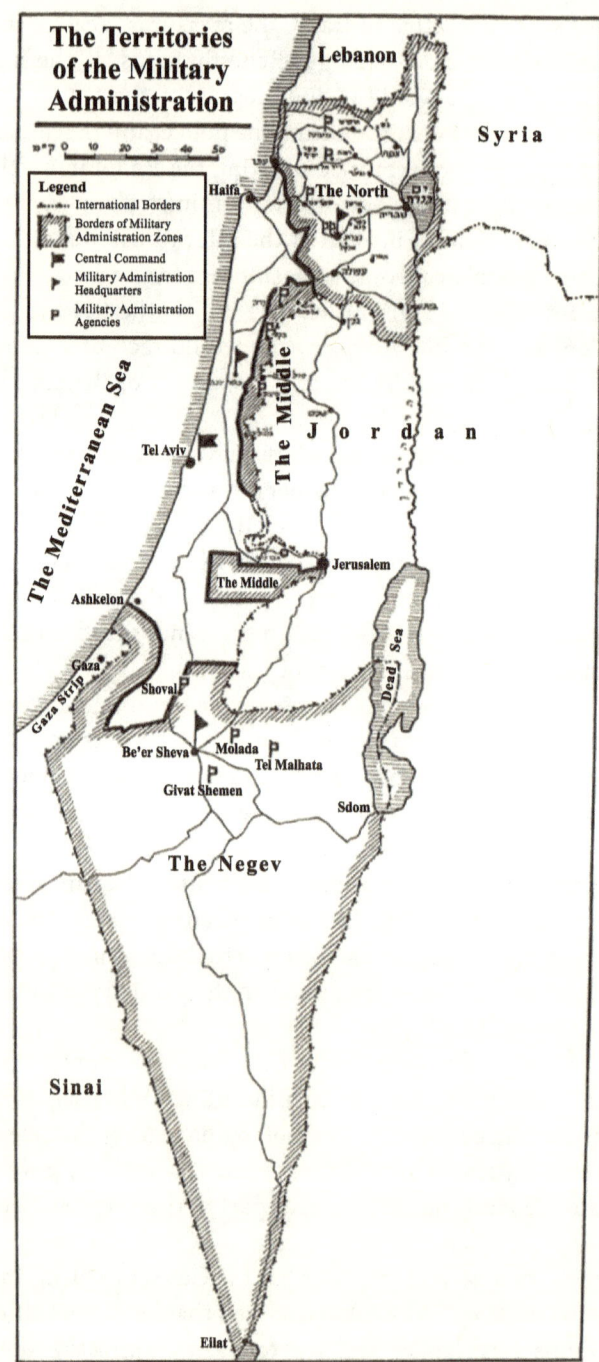

Map 4.3. Military administration boundaries and agencies, 1966.
Source: file GL-17004/4, Israel State Archives [originally in Hebrew].

the Arabs in their daily life.⁵⁸ Map 4.3 shows the military administration territories and its agencies.

The Negev Military Administration authorities and their ability to influence state policy had now suffered another blow. Their role was now more marginal than ever. Their approval of movement permits was no longer required, and their tasks were limited to dealing with minor issues like local disputes and low-level security concerns, which they delegated to the sheikhs.⁵⁹ Their most notable activity was the January 1964 replacement of two ineffectual sheikhs who were opposed by their tribes. In the case of the al-'Atawnah tribe, the sheikh was replaced by his brother-in-law who had led a struggle against him. In the case of al-'Ugbi, the replacement was the brother of a deposed sheikh who had been himself deposed in 1951 at the request of this fractious tribe.⁶⁰

Government Approval of the First Bedouin Localities in the Negev

The rainy winter of 1964 enabled the Bedouin herders to remain in the Negev instead of moving north for pasture, as they had during the long years of the drought. After protracted delays, the issue of Bedouin settlements was finally discussed in the Ministerial Committee for Economic Affairs, to which it had been transferred.⁶¹

At a meeting on January 12, 1964, the committee approved the expropriation of five hundred dunams in the Be'er Sheva area (i.e., Tel Sheva), at the discretion of the Ministry of Finance, for "the establishment of a residential area for the Bedouin."⁶² This was the first government decision to establish a specific locality for the Bedouin in the Negev.

PM Eshkol planned a visit to the Negev, and in anticipation, Bar-Zvi prepared a report in which he explained the role of Bedouin lands, noting that although there were not very many Bedouin in the Sayig, the land there was critical. The Bedouin understanding of this was that the state wished to turn them into laborers and take away their lands, since they did not have the necessary documentation. To assert their claims, they built structures. He also noted that the Bedouin expressed a willingness to accept all solutions so long as they could remain in their current location. In reality, he added, the Bedouin had no place to build legally, so the government's campaign against their illegal building seemed arbitrary, a means of sidestepping the issue.⁶³

Government deliberation over the localities bandied back and forth several times. On March 2, 1964, two months after the decision on Tel Sheva, the Ministry of Finance presented the Ministerial Committee for Economic Affairs with a motion for the approval of three Bedouin localities. One, the future Tel Sheva on the outskirts of Be'er Sheva, was already approved; the second was the future Rahat near Kibbutz Shoval in an area under the influence of the al-Huzayyil tribe; and the third was next to Tel Malhata. Bedouin who wished to settle in cities near the center of the country would be allotted grants to do so.[64] This plan was quite different from the seven localities proposed at the meeting of the interministerial committee only a few months earlier.[65]

The ministerial committee did not authorize the three locations. Instead, on April 19, 1964, they decided to create an Interministerial Directors General Committee "to prepare a decision proposal regarding building sites for the Negev Bedouin," headed by Israel Land Administration, meaning by Weitz, and with the participation of the directors general of the government ministries and the PM Adviser. The committee was charged with the task of drawing up a proposal for Bedouin construction sites within two weeks.[66]

When partial information about the decisions on the establishment of new committees for Bedouin issues reached the press, MK Yusef Khamis submitted a parliamentary question about a rumored secret committee with a secret plan to displace thousands of Bedouin. PM Eshkol answered that a ministerial committee had addressed the issue and would submit its recommendations in the coming weeks.[67]

On July 26, 1964, Weitz presented the Interministerial Directors General Committee recommendations to the ministers. In the first stage, three sites would be authorized in the vicinity of Be'er Sheva, Shoval, and Tel Malhata. In the next stage, with planning completed, steps would be taken to deter illegal construction. The site near Be'er Sheva would be the first in which the building would be carried out, and every Bedouin family that settled there would be eligible to receive a one-half dunam plot of land and a housing unit. Bedouin who preferred to settle in towns north of Be'er Sheva would receive grants.[68] An ensuing interministerial coordinating committee, composed of the PM Adviser and representatives of the ministries, would submit a detailed recommendation, including a budget.[69]

Several objections were made to this proposal. In his last period as minister of agriculture (he resigned in November 1964), Dayan kept insisting that the sites should become suburbs of existing cities and that any Bedouin who received a grant would have to give up an alternative claim to the land. The Ministry of Defense demanded that the locations be determined at or near the current Bedouin sites, and the Ministry of Labor stressed the need to affirm that new illegal structures would be subject to demolition.[70]

On August 16, 1964, the Ministerial Committee on Economic Affairs authorized the immediate building of one hundred housing units, under the aegis of the Ministry of Housing, "as part of Be'er Sheva, in coordination with the municipality and others."[71] It further ordered a report on the implementation of the plans to be submitted within a year. The remaining recommendations of the Weitz Committee were set aside for further consideration. There was no mention as to which Bedouin family would be the first to inhabit these housing units, which would be open to all Bedouin.

In December 1964, the issue of Galilee and Negev Bedouin settlements was brought before the Knesset, this time by MK Tawfik Toubi, the Arab Israeli politician from the Maki (Communist) party. Why were the Bedouin, he asked, placed in settlements and treated like nomads, which they no longer were? What justified their displacement, and according to what law was the process carried out?[72] Aharon Layish, deputy PM Adviser for Arab Affairs, replied that the Bedouin were not being forced to live in settlements and that their settlements in planned localities were the duty of a modern state wishing to provide services. "Arab countries like Syria and Iraq have not refrained from enacting special laws for the concentration and settlement of the Bedouin," he added. "Why is this action appreciated when it is done in a neighboring Arab country but does not receive the same treatment when it is done in Israel?!"[73]

These broader dilemmas remain unanswered: What law has actually been implemented in Bedouin issues, and should Israel act differently from other Middle Eastern countries on the matter?

The miscommunication and lack of coordination between the local and state levels made it difficult to promote a clear policy on Bedouin settlement. One such example was the approval of building plans for the establishment of three localities by the Southern District Planning Bureau on January 18, 1965. The district ratified City Building Plan D 407/4 for constructing localities that would house a thousand families in each of the three. It also determined that during the first stage, half the plots would be developed together with their infrastructure and facilities, with room left for expansion in the future.[74] However, this contradicted the decision of the Ministerial Committee for Economic Affairs, which had approved the establishment of only one locality.

On September 12, 1965, over a year after its initial decision, the ministerial committee agreed to the district's decision to promote two additional sites near Shoval and Tel Malhata, where lenient terms would be granted to lessees.[75] The committee further decided to create two more committees: an interministerial committee, later referred to as the Supreme Bedouin Committee, for the implementation of the plans, which would include the PM Adviser as chair and the Ministries of Housing, Agriculture, Labor, and Interior as well as the Israel Land Administration and the Negev Military Administration, and the second, a Directors General Committee of ministries to decide on additional sites for permanent settlements and their funding, which would include the minister of agriculture as chair and the Ministries of Labor, Housing, Interior, and Finance.[76]

In December 1965, a team of planners tasked with planning the sites near al-Huzayyil and Tel Malhata submitted a report on their progress, noting the urgency of the situation since the "main goal is to find a solution to the problem of illegal construction, which has taken on alarming dimensions, especially this winter."[77] The committee reported that the building of the infrastructures was scheduled for April and identified the lands due to be expropriated for them in the course of 1966.[78]

The promotion of Bedouin localities was the target of much criticism. *Al Hamishmar*'s headings were sarcastic: "Again 'A Plan' for Bedouin Settlement."[79] Gideon Wigard wrote that Jordanian plans for Bedouin settlement had started more than five years earlier, and three years later a special law had been enacted to settle nomadic Bedouin while at the same time Israel lacked a firm policy for its twenty-five thousand Bedouin inhabitants.

In criticizing the plan, the report noted that it provided a solution for only a small segment of the Bedouin population, a solution that was basically experimental and limited in scope, with almost no outreach to the community and hardly any cultural activity. Meanwhile, the Bedouin were discriminated against and were not provided with the services they deserved.[80]

At another meeting in the district planning office for a discussion on how the work on the Bedouin settlement was proceeding, the planners indicated that no enlightening examples had been found elsewhere that might foster a better understanding of the processes of nomadic settlement around the world. The planners asked for advice on the desired profile of the locality, whether to establish an urban settlement that would bridge a developmental gap or whether they should aim at the integration or separation of the Bedouin.[81] No Bedouin were present to provide their own views on the matter, nor were any members of the Negev Military Administration. While these questions remained unanswered, the planners moved ahead and focused on housing for young families, the heads of which would be employed as workers in the vicinity.[82]

Splits, Protests, and the Termination of the Military Administration

From the start, the military administration of the Negev had attributed much significance to Bedouin tribal affiliations. As explained in chapter 2, some tribes were made up of clans and offshoots of tribes that had remained in Israel and were merged by the state into tribal units led by a nominated sheikh. Hence, disputes and calls for tribal separation were to be expected. Appealing to the state with requests gave the Bedouin more freedom and at the same time undermined the existing tribal framework and the authority of the sheikh. In 1963, a group of some eight hundred Bedouin of fellahin origins led by Sliman Mustafa a-Nasasrah, who was affiliated with the influential Abu Rabiʿah tribe, petitioned the Supreme Court for independent status.[83] In pursuance of this, six members of the a-Nasasrah segment sent a formal letter to the Ministry of the Interior in September 1964, requesting to be considered as an independent tribal unit.[84] However, the ministry was willing only to grant the a-Nasasrah the right to have their ID address printed as a-Nasasrah, without the independent tribal status they had requested. The same request was submitted in the name of several other groups of fellahin-Bedouin who were likewise affiliated with influential sheikhs. Bar-Zvi was aware of the severe reactions this was likely to meet from the sheikhs and the long-term consequences on the existing tribal order if someone of non-Bedouin origin were permitted by the state to form a tribal unit on par with genuine Bedouin tribes. Thus, he rejected the petition outright with solemn words about how such a request was liable to prompt similar ones from other factions, leading in turn to a multiplicity of tribes that would result in a significant shock to their society—with all that this implied.[85] Although Bar-Zvi was able to postpone these divisions in 1964, gradually and with the flow of further demands for the separation of fellahin-Bedouin, his views became more ambiguous. In July 1965, another petition was sent by Muhammad Salman a-Zabargah on behalf of 1,500 people, and in December additional petitions were sent by Abu ʿAmmar, Abu Gweder, and Abu ʿAbed. Bar-Zvi noted that these Bedouin wished to separate themselves from the genuine Bedouin.[86] Bar-Zvi explained that although the committee did not encourage separation, the time had come to accept the fact that it could no longer be averted. Requests for separation would have to be considered in accordance with the minimum number of group members and the goals of the state, like their willingness to live in settled communities. A-Nasasrah responded with a letter expressing his willingness in that regard.[87]

By March 1965, cooperation between the military administration and the Bedouin sheikhs was drawing criticism from left-wing parties. An article with the headline "Fraud Perpetrated by Mapai and the Military Administration Revealed to Bedouin," published in *Al-Ittihad*, the Maki party newspaper in Arabic, accused the military administration of restricting the freedom of the Bedouin with the support of sheikhs hired to act against the interests

Figure 4.2. Bedouin women shepherd and flock in the Negev. January 1, 1966. Photographer unknown. *Source: The Government Press Office.*

of their communities. The article also noted that the military administration used bribery to enlist the sheikhs.[88]

As pressure on the government to terminate the military administration mounted, PM Eshkol suggested that it should be done shortly after the elections of November 1965.[89] A few months later, he announced his intention to shut it down within a year.[90]

In early 1966, after two rainy years, the drought returned, and with it the old conflict between herders and cultivators. Issar Harel, in his role as security adviser to the PM, convened a meeting with the police, the Israel Land Administration, and the Ministry of Agriculture, at which a decision was reached to limit the size of the herds and establish patrol units to supervise herders.[91] A few weeks later, and without Negev Military Administration involvement, the IDF closed off large tracts of land previously used for grazing to serve as military training areas. The Bedouin were vocal in their mistrust of the PM, who had announced the easing of military administration restrictions yet at the same time deprived them of their pasturage. Bar-Zvi pleaded their case before the IDF with some success.[92]

As the end of the military administration approached, Bar-Zvi tried to explain the importance of familiarity with Bedouin ways for the development of relations that would serve the country's goals. In his letter to the military administration, he described the interministerial committee for Bedouin settlement as being "almost detached from everyday reality on the ground." The knowledge and experience acquired by the Negev Military Administration were vitally important, he stressed, and "should be fully integrated" in the process of Bedouin settlement since so many delays and problems were liable to arise.[93]

However, as settlement plans proceeded alongside the changes brought about by the dismantling of the military administration, previous forms of relationship and cooperation with the Bedouin were forestalled. The Bedouin publicized their demands and strictures in a series of rallies and petitions calling on the government to freeze its plans until the land problem could be solved.[94] In the course of a large press conference, the sheikhs declared that although they remained loyal to the state, they intended to use every possible method and agency, including the international arena and the UN, in their struggle over land issues.[95] Bar-Zvi's report on the press conference notes that the statements of the prominent sheikhs were extremely sobering, as was the fact that they had kept the matter from the military administration.[96] In an attempt to restore calm, the PM Adviser held a meeting with seventy sheikhs, but without much success.[97] Bar-Zvi was not invited to the meeting and learned of it from the Bedouin.[98] The greatly troubling Bedouin protest was discussed at the Central Committee meeting on June 30, which recommended taking "vigorous activities to inform the general public in a constructive way about the issue of Bedouin settlement and land settlement in the Bedouin areas in the Negev."[99]

Toward the end of his role as the Negev military governor, Bar-Zvi drafted a comprehensive policy proposal for solving Bedouin land and settlement issues. This proposal signaled the start of a new era without the Negev Military Administration. Bar-Zvi explained that if followed, his policy would expedite the government settlement plans. He noted too that the unified front the Bedouin presented in their arguments was merely superficial. And in fact, they were widely diverse. Some Bedouin had been relocated, some had not, and only about half of them had valid claims. Bar-Zvi called for large-scale expropriation and reallocation of land.[100] His plan was not followed.[101]

The continuing strategy of the Bedouin included measures like forming a group opposed to government policy that would establish a committee of sheikhs to represent their issues.[102] While Bar-Zvi was highly concerned about possible ramifications, Harsina regarded the Bedouin protests and the ending of the Negev Military Administration as a constructive turning point in relations between the Bedouin and the state and welcomed the challenges it brought to the fore. He seemed eager to apply Israeli law to the

Bedouin: "The Bedouin have begun to feel the beginnings of an actual state policy, which may (perhaps) reduce the chaos they are accustomed to.... We should not in my opinion, be deterred by their outcry and let the institutions ([Israel Land] Administration and the [PM] Adviser) act on the matter according to the way that law and good order require."[103]

The end of the military administration was declared in December 1966.[104] At that stage, the Bedouin population in the Negev comprised some four thousand families who had built eleven thousand illegal structures, mainly shacks, while thousands of flocks continued to graze in the center of the country.[105]

Discussion and Conclusions

During the first half of the 1960s, the central government and its various ministries gradually assumed control over relations with the Bedouin. The Negev Military Administration continued to adhere to a strategy of cooperation with tribal frameworks as the appropriate way of dealing with the Bedouin. The Sayig was administered by the Negev Military Administration as a separate enclave within the state in which the law accorded with the principles of tribalism rather than those laid down directly by the state. But as the Negev Military Administration gradually lost power, so did the old rules.

Contrary to the Negev Military Administration, the central government viewed Israel and all officials, including government ministers, as a single unit under its control. The Negev was never formally viewed as an independent enclave. There was much more in the area than the Bedouin, and the state had other interests there, particularly in the Arad region. In light of this, all state laws, especially laws concerning land and settlement, were applicable throughout the Negev to the same extent that they applied in other areas of the country.

Yet once the central government began to promote settlement plans, state laws dealing with issues of illegal construction and landownership led to confrontations with Bedouin sheikhs who demanded formal recognition of their land rights.

Moreover, state initiatives served to reaffirm the sheikhs' leadership status and unity of the tribes. This was particularly necessary for the sheikhs, considering the weakening of tribal frameworks during the drought and the dispersal of many of them to different areas and walks.

The tension between the state, which sought to apply its planning regulations and laws, versus the principles of tribalism, stood in opposition to yet another aspiration of the state—that is, the avoidance of confrontation. Thus, state practice, as expressed in the decisions of the ministerial committee of the 1960s, gradually progressed through a process of trial and error, led by events such as illegal construction, rather than leading events by means of timely plans.

Both the military administration and the state tried to avoid confrontation. However, while the military administration did so as part of a broad and conscious strategy of forming alliances with the tribes, the state had no such strategy. Declaratively, the state announced the dismantling of tribalism, which drove antagonism and resentment toward it, but in practice it surrendered to tribal norms when needed to restore the calm.

It was during this period that the gap between intention and implementation widened. As we shall see in the next chapter, Harsina was completely wrong in his assertion that ending the military administration would bring the Israeli rule of law to the Negev.

PART III

5

NEW INSTITUTIONS—
OLD ALLIANCES, 1967–71

> One must be very careful about demands which
> could be interpreted as demanding changes in the
> Bedouin way of life or social structure. Presumably,
> the policy is that the Israel Land Authority will not
> dive deeper or cause any shocks in this regard.
>
> *Shulamit Levi, State Comptroller*
> *Office, 1967*

In late 1966, at a particularly sensitive time, the military administration came to an end. First steps had been taken by the government to promote the establishment of three Bedouin sites in the Negev: Tel Sheva, Kseyfah, and the area near Shoval. This might have signaled the start of Harsina's hoped-for era of a full application of Israeli law, but it was not what happened. The powers and responsibilities of the military administration were transferred to other agencies. The Bedouin tribal framework also remained as it had been, with each family formally affiliated with a tribal unit, under a nominated sheikh. The latter continued to function as mediators between the state and Bedouin citizens in various spheres of life such as land allocation; mail addresses; birth, death, and marriage registrations; and so forth.

Approval of the tribal framework was qualified to some degree by the state comptroller, whose role was to review the legality and ethicality of public institutions. In his report, published in 1967 for the previous year, the comptroller expressed some concern about the arrangements with the sheikhs regarding the allocation of lands to them as mediators rather than according to the procedure. While indicating the legal problems involved, he was reluctant to censure the sheikhs' mediation. In the internal record that preceded the final report, Shulamit Levi of the comptroller's office explained, "One must be very careful about demands which could be interpreted as demanding changes in the Bedouin way of life or social structure. Presumably, the policy is that the Israel Land Authority will not dive deeper or cause any shocks in this regard."[1]

In his final report, the comptroller was satisfied with a vague recommendation noting that "here it is necessary to maintain as many accepted customs as possible and at the same time to institute arrangements for which a state administration can take responsibility."[2] He did not specify how two such contradictory clauses could accommodate each other.

Institutional Duties and Responsibilities

Once the military administration was abolished, the security dimension of its executive tasks was transferred to the police and the Southern Command of the IDF.[3] The police took over the military administration's responsibility for granting permits as well as its physical facilities and opened a new police station in Arad.[4] Members of the Mapam party criticized the police for their dilatory and cumbersome handling of Arab matters and for their harshness and lack of transparency compared to the military administration.[5] The military administration had taken broad discretion and implemented tailor-made regional policies while the police department was a bureaucratic body and showed less flexibility. Toledano, when asked about this, explained that the frustration of the Arabs was also due to police strictness in enforcing the law and their unwillingness to turn a blind eye as the military administration had.[6]

The powers of the military governors that were based on the Defense (Emergency) Regulations of 1945, including the authority to restrict various rights and limitations on the free movement of the Bedouin, were now transferred to the IDF Southern Command.[7] The latter had formed a new unit headed by a lieutenant colonel: Assistant Military Commander in the Southern Command (hereafter Assistant Military Commander).

Although the title does not suggest it, it was in fact an operational field unit tasked with working alongside police in order "to maintain the proper course of life for the Bedouin in the Sayig."[8] Like the police patrols, this unit too had patrols charged with demonstrating Israeli rule, preventing the formation of nationalist cells and hostile sabotage activities, barring the Bedouin from entering prohibited areas, driving out trespassers, maintaining contact with the population, and collecting information that could help avert hostilities.[9]

The PM Adviser also played a central role that extended to Bedouin settlements. Shmuel Toledano retained his position, and Joseph Ginat and Uri Mor were his main representatives in Bedouin affairs.[10] Toledano's ties with the PM and his part in the Central Committee gave him influence, but the PM Adviser had no executive power and no means of implementation. Toledano's success in promoting policy was based on his ability to motivate others, which was done by convening meetings and leading interministerial forums. Toledano continued in his role as chair of the Supreme Bedouin Committee, which was established by the government in 1965 as the highest level interministerial forum for decision-making and supervision of Bedouin settlement.[11] At the local level, a representative of the PM Adviser replaced the Negev military governor as chair of the Negev Regional Committee, which had been established in the 1950s to discuss security issues.[12] A representative of the PM Adviser replaced the military governor also in the Lease Committee, another old committee for land allocation.[13]

The Return of the Drought

In early 1967, after two rainy seasons, and just as the PM Adviser's office was beginning to advance the settlement process, the drought returned, and Bedouin herders started moving northward.[14] In January 1967, Bedouin tents were scattered widely, everywhere from Beit Kama in the south to Haifa in the north.[15] Large encampments appeared in the Lod-Ramleh area, and some 3,300 individual Bedouin were counted around Tel Aviv, in the Moledet neighborhood of Hulon, in Herzliya, and in Bnei Brak. Security forces worried about the tents pitched near military bases like Tel HaShomer (see map 5.1).[16] Tens of thousands of sheep were counted, about forty thousand head in the strip between Rosh Ha'Ayin and the Jerusalem Corridor alone. Many Bedouin encamped in the sand dunes near Rishon LeZion, Palmahim, and Ashdod, as well as in the hills around Rehovot and Gedera. At this time, too, scores of tents were left empty in the Negev with a single guard.[17]

Once again, the future of the Negev Bedouin was in question. The Central Committee raised doubts as to whether Bedouin settlements in the Negev were a viable solution.[18] On February 9, 1967, it was decided "that action should be taken on a number of levels including the establishment of Bedouin towns in the vicinity of Gedera, Ramleh, etc."[19] But soon after, on March 9, the decision was reversed, and actions were ordered to return all Bedouin to the south.[20] Although the Central Committee did not indicate any reason for this reversal, presumably, as on previous occasions, it involved complaints by the local Jewish population in the central region against the Bedouin herders.

As Ginat noted, so long as the Bedouin continued to encamp outside the Sayig, "the advancement of the housing projects and the building of new sites [in the Negev]" would be prevented.[21]

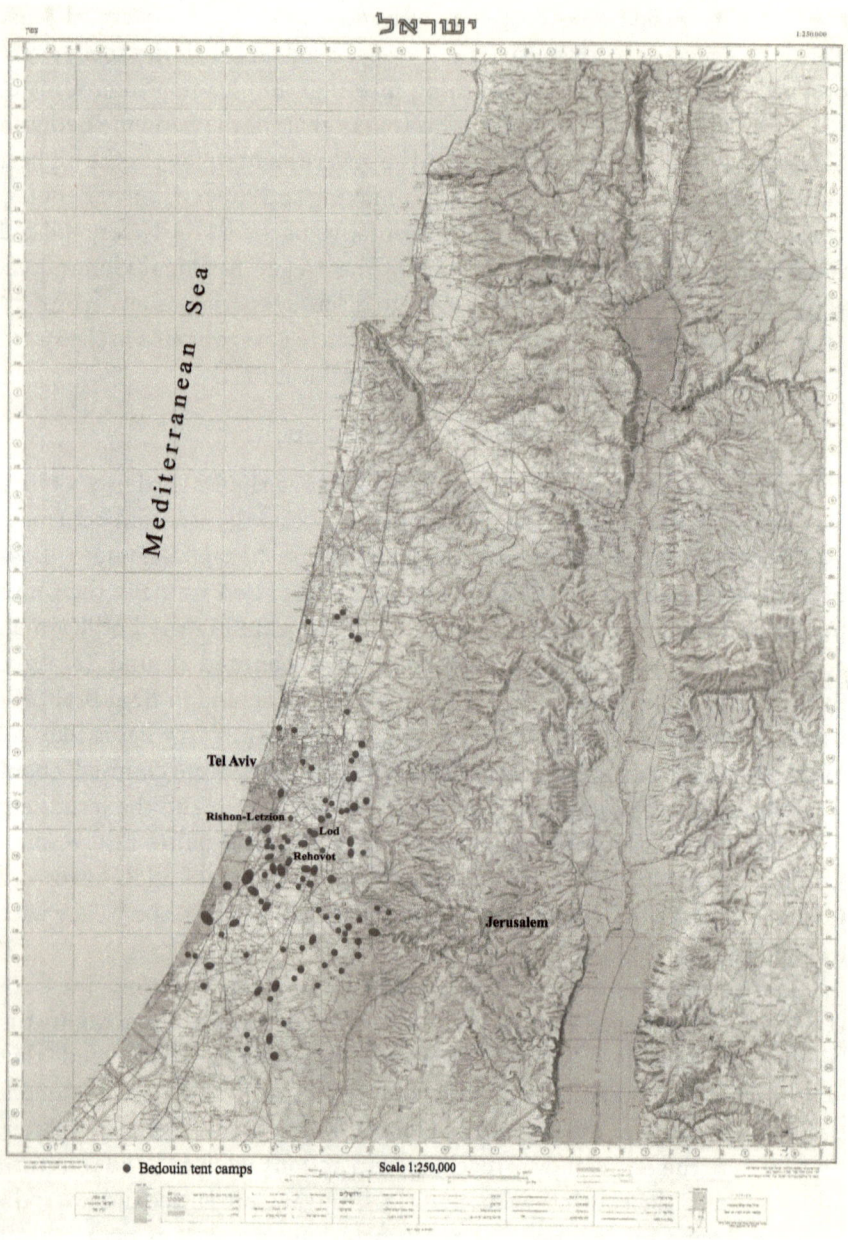

Map 5.1. Survey of Bedouin tents, attached to Joseph Ginat, "Review," March 20, 1967. *Source: file GL-13909/1, Israel State Archives [originally in Hebrew].*

Tribal Status and the Promotion of Bedouin Settlements

State authorities, led by the PM Adviser, maintained good relations with the Bedouin leadership as well as with the previous tribal framework. However, they were much less effective in using it to the benefit of the settlement process, and their efforts in many instances turned out to be unproductive. One such case occurred in May 1967, when the authorities finally gave the fellahin-Bedouin of a-Nasasrah, joined by the al-'Amur families, an independent tribal status detached from Sheikh Abu Rabi'ah, with whom they were affiliated. This status was granted to them after years of requests, upon their declaring their willingness to settle in an orderly way.[22] This was the first time a fellahin-Bedouin group had gained an independent status, and the PM Adviser explained that it would help contest Abu Rabi'ah's negative position on settlement.[23] However, in practice their declaration was of no avail since the land for the nearby site, Kseyfah, although confiscated, was de facto subject to the control of Abu Rabi'ah, from whom they had declared themselves independent.

Another example was an attempt by the PM Adviser to nominate new sheikhs according to their potential contribution to the settlement process. Such was the case of the nominated sheikh, a replacement for the deceased Sheikh 'Awwad Abu Rgayyig. The Abu Rgayyig tribe, the largest in terms of its members, was in fact an amalgamation of various tribes scattered around the Be'er Sheva Valley. The death of Sheikh Abu Rgayyig gave rise to disputes over leadership, along with requests for splits and divisiveness within the tribe.[24] In February 1967, the Negev Regional Committee discussed options for replacing sheikhs. Ginat, the chair of the meeting, promoted the idea of replacing Abu Rgayyig in accordance with "the willingness of each candidate to contribute to the success of the sites and organize people who would join the site."[25] All but three of the Negev sheikhs put pressure on the authorities to nominate Ibrahim Abu Rgayyig (also known as Dweyhi), who took a negative position on settlement.[26] The authorities surrendered to the pressure of the sheikhs. Sheikh Ibrahim Abu Rgayyig's position had an acutely negative effect; as a result, soon after, the authorities were unable to populate the town of Tel Sheva.

The Six-Day War (June 5–10, 1967)

On June 5, 1967, Israel began what came to be known as the Six-Day War, a preemptive strike on the combined Arab forces mounted against it. This followed Egypt's closing of the Straits of Tiran to Israeli ships in May 1967, the expulsion of the UN Peace Keeping Force from the Israeli-Egyptian border, and the movement of the Egyptian army toward the border. As the war began, Israel reimposed the military administration over the Arabs.[27] Between June 5 and 10, the IDF succeeded in capturing the Golan Heights from Syria, East Jerusalem; Judea and Samaria, known as the West Bank, from Jordan; and the Sinai Peninsula and Gaza Strip from Egypt.[28]

The war had a strong impact on the Negev Bedouin and the economic and demographic circumstances of their life. The opening of the borders with the West Bank, Gaza, and the Sinai Peninsula brought new markets and united families that had been separated in 1948.[29] The arrival of cheap labor from the West Bank and Gaza Strip meant that the Bedouin were less in demand as laborers, but their Israeli citizenship, bilingualism, and connections with people on the other side paved the way to their involvement in manpower contracting, construction, and transportation. The Bedouin enjoyed improved economic conditions and new occupations, although the profitability of other subsistence activities, mainly herding and smuggling, was in decline.[30]

While general restrictions on the movement of Arabs were terminated soon after the Six-Day War, the Bedouin still required daily permits for movement to the center of the country.[31] The measure was intended to decrease the number of Bedouin herders outside the Sayig and to encourage their settlement in the Negev.[32]

The new borders enabled Bedouin men from the Negev to marry women from the West Bank and Gaza.[33] It also intensified polygamy, a phenomenon that was marginal until then. The marriage of a Bedouin bride involved a dowry payment to her family, which was substantially lower in the case of non-Israeli women, due to the differences in the economy and standard of life. The PM Adviser estimated in November 1968 that about two thousand marriages had taken place with non-Israeli women,[34] many of whom were not accustomed to living in tents. This contributed to an increased building of shacks, which were less expensive than tents thanks to the cheap materials now obtainable from the West Bank and Gaza.[35] Overall, construction grew by 30 percent within the first three years after the war, from about 1,000 in 1966, to about 1,300 in 1969.[36]

While most of the shacks and huts were built of cheap materials and easily disassembled and rebuilt elsewhere, some were made of stone blocks. The latter could not be relocated and were perceived by the authorities as attempts to establish a fait accompli contrary to the policy of orderly planning.[37] An example of this was the building of a dozen or so two-to three-room residential blocks in 1968 at the Shoval [Rahat] site by members of the al-Huzayyil tribe associated the family of the sheikh. These Bedouin disregarded court orders and calls by the authorities to negotiate legal building permits on the grounds that "they do not recognize the expropriation of the land and consider themselves to be its legal owners."[38] The state preferred to demolish only a few of these houses and reach an agreement with Sheikh al-Huzayyil, granting him special rights, in order to keep him from interfering in the development of the site.[39]

"Kazzaz's Army"

A prominent manifestation of the tribal-state alliance, not connected with the settlement process, was the military initiative of creating a tribal army unit. In September 1968, Sheikh ʿAwdah Abu Muʿammar, together with Lieutenant Colonel Nissim Kazzaz, the assistant military commander, established a unit of Bedouin trackers and cameleers. These Bedouin were recruited by Sheikh Abu Muʿammar and were "under his supervision."[40] Sheikh Abu Muʿammar was the closest Bedouin ally and supporter of a Jewish state prior to 1948 and the only Bedouin to receive a medal for his contribution to Israel's security in the War of Independence.[41] The mission of the Bedouin unit was to fight against infiltrators in the Arava.[42] The trackers, who numbered no more than seventy, were not drafted into the IDF and were paid on a daily basis. In light of their successes in locating and capturing infiltrators and weapons, "they were given control of an area from Mitzpe Ramon to about 100 km south."[43] According to Kazzaz, the unit was nicknamed "The Kazzaz Army" by his fellows in the IDF. Though the unit was dismantled shortly after Kazzaz left his position in 1970, the fact that there was a small corps of Bedouin nonconscripts tasked with army missions under a tribal sheikh enhanced the tribe's perception of its military unit as separate from the state.

Tel Sheva

The decisions of the Population Committee regarding the sheikh's role in Tel Sheva and all future settlements demonstrate the path that began with confrontations over the settlements themselves and ended with extraordinary attempts by the authorities to achieve an alliance with a prominent sheikh.

Tel Sheva was one of three sites in which the government decided in 1965 to create orderly settlements for the Bedouin.[44] Then, in 1966, lands were confiscated to make them formally available for that purpose. Such towns were supposed to be heterogeneous and introduce the Israeli modern way of life to the Negev Bedouin. Once settled, each Bedouin would get his own address and become a free individual independent of the sheikh and his tribal unit. While settlement was a desirable target from the perspective of the state, it was not seen as such by the sheikhs and the leadership of the tribes. Settlement was against their interests and traditions and seemed to threaten their claims to land rights. Hence, it is not surprising that they strongly objected to it.

The overall development, planning, and construction of housing in Tel Sheva was put into the hands of the Ministry of Housing, headed by Mordechai Bentov of the Mapam party, the coalition party closest to Bedouin issues.[45] The detailed blueprints were drawn up by the architect Arieh Peled, then an employee of the Ministry of Housing.[46] The town was designed in a modern style with a grid street plan, similar to the standard layout for Israeli development towns like Dimona, Arad, and Yeruham.[47] Any Bedouin could settle in the town, which included a commercial center, stores, and cafés to attract young families looking for a modern way of life[48] (see map 5.2).

In November 1967, the blueprints were approved by the Southern District Planning Committee.[49] They covered a total of 206 dunams for 220 residential units, public areas, and public buildings.

The Ministry of Housing recruited architects to design uniform model homes that would accommodate and incline the Bedouin to modern living while addressing specific aspects of their traditional life. After consultations with Bedouin who expressed interest in settling there, the homes were designed with wide courtyards so that the women would not be seen from the street and two entrances: a front entrance facing the street and leading to the men's area used for hosting, and a back entrance leading to the kitchen courtyard, the bedrooms, and the bathroom for use by the women and the rest of the family.[50]

Toward the end of 1967, Zvi Gluzman, then in charge of minority housing at the ministry, reported to the High Bedouin Committee that twenty-two housing units and public buildings were nearing completion, that Bedouin had registered for twelve housing units, and that more and more of them showed an interest in populating the town.[51]

In March 1968, the High Bedouin Committee approved the building of another twenty-eight houses in Tel Sheva and developed the infrastructure for one hundred more plots, half of them to accommodate temporary shacks for those subject to demolition orders. The High Bedouin Committee decided to start advertising the town as well.[52] It was presented in glowing colors as revolutionary and progressive.

In November 1968, Ginat described Tel Sheva as a great success. Bedouin from mixed tribes had registered for housing and the "demand exceeds the supply." He assumed that in time the Bedouin pursuit of modern housing would increase.[53]

But the euphoria did not last long. In early 1969, the actual process of populating Tel Sheva met with certain problems. Some Bedouin had begun to speak against the housing format and argued that it did not suit their lifestyle, that the houses were built too close together, and lacked the open space

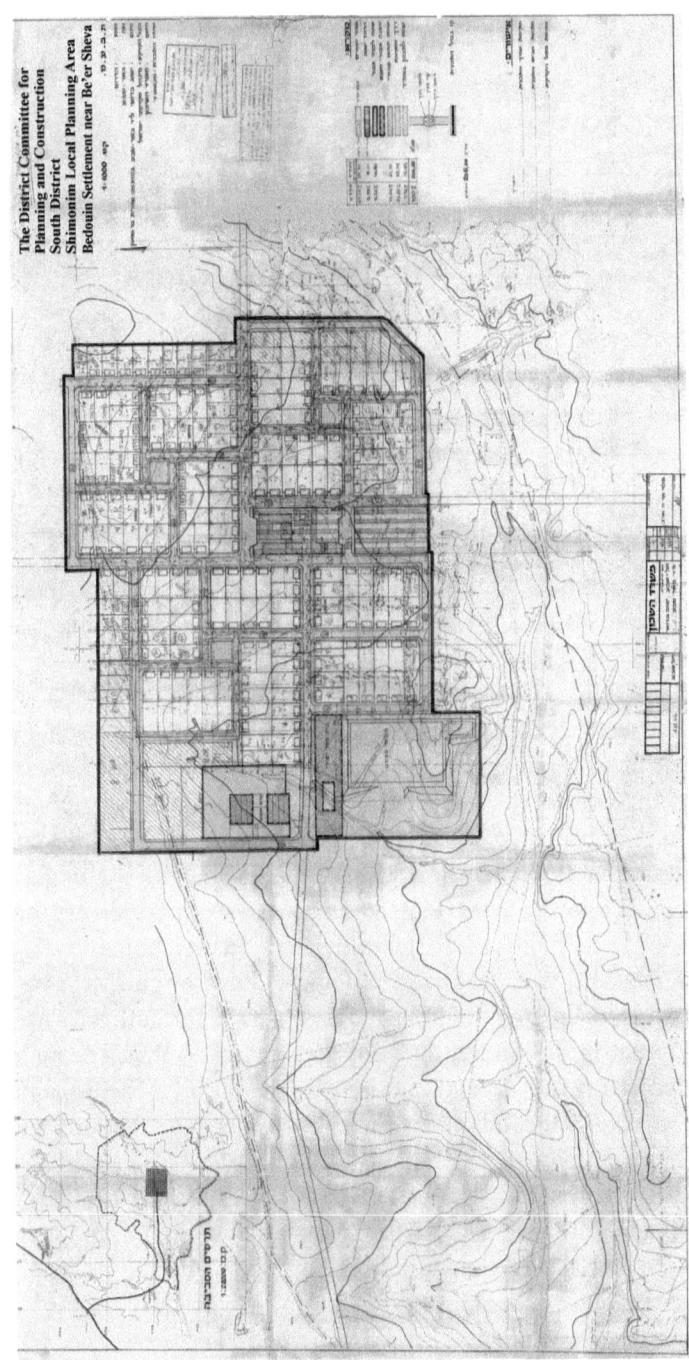

Map 5.2. Tel Sheva detailed plan, 1968, 137/03/7. *Source: Ministry of Interior [originally in Hebrew].*

Figure 5.1. Official inauguration ceremony of Tel Sheva, June 4, 1969. *Photo: Fritz Cohen. Source: The Government Press Office.*

they were used to.[54] The newspaper *Lamerhav* reported that some had canceled their plans to move to the town, claiming that the prices were higher than agreed and that the Bedouin should own their houses, not lease them long-term.[55] But most concerning of all was the pressure the sheikhs put "on candidates not to enter the housing."[56] The difficulties in populating Tel Sheva made the government rethink and delay the promotion of other sites.[57]

Still, in January 1969, the first families entered their homes in Tel Sheva.[58] The earliest to settle were of mixed Bedouin-fellahin origin. Most were young wage workers. Following publications that blamed the authority for difficulties in populating Tel Sheva, the PM Adviser argued that "the main reason for not occupying the last eight houses [in Tel Sheva] is the influence of the sheikhs on potential candidates. The tribal leaders and factions are putting pressure on candidates not to enter the housing."[59]

Progress on construction in Tel Sheva was relatively swift.[60] In June, the glorious inauguration of Tel Sheva was celebrated with the completion of infrastructure for a total of one hundred plots and an additional one hundred in the process of planning and authorization[61] (see fig. 5.1).

Bentov, the housing minister, cut the ribbon and pronounced Tel Sheva a major success with both practical and symbolic dimensions. "The Negev Bedouin are starting to march forward in time, and integrate in the development of the State and raising the standard of living together with the

Figure 5.2. 'Abdul Qader Ibn Bari watering his vegetable garden in the backyard of his house in Tel Sheva. *Photo: Fritz Cohen, June 10, 1969. Source: The Government Press Office.*

rest of the citizens, Jews and Arabs of Israel," he said. To this he added, "We showed the world and try to show here also, how to turn a wasteland into a blooming settlement." He concluded his speech with the Mapam slogan: "Let's see this modest enterprise here be as one of the stones to build peace and brotherhood for the future to come."[62]

The national press office made efforts to promote positive media coverage that presented Tel Sheva as a revolutionary wonder. Photos of Bedouin watering their gardens, taking showers, and opening the refrigerators in their new homes were distributed in order to boost the Bedouin's motivation to settle[63] (see fig. 5.2).

In July, Deputy PM Yigal Allon showed his strong support on a visit to Tel Sheva as he strode hand in hand with Hadi Hamid Abu Taha, leader of the first families to settle there (see fig. 5.3).

New Institutions—Old Alliances, 1967–71   135

Figure 5.3. Deputy PM Yigal Allon hand in hand with Hadi Hamid Abu Taha in the commercial center of the newly established town of Tel Sheva, July 13, 1969. *Photo: Fritz Cohen. Source: The Government Press Office.*

However, in reality, the situation was not at all as it was presented. In October 1969, protests against Bedouin settlers escalated. Members of the Abu Rgayyig tribe attacked them, and four of Abu Taha's men, affiliated with the Tarabin tribe, submitted a complaint to the police on behalf of twenty-two Tel Sheva residents claiming that the Abu Rgayyig men, who opposed the government policy of settling Bedouin in Tel Sheva, "arrive every day to hit and beat our children and threaten our wives, for no reason whatsoever. The intention is that we leave the place and return to our tents, and do away with the government policy.... If we cannot live in peace during days and nights, and if they come at nights to attack and threaten us, and we receive no protection from the Israeli government, we will have no choice but to abandon our houses, and get the peace and quiet of our former tents."[64]

The Abu Rgayyig perpetrators were caught and prosecuted, but this was not enough to restore calm, and Bedouin were still fearful of moving to the town. The acts of Abu Rgayyig tribe members against the Tel Sheva settlers reflected their leader's opposition to the government plans. The process that had been set in motion without their explicit consent involved both people and areas that they perceived as subject to their control.

The Land Settlement Process

Sheikh Abu Rgayyig was not alone in his objection. Other sheikhs and leaders tried to halt the settlement policy. Some conditioned their support on solving their own land problem—that is, granting them ownership before advancing with any settlement plans.[65] They were unwilling to accept a policy that gave the state legal rights to expropriate lands for Bedouin towns. They were likewise dissatisfied with the state's promise that their settlement in the towns would not affect their previous legal status to land claims.[66] As claimants, they believed, they were entitled to decide who would and would not be allowed to live on the land.

The link between the settlement process and landownership was an ongoing challenge. Following earlier decisions to reach an agreement on ownership titles as a prerequisite for Bedouin settlement, the Ministry of Justice began the formal process.[67] See in map 5.3 the declaration and attached map.

The Bedouin were called by the land registrar to submit their formal ownership claims and put forward several thousand of them.[68] Some of the sheikhs had ownership claims to thousands of dunams. In early 1969, seventeen of the claims to lands in Gaser a-Sirr near Dimona, submitted earlier by the al-Hawashlah families, were sent by the registrar to be decided by the Be'er Sheva District Court.[69] These cases were supposed to provide a legal precedent that the authorities hoped would help them reach agreements in future.[70] But the court proceedings took years.[71] The PM Adviser's office described the processing of Bedouin issues as lackadaisical.[72] Sheikhs had been far from satisfied with the change in their land holdings before their claims were approved. A large delegation of Bedouin sheikhs met with Allon and called for solutions, linking future settlement with a solution to their land claims.[73]

Toledano, the PM Adviser, continued to seek solutions that would save the settlement process. He published a booklet that called for making compromises with the Bedouin over their claims to land in order to facilitate the move to towns and explained that their opposition to settlement was due to their fear of change. To the changes brought on by the settlement process were added changes in Bedouin professions and the effect of a democratic regime that allows all citizens to apply directly to government institutions without the need for mediation. Toledano's booklet stated that "there is a natural opposition on the part of the sheikhs who incite against settlement in the towns for fear of losing influence."[74] The booklet expressed the need to accelerate the implementation of the policy while noting that unless the settlement process was planned in advance, "we will not be able to move them

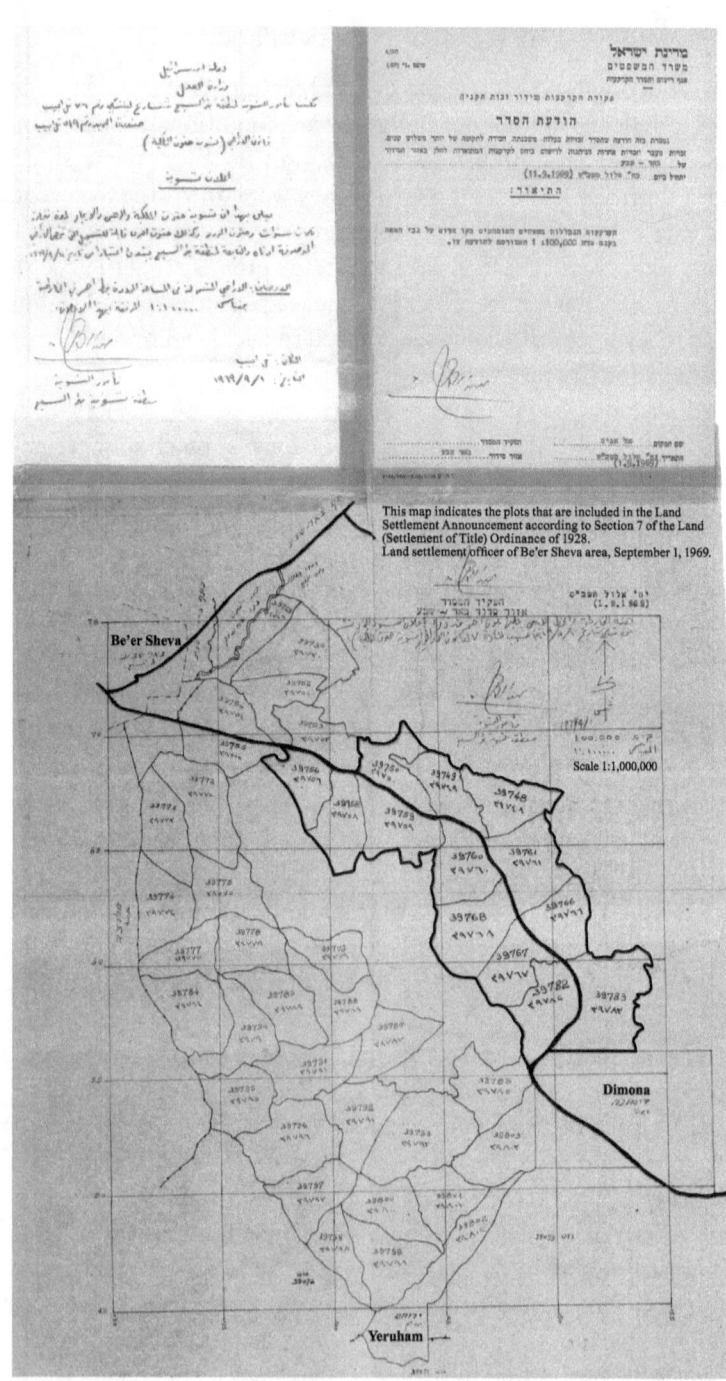

Map 5.3. Announcement of land settlement process. 1969. *Source: Land Settlement Department. Ministry of Justice [originally in Hebrew].*

from the towns they have built on their own, and at the same time the question of settlement of the lands where these town were built by the Bedouin will be exacerbated."[75]

Another attempt by the PM Adviser was focused on the need for sufficient coordination between authorities.[76] Following Toledano's recommendation, the High Bedouin Committee decided to form a subcommittee as the local address for Bedouin settlement issues.[77] At its first meeting in September 1969, the subcommittee suggested that future towns would segregate the tribes.[78]

To help promote the settlement process, Reserve Lieutenant Colonel Amos Yarkoni ('Abd al-Majid Khadher al-Mazarib), himself a Bedouin from the Galilee, was asked to join the Ministry of Housing.[79] At a meeting of the planning team, he stressed the need for police patrols to protect settlers who might wish to enter the settlements but are afraid to do so. "A Bedouin remains a Bedouin even if he builds a house," he said. "The structure will be preserved even if everyone lives in houses. The sheikhs are not interested in moving to settlements, out of fear about having their authority undermined, out of Bedouin inherent opposition to any form of rule, out of conservatism and the fear that the tribal framework will fall apart."[80]

Half a year later, in December 1970, the settlement process was in a near-total state of stagnation. Most of the Tel Sheva houses stood empty. The High Bedouin Committee convened a meeting and decided to return its mandate to the government unless a fundamental improvement came about within six months.[81] Since this committee was the leading forum for Bedouin issues, such an eventuality would indicate the total failure of the government settlement strategy. In the course of the following months, and facing such a possibility, great efforts were made to find a way to break through the deadlock.

The Sheikh ʿAwdah Mansur Abu Muʿammar Proposal

In order to escape this predicament, they needed help from their best ally, Sheikh Abu Muʿammar. Shortly after January 1971, the Negev Regional Committee met to discuss a new proposal for solving the problem of Tel Sheva, which emerged from a collaboration between Amos Yarkoni and Sheikh Abu Muʿammar. This committee was initially a restricted forum for security coordination, but since the meeting in January, it had taken the lead in an overall exchange of information and the coordination of all local representatives of government ministries in the Bedouin sector.[82] The fact that a security committee became the principal body for settlement issues symbolized the failure of the civil bodies to deal with the Bedouin.

The initial proposal undertaken by the committee included the purchase by the 'Azazmah families of all twenty-seven houses in the second stage plans for Tel Sheva and the sheikh's call to all his affiliates to settle in the town in accordance with certain conditions: 1) Improved financial terms for housing; 2) Sheikh Abu Mu'ammar would be allotted two hundred dunams in the planned setup for his encampment and his *shigg*, the traditional hospitality tent; 3) In addition he would be allotted two stores and the coffeehouse in the commercial center, plus an option to purchase the area in the center designated for additional stores; 4) The name of the locality would be changed to "Tel Sheva—'Azazmah."[83]

Such proposals, if accepted, would change the character of the town in many respects. First and foremost, Tel Sheva would be restricted to a single tribe under the control of a current and future sheikh who would receive the "keys to the city."

Desperate, and with no other options, the Negev Regional Committee favored the proposal. The only objections came from Shayek of the Israel Land Authority, who was uneasy about the intention to grant lands to the sheikh without proper procedure.[84] However, Yarkoni, backed by the committee and the PM Adviser, continued to promote the deal.[85] Uri Mor agreed that the demands should be complied with as far as possible.[86] Optimistic about finalizing the deal, the Ministry of Housing produced a timeline to expedite the settling of 250 families in Tel Sheva by the end of December 1971.[87]

The Population Committee

In February 1971, the High Bedouin Committee met and decided to form a Population Committee, a turning point in Bedouin settlement. The main mission of this committee, which had been proposed already in September 1969 by the subcommittee, was to help populate the towns. Based on the sheikhs' opinions, the Population Committee would screen the different tribes and tribal segments and decide on eligible candidates for each. This meant a transition from the concept of towns as open to all Bedouin, with free, modern, and democratic spaces, to towns as tribal territories under the control of the sheikhs. Furthermore, initially, the move of the Bedouin to orderly settlement was a means of achieving various goals, chief among them introducing modernity—that is, the possibility of providing modern services to citizens in the fields of education, health, and welfare, tasks that were extremely difficult among nomadic populations; second was the introduction of Israeli law and its principles, and the abolition of conflicting norms such as blood feuds and subordination to collective tribal responsibility.

The decision to establish the Population Committee, which was specifically designed to give weight to tribal considerations within the settlement process, contradicted the second goal. Thus, the establishment of the committee largely disregarded settlement as a means of strengthening Israeli law and regarded it rather as an end in itself. This preference for the settlement mission over Israeli law led the government to set aside its liberal principles, such as equality and individual freedoms. In practice, from that decision onward, all Bedouin towns were segregated, and their individual populations were not free but subject to tribal affiliation. As a result, the planning for other towns was delayed until further discussions with the sheikhs could take place. As for Tel Sheva, it was determined that "approval of candidates for settlement on the site will be done by the above-mentioned Population Committee after receiving the opinion of Sheikh ʿAwdah [Abu Muʾammar]."[88] Although the authorities were willing to accommodate the sheikhs' demands, the negotiations faced further obstacles.

In March 1971, Toledano stressed that they "must find a way, even if it deviates from protocol, of encouraging him to settle in the town."[89] Toledano explained that the harassment of families settled there would cause them to leave, and the presence among them of a figure like Sheikh Abu Muʿammar would symbolize the changing trend. He expressed the fear that the collapse of Tel Sheva at this early stage would spell the failure of the entire settlement project. Tel Sheva, he noted, exemplified both the willingness of the tribes to live in settled communities and the authorities' ability to protect them from harassment.

In April, Shneʾur Peleg, deputy to the director general of the Ministry of Housing stated that "any further delay in populating the finished houses and developed lots in Tel Sheva, might disrupt all plans to resolve the problem of Bedouin concentrations and settlements in the Negev." The committee would have to lean toward Sheikh Abu Muʿammar, he suggested, "even if the solution goes against what has thus far been considered acceptable by the population."[90]

But in July, when it was reported that Sheikh Abu Maʾamar had not lived up to his commitment to settle with his tribe in Tel Sheva, Toledano invited the sheikh to a meeting in order to determine whether he was sincere.[91]

Meanwhile, scores of houses in Tel Sheva were still empty, and the authorities approved the sale of some of these to Arab teachers from outside the Negev.[92] Harassment of settlers in Tel Sheva by Bedouin affiliated with Abu Rgayyig continued. This time they uprooted trees planted on the sidewalks of Tel Sheva and pitched their tents across the town lots, preventing their allocation to others.[93]

The negotiations finally came to a close in December 1971, and Sheikh Abu Muʿammar sent a letter with his updated terms. "I was happy to hear about your proposal to concentrate Bedouin in permanent housing under comfortable conditions and I will be happy to make efforts to bring most members of the ʿAzazmah tribe with me to a permanent site."[94] He moved on to describe his updated terms, some of which were not new but were now more specific. These included the demand to rename the town the ʿAzazmah Village, to make applications subject to his approval, to receive a signed contract for an area of two hundred dunams and permission to purchase all the cafés and shops not yet sold in the commercial center, and to designate a special area for the establishment of light industries like knitting factories, training programs for mechanics, and a permanent guard unit to maintain order and security in Tel Sheva. Another demand pertained to returns on investments he had made in Sagiv, where he currently lived. He also introduced a new option: if his conditions were not met, the authorities would have to plan a village for him and his tribe in Sagiv, where he would get to decide who would be allowed to settle. Eager to finalize the issue and populate Tel Sheva, Toledano drafted an answer accepting nearly all of Abu Muʿammar's terms, stipulating only that the sheikh's people would be obliged to purchase thirty houses and at least two hundred residential lots.[95] Toledano's unsent answer is preserved in the file. There is no indication as to why it was never sent. By 1978, only twenty-seven Bedouin families were still living in the town.[96]

During the following years, Sheikh Abu Muʿammar and his tribesmen received a separate town where they camped in Sagiv. Other influential sheikhs, such as Abu Rabiʿah, al-ʿAtawnah, al-Asad, and others who were not willing to move elsewhere, remained where they were and were granted their own option to settle if they so desired, in segregated neighborhoods. Other less influential groups, and those who settled in certain problematic areas, had to relocate to several established settlements.

Discussion and Conclusions

As of 1967, Israel established a framework of institutions and forums to replace the military administration that were found to be far less effective in addressing the Bedouin issues in general, and the settlement mission in particular. The return of the drought followed by the Six-Day War likewise complicated settlement efforts.

During that period, the PM Adviser who led the settlement process had tried, like his predecessor, to make use of the tribal system but was far less effective. The state was eager to promote Bedouin settlement in modern towns that could be used as a platform for the transformation of traditional collective tribal life to a communal life of free individuals. Bedouin tribal leaders opposed this policy for various reasons, including their apprehension that it undermined their land claims, eroded their power, and so forth. Since the government was unwilling to confront them, it had to find a way to bypass their opposition. Here again, the government's only recourse was to continue using the tribal hierarchy and its power base relations.

While facing sheikhs who opposed the settlement process, Israel could either confront them and implement law and order using housing demolition and force or else align with the sheikhs and the tribal mechanisms. The decision was to use only marginal force. The alliance with Sheikh Abu Muʻammar and the willingness to accept his extreme and unequal terms were a clear and deliberate deviation from the Israeli democratic values and the rule of law.

The events that took place during the early days of Tel Sheva supported by the Bedouin High Committee foreshadowed times to come in other localities. More towns with segregated communities were built after the sheikhs' demands were met. This distanced them from certain advantages offered by liberal democracy. Bedouin life in the Negev, especially within the localities, was and still is highly affected by tribal considerations and hierarchies. These include strict rules of honor that limit women's rights and freedoms, the threat of blood revenge, and the inability to use large portions of state-owned lands that are de facto controlled by other Bedouin.

CONCLUSION
The Question of Functional Alliances

I began this book with the story of the state's attempt to plant trees in the Negev and how this attempt deteriorated into disruptive clashes, which ended once the state drew back and halted further planting. The typical analysis of this event puts it within the Jewish-Arab conflict—that is, the Jewish state taking over Arab lands. Based on an in-depth analysis of thousands of archival documents, this focus on Israel's Jewishness as the dominant prism to study the Bedouin-Israel relationship while ignoring the fundamental challenge that tribalism poses on all states is too narrow and misleading. The key factor is Israel's framework as a *state* versus as a *tribe*. Indeed, Israel's identity as a liberal democracy and as Jewish is relevant, but only as an addition to the inherent challenge that exists to all entities that are states and not tribes. Hence, this study is about similarities rather than differences.

In Israel, like other states, Bedouin collective identity and deep commitment to their blood group override their potential attachment, loyalty, and commitment to the state. In addition, the Bedouin tend to follow their own traditions and norms, even if those differ from the written laws formulated in modern states, whether Muslim or Jewish. Tribal societies, shaped by the harsh desert conditions, are robust and resilient against attempts to change them and impose different norms. Hence, those leaders who sought a peaceful and glorious Bedouin transformation failed.

The Bedouin pose a challenge no matter where they live in the Middle East, and the countries they inhabit are divided in their approach to tribalism. While some have chosen a path of cooperation, others act to dismantle their nomadic way of life. Judging by academic publications and media reports, one might suppose that the State of Israel has always been in conflict with the Bedouin of the Negev, but is this entirely true? I wondered, and has there ever been an official government policy on the matter?

The answer I found is that Israel has never been unified or consistent in its approach to tribalism. During the early decades of the state, different authorities promoted different policies, some seeking to uphold Bedouin tribal life, others opposing it. There was, furthermore, a large discrepancy between their stated policy, which usually favored Bedouin integration into Israeli society and the abolition of tribalism, and the policy implemented by the local authorities that acted to preserve it.

Throughout most of the period considered here, the Bedouin of the Negev lived under military rule, the long-term policy of which was to dismantle tribalism and free the Bedouin to live as individuals, entitled to the rights conferred by liberal democratic values and integrated into the Israeli society. This conclusion is based on an analysis of statements by government ministers and representatives regarding their intention to apply Israeli law in a way they believed was necessary and right for the Bedouin, as it was the duty of a modern state to improve their living conditions and bring them economic and social benefits. This approach was shared by members of all parties and reflected the worldview that the Bedouin as individuals would be free to make decisions and would be released from subordination to their tribal framework and the yoke of the sheikhs. Even the left-wing Mapam party did not explicitly reject the vision of Bedouin modernization and transformation. A case in point is the speech delivered by Minister Mordechai Bentov of Mapam at a ceremony marking the inauguration of Tel Sheva, in which he applauded this venture, which offered a modern way of life to all Bedouin, regardless of origin. A point to note is that integration and to some extent even assimilation were perceived as desired not only toward Bedouin but also toward other groups of Jews that came from non-European states, mainly from Arab countries.[1]

However, the actual policy implemented by the military administration and others who came into contact with the Bedouin on a daily basis was quite the opposite of the one proclaimed. With limited resources and not enough employees, they were required to provide the Bedouin with essential services and maintain stability in the area. The long-term effects of their work were not scrutinized, and the tools at their disposal were inadequate for the job. The Negev Military Administration, the dominant factor for most of the period under consideration here, was a temporary body, challenged and reexamined every few years. Such a temporary situation prompted the focus on short-term accomplishments. In the immediate aftermath of the 1948 war, it formed alliances with the sheikhs and adopted various tactics to achieve its goals, restructuring tribal frameworks and reinforcing tribal leadership. This, it was hoped, would enable the Bedouin to conduct their lives according to their customs insofar as possible, to establish tribal courts in accordance with customary law, and to create alliances. These alliances continued in the de facto absence of Israeli legal framework even after the military administration was abolished. For instance, the Bedouin Tracker Unit was established in 1968 as an unofficial military unit subordinated to Sheikh Abu Muʿammar.

The Negev Military Administration not only promoted alliances but also acted to prevent state initiatives that might lead to confrontation with the sheikhs. Indeed, hostilities did break out from time to time but mostly in cases where the administration failed to deflect pressures from above, as when the state promoted land settlement in the 1960s. Other such confrontations occurred in the period leading up to the Sinai Campaign when certain sheikhs were found to be aiding infiltrators and the administration decided to curtail their powers. However, most of the time, the Negev Military Administration succeeded in keeping the peace among the Negev Bedouin.

During the first decades of the state, Israel sought temporary solutions rather than long-term policies. Shortly after the war of 1948, proposals to establish agricultural villages and turn the Bedouin into fellahin were abandoned. According to Michael Hanegbi, moving the Bedouin to the eastern Negev without running water, as was done, would thwart a long-term solution. Such was also the case regarding land allocation throughout the 1950s and 1960s, when demands for direct allocation of land to individual Bedouin, rather than via their sheikhs, were repeatedly denied. This occurred as well when the state chose not to complete the legal procedure for registering lands in the Negev, as it became clear that Bedouin claimants did not have the required proof of ownership. As evident from the last episode discussed in the book, this was the point at which the state gave up on the hope of promoting modern, open Bedouin localities and established instead a "populating committee," a platform that enabled the sheikhs to control admittance to the settlements.

It is worth noting that although the military administration of the Negev together with local officials implemented a policy of alliances, they did not glorify it or regard it as an appropriate long-term solution, nor did they call for the preservation of tribalism as an autonomous social framework in Israel. In fact, they too were critical of various elements in tribalism and did not hide their displeasure at the lack of equality in the sheikhs' treatment of their people, especially in matters of resource allocation. Nevertheless, the administration found it necessary to accommodate tribalism so as not to undermine the prevailing order that had for so many years existed in Bedouin society and, if upset, might lead to conflicts with the sheikhs who controlled most of the material and symbolic capital. The decision to form alliances was thus a practical short-term necessity and not one anchored in ideology.

Figure Conclusion 1. PM Levi Eshkol with Sheikh Salman al-Huzayyil and Sheikh ʿAwdah Mansur Abu-Muʿammar during a visit in Beʾer Sheva. August 4, 1965. *Photo: Fritz Cohen. Source: The Government Press Office.*

As noted, there were reasons why the military administration of the Negev and its successors chose to preserve tribalism. But this begs the question as to why the central government, to which the local administration was subordinated, did not enforce a long-term policy of dismantling tribalism. Or, in other words, how did it happen that despite the statements and views of government ministers and officials regarding the importance of implementing the law and the principles of democracy in the Negev, their initiatives were continually shelved?

There is no single answer to that question. Instead, I wish to offer several reasons that, taken together, may provide a possible explanation. First, despite the many declarative statements Israel made in favor of dismantling tribalism and applying democratic principles and law and order in the Negev, the government was not in fact seriously determined to do so. There are several expressions of this ambivalence that do not reflect a consistent policy—for example, Israel's initial acknowledgment of Bedouin tribalism when, in 1948, it offered to form an alliance with certain tribes and allow them to return to the Negev but rejected the appeals of other tribes, thereby treating them not as individuals but as groups.

Likewise, the government received reports about how things were proceeding in the Negev and was aware that Israeli law was not being applied there, but it closed its eyes to this and chose not to intervene. A notable case in point was the discovery by the state comptroller's office in its 1967 audit that lands were being allocated to the sheikhs directly rather than to the Bedouin themselves and the comptroller's consequent decision not to intervene. Moreover, the government's statements of purpose with regard to the dismantling of tribalism were made haphazardly, in reaction to either extraneous circumstances like drought and war or the nomination of new "players": institutions or individuals.

Furthermore, the government's stated policy often appeared to lead in different and even contradictory directions: to turn the Bedouin into fellahin or else urban dwellers, to settle them in the Negev or else in the center of the country, etc. Nor did the government initiatives provide enough resources and measures to secure implementation.

A second explanation is that difficulties arose every time someone came up with an initiative to implement Israeli law as a means of detracting from the power of tribalism, a means that ultimately led to conflict. Conflict management involved a considerable investment of public resources, risk taking, and government attention. According to this explanation, Israel's difficulty or unwillingness in confronting the Bedouin population in the early decades was due to other acute challenges like a succession of wars, massive immigration and absorption, and economic, political, and social turbulence that the government was forced to address. These challenges did not leave enough room to embark on an elective confrontation that was not existential. Moreover, the physical remoteness and social marginalization of the Bedouin made their difficulties less visible on the agenda. By the end of this period, the Bedouin population had reached a maximum of about forty-five thousand people. Indeed, the Negev was not central to the Israeli agenda and not important enough to fight for or engage in conflict over their internal issues.

Third, Israel's reluctance to confront tribalism, even at the price of its principles, may be related to its core values as a liberal democratic regime. Democracy is a social system based primarily on individual consent, on the freedom to make decisions.[2] Unlike Western societies that are based on an amalgam of individuals all entitled to equal rights, tribal societies are based on an amalgam of groups where the rights of individuals are based on kinship. They lack gender equality, and personal freedom is determined by tradition and group affiliation. It does not alter as a result of formal elections.[3] Hence, when a liberal democratic society encounters a group whose basic values clash with its ideals, the principle of consent is absent, and this undermines the state's ability to fulfill the purpose of applying its laws. Thus, by its very nature, democracy is ill equipped to confront tribal groups.

Fourth, as we have learned from the experience of neighboring countries, it is anything but easy to apply the law of the state to the Bedouin. Implementing state regulations requires dedication, consistency, and a willingness to tackle long, drawn-out conflicts. None of the attempts to eradicate tribalism and integrate the Bedouin fully into society have succeeded. Arab states that chose to confront tribalism found themselves in a state of persistent struggle while those who sought peace and calm had to accommodate tribalism.[4]

While dealing with the Bedouin was found difficult for Arab Muslim regimes, in Israel it was even more complicated. The different language, religion, democratic regime, and liberal norms, as well as its relatively small size, made it harder to accommodate Bedouin tribalism. Due to Israel's Jewish identity, any initiative that involved a change in the Bedouin way of life by settling them, dismantling tribalism, or interfering with their social hierarchy was perceived as part of the broader Jewish-Arab conflict. Israeli land and settlement initiatives were marked as Jewish attempts to grab Arab lands and suppress their human rights. Different from Arab states, the freedom of speech in Israel also aided in promoting an open public debate in the Knesset and the media. One notable example is in a meeting in 1964 to discuss Bedouin issues. Layish, the deputy to the PM Adviser for Arab Affairs, referred to a promotion of a settlement law for the Bedouin and expressed frustration while asking why similar actions toward Bedouin settlement, when done by neighboring Arab countries, were appreciated.[5]

The combined identity of Israel as both a Jewish state and a liberal Western democracy contributed to the challenge. Being the only Jewish nation-state surrounded by Arab countries that showed fundamental hostility against it made the idea of giving formal accommodation to Arab and Bedouin narratives within its declared ethos unrealistic.

Israel was willing to grant its Arab population only minor cultural recognition in their language and jurisdiction over their domestic and religious issues. Formal accommodations of tribal collective nonliberal norms, let alone acceptance of their internal hierarchies, were impossible to adopt as they contradicted democratic ideology. However, at the same time, Israel's combined identity exposed it to internal and external scrutiny. Unlike other Arab states in the region, with its free speech, Israel's actions constantly faced public criticism, which had a chilling effect on the motivations of those involved.

Another challenge for Israel during the period under discussion was that as a nascent state consisting largely of immigrants from nondemocratic countries, Israel lacked a consistent theory to deal with such a challenge, particularly in a region where it had no democratic neighbors with a Bedouin population to lead the way.

With these conclusions in mind, further research is needed on the link between the military administration, tribalism, and human rights. Previous studies of the military administration have focused on it mainly as a system that withheld civil rights endowed by liberal democracies. This is true, but it is also misleading. There is a significant difference between the military administration's operations in the Negev and the rest of the state. Although it withheld individual human rights from the Negev Bedouin, the Bedouin enjoyed many collective rights denied under individually focused human rights regimes. Regardless of the morality in question, introducing modern democratic values means breaking up long-standing Bedouin traditions. Bedouin tribalism was never similar to Western democracy, nor was it a liberal system in which individuals were considered equal in rights. Women were neither equal to men nor free to move about and make decisions. According to the tribal system, fellahin-Bedouin and Afro-Bedouin were equal neither to one another nor to the genuine Bedouin, and it was acceptable for sheikhs to get a bigger share of the pie (or the land). Individuals were not autonomous decision-making units but functioned as part of a collective group. As this study shows, they were able to live according to their customs and tradition in a designated territory, with limited intervention in their daily life. This is not to say that Bedouin life was ever easy—quite the contrary. The Bedouin endured enormous challenges, many of them inflicted by the state. Distinguished from other Arabs, they afford us a perspective to see beyond the oversimplified one that characterizes much academic writing on the military administration.

Another insight is the role of Bedouin land rights in Israeli policy. When I started writing this book, I gave it a working title that included the word *lands*. In this, I followed previous studies, including my own, that focused on lands. However, the more archival documentation I came across and analyzed, the more it became apparent to me that during the first decades of the state, the question of landownership was important, but not to the exclusion of other issues. Indeed, decisions were made to move the Bedouin to the eastern Negev and later from one part of the Sayig to another, yet this was only part of the other changes proposed for the region. Furthermore, the documentation in my analysis does not support the argument that such decisions were made out of fear that the Bedouin would be legally awarded ownership of the land, as some scholars have suggested. Quite the opposite. Most established authorities in both the central and Negev regions held that the Bedouin would lose their claims in courts. Hence, they were satisfied with the alternative of allocating state lands to them. If taking over Bedouin lands had been Israel's main intention at the time, it could have accomplished this quite easily, at least from a legal point of view. The legislation was in place, and so was the legal system for registering lands, as was done elsewhere in Israel. And during Israel's early decades, as I have demonstrated, Israel refrained from using its powers to register lands and repeatedly shelved such initiatives in the wake of Bedouin pressure.

Landownership became a critical issue only in the 1970s, when the state promoted its initiative to establish Bedouin settlements. But this was part of a broader change in Israel's focus.

The experience of Middle Eastern states showed that relative peace and calm with Bedouin tribes were mainly achieved when states maintained the balance of power between tribal families, allowed measures of political independence to apply tribal norms, and incorporated tribal values in national ethos.[6] The current study shows that this is also true in the case of Israel. Time and again, calm was temporarily retrieved only upon Israel's willingness to accommodate tribal norms and allow the intertribal balance.

The complete history of the establishment of new Bedouin towns, the development of Bedouin landownership claims in courts, and the promotion of land policy compromises deserve a separate study, as do other developments that have occurred since in the Negev, Bedouin society, and state-Bedouin relations. Despite many changes, the policies that evolved during the first decades of the state shaped the lives of the Bedouin of the Negev and remain critical for understanding what ensued.

EPILOGUE

My account of Israeli-Bedouin relations breaks off at a transformative moment, the start of an accelerated phase in the building of Bedouin towns after Israeli leaders abandoned the notion of using urbanization to abolish tribalism. From that stage on, the new Bedouin towns were planned as segregated tribal territories.

Israel's ambiguous relations with tribalism continued and gradually caused more misunderstandings. The de facto accommodation of tribalism had long-lasting effects. The old pact with Bedouin leaders, which had been helpful at first, included only high-level sheikhs and their associates. By choosing the sheikhs as allies and mediators and not promoting direct relations with each individual Bedouin, a chasm formed between the state and individuals. The Bedouin thus continued to be exploited by the sheikhs and tribal leaders who controlled many aspects of their daily lives, including the allocation of lands, permits, and personal mail. This created more resentment against Israel, which in theory declared freedom and equality for all but in practice took no steps to implement it. The Bedouin's perception of the regime as weak and hypocritical only heightened antidemocratic and anti-Israeli attitudes.

Beginning in the 1970s, Israel introduced several comprehensive plans for the Bedouin community. In 1976, the government adopted the conclusions of its committee of experts and offered what they viewed as generous compromise solutions to Bedouin land claimants "beyond the letter of the law"—that is, more than those offered by state legislation. Nearly all the Bedouin claimants held otherwise, however, and rejected the offers with loud protests. Pursuant to the Peace Treaty with Egypt in 1979, Israel was forced to evacuate the Sinai Peninsula and rapidly relocate three airbases to the Negev. A location that suited airbase topography was found in Tel Malhata, in the eastern Negev. Within several months, a new law was enacted. Two new Bedouin towns, Arara BaNegev and Kseyfah, were established, and compensation was offered to about seven hundred families from the region to facilitate their resettlement there. This was the only instance of such a comprehensive plan, and its successful implementation may be attributed to the urgent need to forge a peace treaty with an Arab state. In the 1980s and '90s, more Bedouin towns were built, but not much progress was made with regard to land issues and law enforcement. By the twenty-first century, there were seven Bedouin towns in the Negev, and then–Prime Minister Ariel Sharon initiated and promoted a new government plan that would include legislation, large investments in infrastructure, and an improvement in the social-economic situation of the Bedouin. Unfortunately, a few years later, Sharon suffered a stroke and left the office. In 2007, former Supreme Court justice Eliezer Goldberg was appointed head of a committee to recommend a Bedouin settlement policy, upon which I was called to sit as an expert in matters of fact and law. The committee comprised representatives of the public, including two Bedouin land claimants, and government officials. After an extensive public hearing, the Goldberg Committee submitted a report that included a majority recommendation calling for quick implementation through new legislation and stressed the need to enforce the laws of the state.

However, instead of following the Goldberg Committee's majority recommendations, the government appointed an Implementation Committee headed by Udi Prawer from the PM's office. This committee sought to provide a better plan than the one proposed by the Goldberg majority, one that would arguably be more generous and would lead to a broad agreement among the Bedouin. In practice, due to a lack of understanding and knowledge, combined with legal dictation, the committee's report was inadequate, incomprehensible, and impossible to implement. The compensation this committee offered was higher than those offered by Goldberg, yet it did not fully accept the Bedouin claims. The committee's insistence that their offers were benevolent was rejected outright, and instead of bringing about a broad agreement, they drew a great deal of anger. The Bedouin claimants protested inter alia that they had not been heard in the course of the discussions. In an attempt to calm things down, the government appointed Minister Benny Begin to breach the impasse with the Bedouin, who had by then begun rioting. Begin, who had good intentions, conducted a public hearing and suggested that the sum of the compensation should be increased. He did not comprehend that the Bedouin's demand to be recognized as sole owners of the claimed lands was nonnegotiable and that the right-wing parties would never support such a move. Once again, as in the first decades of the state, the government preferred to restore the peace by shelving those elements that focused on the implementation of the land law.

Half a century has passed since the period discussed in this book, and the situation of the three hundred thousand Bedouin who live in the Negev today has changed in many respects. Housing replaced tents, and traditional instruction by the sages of the tribe was replaced by formal schooling. A variety of professions opened up to them. No longer limited to herding or physical labor, with academic education, they work as lawyers, doctors, high-tech entrepreneurs, and businessmen.

Nevertheless, tribalism still dominates the Bedouin way of life and continues to be an integral part of their identity, preventing many of them from fully benefiting from the advantages that the democratic State of Israel offers its citizens. There is not a single Bedouin town today free of tribal restrictions and open to all Bedouin who wish to live there. Tribalism predominates in every Bedouin locality and controls most areas of life. Tribal loyalty dictates public elections and prevents democratic norms. A prominent example is the elections for the Bedouin local authorities, which are decided in advance within the framework of agreements between tribes and extended families. These agreements are based on a tribal commitment to provide a certain number of voters according to the size of the group. All members have to follow tribal decisions on the matter. Tribal loyalty also dictates local appointments to public positions, regardless of qualifications.

Furthermore, the ongoing conflict over landownership and the gap between state law and Bedouin norms make large portions of land, even if formally owned by the state, to be de facto controlled by Bedouin lineage groups. The latter use tribal norms—that include threats of physical harm—to prevent other Bedouin from entering the disputed territories. Streets are often blocked to prevent rival families from entering. Blood feuds persist as a means of settling disputes, as do honor killings, which threaten the lives of women suspected of "inappropriate behavior." Honor, land, and women are among the main generators of violence and contribute to the booming market for illegal weapons. Today, tribal disputes erupt not only in Bedouin localities but occasionally in the streets of Be'er Sheva, the capital of the Negev, which contributes to a growing sense of lawlessness. This creates fear in the general public and further distances the Bedouin from integrating into Israeli society.

More than ever, the need for consistency in governance should be on the agenda of the political parties. Whether we are at a critical point at this juncture, only time will tell.

APPENDIX 1:
TABLE OF CONSONANTS

Arabic Orthography	Transcription	
	Book Version	Phonetic
ء	ʾ	ʾ
ب	b	b
ت	t	t
ث	th	ṯ
ج	j	ǧ
ح	h	ḥ
خ	kh	x
د	d	d
ذ	dh	ḏ
ر	r	r
ز	z	z
س	s	s
ش	sh	š
ص	s	ṣ
ض	dh	ḍ
ط	t	ṭ
ظ	dh	ḍ
ع	ʿ	ʿ
غ	gh	ġ
ف	f	f
ق	g	g
ك	k	k
ل	l	l
م	m	m
ن	n	n
ه	h	h
و	w	w
ي	y	y

APPENDIX 2:
BEDOUIN GROUPS

	Transcription	Arabic Orthography
Book Version	**Spoken Phonetic Transcription**	
Abu 'Abdun	*Abu ʿAbdūn*	أبو عبدون
Abu 'Abed	*Abu ʿĀbed*	أبو عابد
Abu 'Ammar	*Abu ʿAmmār*	أبو عمّار
Abu Blal	*Abu Blāl*	أبو بلال
Abu Grenat	*Abu Grēnāt*	أبو قرينات
Abu Gweder	*Abu Gwēdir*	أبو قويدر
Abu Jwe'ed	*Abu Ğwēʿid*	أبو جويعد
Abu 'Omrah	*Abu ʿUmrah*	أبو عمرة
Abu Rabi'ah	*Abu Rabīʿah*	أبو ربيعة
Abu Rgayyig	*Abu Rgayyig*	أبو رقيّق
Abu Sittah	*Abu Sittah*	أبو ستّة
Abu Siyam	*Abu Ṣiyām*	أبو صيام
Abu Srihan	*Abu Srīḥān*	أبو سريحان
Abu Sukut	*Abu Sukūt*	أبو سكوت
al-Afinish	*alʾAfīniš*	الأفينش
Ahaywat	*alʾAḥaywāt*	الأحيوات
'Alamat	*alʿAlāmāt*	العلامات
al-Asad	*alʾAsad*	الأسد
al-A'sam	*alʾAʿsam*	الأعسم
al-'Atawnah	*alʿAtāwnah*	العطاونة
al-Gawa'in	*alGawāʿīn*	القواعين
al-Hawashlah	*alHawāšlah*	الهواشلة
al-Huzayyil	*alHuzayyil*	الهزيّل
al-'Ugbi	*alʿUgbi*	العقبيّ
a-Sufi	*aṣṢūfi*	الصوفي
a-Zabargah	*azZabārgah*	الزبارقة
'Azazmah	*al-ʿAzāzmah*	العزازمة
Dhullam	*aḍḌullām*	الظلّام

	Transcription	Arabic Orthography
Book Version	**Spoken Phonetic Transcription**	
Hanajrah	alḤanāǧrah	الحناجرة
Jarawin	alǦarāwīn	الجراوين
Jubarat	alǦubarāt	الجبارات
Mas'udin al-'Azazmah	Mas^cūdīn al^cAzāzmah	مسعودين العزازمة
Sager al-Huzayyil	Ṣagir alHuzayyil	صقر الهزيّل
Sa'idiyyin	as-Sa^cidiyyīn	السعيديّين
a-Sane'	aṣṢāni^c	الصانع
Sarahin	asSarāḥīn	السراحين
Tarabin	atTarabīn	الترابين
Tiyaha	atTiyāha	التياها

APPENDIX 3:
PERSONS (BEDOUIN)

Transcription		Arabic Orthography
Book Version	**Spoken Phonetic Transcription**	
ʿAbdallah Abu Sittah	ᶜAbdallah Abu Sittah	عبد الله أبو ستّة
ʿAbd al-Qadir Ibn Barri	ᶜAbd al-Qādir Bin Barri	عبد القادر ابن برّيّ
ʿAbd Abu Rgayyig	ᶜAbd Abu Rgayyig	عبد أبو رقيّق
Ahmad Abu Taha	Aḥmad Abu Ṭah	أحمد أبو طه
ʿAli Abu Ghanem	ᶜAli Abu Ġānim	علي أبو غانم
ʿAli Abu Madun	ᶜAli Abu Madūn	علي أبو مدون
ʿAli Salman Abu Grenat	ᶜAli Salmān Abu Grēnāt	علي سلمان أبو قرينات
ʿAwdah Mansur Abu Muʿammar	ᶜAwdah Manṣūr Abu Muᶜammar	عودة منصور أبو معمّر
ʿAwwad Abu Rgayyig	ᶜAwwād Abu Rgayyig	عوّاد أبو رقيّق
Farhan Abu Yihya	Farḥān Abu Yiḥya	فرحان أبو يحيى
Farhan al-Baz	Farḥān alBāz	فرحان الباز
Freih al-Musaddar	Frēḥ al-Muṣaddar	فريح المُصدّر
Freih Salim al-Aʿsam	Frēḥ Salīm alʾAᶜsam	فريح سليم الأعسم
Gharem Abu Ghalyun	Ġārim Abu Ġalyūn	غارم أبو غليون
Hadi Hamid Abu Taha	Hādi Ḥamīd Abu Ṭah	هادي حميد أبو طه
Hammad Khalil Abu Rabiʿah	Ḥammād Xalīl Abu Rabīʿah	حمّاد خليل أبو ربيعة
Harb Abu Rgayyig	Ḥarb Abu Rgayyig	حرب أبو رقيّق
Hasan Abu ʿAbdallah	Ḥasan Abu ᶜAbdallah	حسن أبو عبدالله
Hasan Abu ʿAbdun	Ḥasan Abu ᶜAbdūn	حسن أبو عبدون
Hasan Abu Jaber	Ḥasan Abu Ġābir	حسن أبو جابر
Hasan Abu Rabiʿah	Ḥasan Abu Rabīʿah	حسن أبو ربيعة
Hasan Abu Rgayyig	Ḥasan Abu Rgayyig	حسن أبو رقيّق
Hasan al-Efranji	Ḥasan alʾIfranği	حسن الإفرنجي
Hasan ʿId Abu ʿAbdun	Ḥasan ʿĪd Abu ᶜAbdūn	حسن عيد أبو عبدون
Hasan Salem a-Nasasrah	Ḥasan Sālim anNaṣāṣrah	حسن سالم النصاصرة
Hlayyel ʿAsi Abu ʿOmrah	Hlayyil ʿĀṣi Abu ᶜUmrah	هليّل عاصي أبو عمرة

Transcription		Arabic Orthography
Book Version	**Spoken Phonetic Transcription**	
Ibrahim Abu 'Abdun	*Ibrāhīm Abu ᶜAbdūn*	إبراهيم أبو عبدون
Ibrahim Abu Rgayyig	*Ibrāhīm Abu Rgayyig*	إبراهيم أبو رقيّق
Ibrahim Abu Sittah	*Ibrāhīm Abu Sittah*	إبراهيم أبو ستّة
Ibrahim Abu Taha	*Ibrāhīm Abu Ṭah*	إبراهيم أبو طه
Ibrahim al-'Ugbi	*Ibrāhīm alᶜUgbi*	إبراهيم العقبي
Ibrahim a-Saneʿ	*Ibrāhīm aṣṢāniᶜ*	الحجّ إبراهيم الصانع
'Id Abu Rabi'ah	*ᶜĪd Abu Rabīᶜah*	عيد أبو ربيعة
'Id Ibn Hdheirah	*ᶜĪd Bin Xḑērah*	عيد بن خضيرة
Muhammad Abu Taha	*Muḥammad Abu Ṭah*	محمّد أبو طه
Muhammad Mheisen Abu Jwe'ed	*Ḥasan Mhaisen Abu Ǧwēᶜid*	محمّد محيسن أبو جويعد
Muhammad Salman a-Zabargah	*Muḥammad Salmān azZabārgah*	محمّد سلمان الزبارقة
Musa Abu Rashid	*Mūsa Abu Rāšid*	موسى أبو راشد
Musa a-Surani	*Mūsa aṣṢurāni*	موسى الصوراني
Musa Hasan al-'Atawnah	*Mūsa Ḥasan alᶜAṭāwnah*	موسى حسن العطاونة
Mustafa Abu Midyan	*Muṣṭafa Abu Midyan*	مصطفى أبو مدين
Nayif Abu Rgayyig	*Nāyif Abu Rgayyig*	نايف أبو رقيّق
Razi Abu Taha	*Ġāzi Abu Ṭah*	غازي أبو طه
Salam al-Breiqi	*Salām alBrēygi*	سلام البريقيّ
Salamah Abu Ghalyun	*Salāmah Abu Ġalyūn*	سلامة أبو غليون
Salamah Ibn Sa'id	*Salāmah Bin Saᶜīd*	سلامة بن سعيد
Salamah Sager al-Huzayyil	*Salāmah Ṣagir alHuzayyil*	سلامة صقر الهزيّل
Salman a-Shteywi Abu Blal	*Salmān ašŠtēywi Abu Blāl*	سلمان الشتيوي أبو بلال
Salman al-Huzayyil	*Salmān alHuzayyil*	سلمان الهزيل
Salman Muhammad al-A'sam	*Salmān Muḥammad alᴈAᶜsam*	سلمان محمّد الأعسم
Shawkat a-Sufi	*Šawkat aṣṢūfi*	شوكت الصوفي
Sliman al-Atrash	*Slimān alᴈAṭraš*	سليمان الأطرش
Sliman 'Id a-Sane'	*Slimān ᶜĪd aṣṢāniᶜ*	سليمان عيد الصانع
Sliman Muhammad al-'Ugbi	*Slimān Muḥammad alᶜUgbi*	سليمان محمّد العقبي
Sliman Mustafa a-Nasasrah	*Slimān Muṣṭafa anNaṣāṣrah*	سليمان مصطفى النصاصرة

NOTES

INTRODUCTION

1. Civil Case 13723-11-20 *Saliman Mansur al-Atrash vs. Israel Land Authority*, Appeal for Declaratory Ruling.
2. K. Uzan, "While Israel Is Trying to Correct Past Injustices, It Is Better That Those Who Do Not Understand What Is Happening in the Negev, Do Not Speak Out on the Issue," *Maariv*, January 23, 2022, https://www.maariv.co.il/journalists/Article-892813.
3. Kann News (@kann news), "The riots in the Negev—Internal Security Minister Omer Bar Lev to @liat_regev," Twitter, January 13, 2022, https://twitter.com/kann_news/status/1481607320496918531.
4. G. Levi, "What Is Wrong with a Bedouin Negev?," *Haaretz*, January 13, 2022, 2.
5. S. Attila, "Joint MK: 'Arabs from the Negev Do Not Plant Trees in Tel Aviv.' Mayor of Arad: 'Stone Throwers—Terrorists,'" *YNet*, January 16, 2022. https://www.ynet.co.il/news/article/rydjbpb6y.
6. Doughty, *Travels in Arabia Deserta*; Musil, *Arabia Petrea Edom*.
7. Epstein, *HaBedu'im*; Al-'Araf, *Bedouin Love, Law and Legend*.
8. Shimoni, *Araviye Eretz Israel*, 120–35.
9. Braslavy, *HaYad'ata Et HaAretz*, 257–73.
10. His contribution as a state official is discussed in chapter 2.
11. Marx, *Bedouin of the Negev*. Other scholars who wrote about the Bedouin include Helmut V. Muhsam in his demographic study *Bedouin of the Negev*; Tuvia Ashkenazi, *HaBedu'im*, on Bedouin beyond the Negev; and Moshe Sharon in his historical study of the Bedouin in the eighteenth and nineteenth centuries, *HaBedu'im BeErets Israel BeMeot HaShmone Esre VeHaTsha Esre*.
12. Kressel, *Pratiy'ut LeUmat Shivtiyut*.
13. Bar-Zvi, "Meafyenem Shel Hayei HaBedouim BaNegev BeTerem Hitnahalut"; Ben-David, *HaBedu'im BaNegev*.
14. Bailey, "Negev in the Nineteenth Century"; Bailey, "Dating the Arrival of the Bedouin Tribes"; Bailey, "Reply to F. Stewart's"; Bailey, "Review"; Stewart, "Boundaries in Central Sinai and the Southern Negev"; Stewart, "Notes on the Arrival of the Bedouin Tribes in Sinai."
15. Falah, "Development of the 'Planned Bedouin Settlement'"; Falah, "Israelization of Palestine Human Geography"; Falah, "Israeli State Policy toward Bedouin Sedentarization in the Negev."
16. Shamir, "Suspended in Space," 232.
17. Marx and Meir, "Land, Town Planning"; Meir, *HaMetah Beyn Bedu'ey HaNegev LaMedina*; Meir, *As Nomadism Ends*; Krakover, "Demographic Examination of the Bedouin Settlement"; Zivan, *Yaḥasey Yehudim VeBedu'im*; Porat, "Mediniyut HaPituah." References to

the Negev Bedouin are also found in geographer Avshalom Shmueli's writings on the Bedouin of the Judean Desert, *Ketz HaNavadut*, and historian and orientalist Gabriel Baer's *Population and Society in the Arab East*.

18. Dinero argued that polygamy among the Negev Bedouin is an anticolonialist act of resistance against the Israeli Zionist agenda. Dinero, "Women's Roles"; Abu-Rabiʻah, "Bedouin Refugees in the Negev"; Abu Rabiʻah, "Negev Bedouin"; Shmueli and Khamaisi, *Israel's Invisible Negev Bedouin*; Rudnizky and Abu Ras, *Bedouin Population in the Negev*; Yiftachel, "Ethnocracy"; Fenster, "Ethnicity and Citizen Identity"; Parizot, "Counting Votes That Do Not Count"; Noah, *HaKfarim SheHayu VeEinam*; Tzfadia and Roded, *Mabat Hashvaʻati*.

19. Frantzman, Yahel, and Kark, "Contested Indigeneity," 88–89.

20. Among scholars who do not adhere to political correctness are Kark, Franzman, Galilee, Kressel, and Mintzker as well as Yahel and, more recently, Oz and Dekel.

21. Kedar, Amara, and Yiftachel, *Emptied Lands*.

22. Khoury and Kostiner, *Tribes and State Formation in the Middle East*, 15.

23. Rabi, *Tribes and States*, 4.

24. Ibid., 2.

25. Ibid., 4.

26. See also Sussar and Duygo, *Emergence of the Modern Middle East*.

27. Chatty, *Nomadic Societies in the Middle East and North Africa*.

28. Salzman, *Pastoralists*, 103–24.

29. Khazanov, *Nomads and the Outside World*, xlii.

30. Salzman, *Culture and Conflict in the Middle East*, 11; Marx, "Tribe as a Unit of Subsistence," 344; Bar, *Arviye HaMizrah HaTikhon*, 140; Stendel, *Arviye Israel*, 163.

31. Khazanov, *Nomads and the Outside World*, 198–227; Khazanov, "Nomads in the History of the Sedentary World," 1–23.

32. Stewart, "Customary Law among the Bedouin," 241, 245.

33. Salzman, *Pastoralists*, 12.

34. Marx, "Tribe as a Unit of Subsistence," 355; Stewart, "Structure of Bedouin Society in the Negev," 268; Salzman, *Culture and Conflict in the Middle East*, 11–13.

35. Ekeh, "Social Anthropology and Two Contrasting Uses of Tribalism in Africa," 660.

36. Fukayama, "Against Identity Politics"; Davis, "Tribalism and Democracy."

37. Suwaed, *Historical Dictionary of the Bedouins*, 10.

38. Stewart, "What Is Honor?," 13–28.

39. Stewart, "Customary Law among the Bedouin," 241.

40. Yahel and Abu-Ajaj, "Tribalism, Religion, and the State in Bedouin Society," 64–65. The first mosque was built by Bedouin in 1976.

41. Marx, *Bedouin of the Negev*, 32; Suwaed, "HaBeduʼim BeEretz Israel," 94.

42. Stewart, "Customary Law among the Bedouin," 241–44.

43. Marx, "HaMivne HaHevrati Shel Beduʼey HaNegev," 393–409; Marx, *Bedouin of the Negev*, II; Braslavy, *HaYadʼata Et HaAretz*, 236; Kressel, Ben-David, and Abu Rabiʻa, "Changes in Land Usage by the Negev Bedouin," 43–44; Shimoni, *Arviye Eretz Israel*, 131.

44. Al-ʻAref, *Bedouin, Love, Law and Legend*, 86–92; Stewart, "Customary Law among the Bedouin," 256; Bar-Zvi, "Meʼafyenim Shel Haye HaBeduʼim BaNegev BeTerem Hitnahalut," 626.

45. Salzman, *Culture and Conflict in the Middle East*, 165.

46. For further reading on Bedouin women, see Abu-Rabia-Queder, "Paradox of Professional Marginality among Arab-Bedouin Women"; Huss, "Tziyurim KeTriger LeNerativ Shel Metzuka Hevratit BeKerev Nashim Beduʼiyot Mudarot"; Abu-Lughod, *Do Muslim Women Need Saving?*

47. For further reading on polygamy, see *Summary Report—The Ministerial Committee for Dealing with the Negative Consequences of Polygamy*, July 2018; Abu-Rabia, "Law on the Books

Versus the Law in Action"; Al-Krenawi, Slonim-Nevo, and Graham, "Polygyny," 195; Yahel, "Lo Huki Akh Mishtalem." Although Islamic law restricts the number of wives permitted to four, some Negev sheikhs had more, most notable among them Sheikh Salman al-Huzayyil with thirty-nine wives and more than seventy children.

48. Kressel and Aharoni, *Egyptian Émigrés in the Levant of the nineteenth and 20th Centuries*, 208–209.

49. Ben-David, *HaBedu'im BeIsrael*, 45.

50. Kressel, Ben-David, and Abu Rabi'a, "Changes in the Land Usage by the Negev Bedouin," 35–37.

51. Alon, "Tribal Shaykhs," 78–79; Ben-David, "HaBedu'im BaNegev," 411.

52. See chapter 2.

53. Bailey, "Dating the Arrival of the Bedouin Tribes," 20–49; Muhsam, *Bedouin of the Negev*, 24–26; Stewart, "Notes on the Arrival of the Bedouin Tribes in Sinai," 106.

54. The League of Nations granted Britain a mandate for Palestine on August 12, 1922. C.529.M. 314.VI.

55. Marx, "Tribe as a Unit of Subsistence," 345; Shmueli, *Ketz HaNavadut*, 255. The majority of the Bedouin continued to live in movable tents up to the 1960s (see chap. 3).

56. Ben-Arieh and Sapir, "Reshita Shel Be'er Sheva," 62–63; Luz, "Yetsirata Shel Be'er Sheva HaModernit," 180, 189; Ben-David and Kressel, "The Bedouin Market," 3.

57. Cohen-Hattab, *Nekudot HaMishtara HaBritiyot BaNegev*, 26.

58. Bedouin Control (Application of Ordinance) Order, 1942 implemented the order to Negev tribes, August 20, 1942, Palestine Gazette; Frantzman and Kark, "Bedouin Settlement in Late Ottoman and British Mandatory Palestine," 71.

59. Collective Punishments Ordinance, 1926, *Laws of Palestine 1*, 147 (Robert Harry Drayton, 1934). For Bedouin tribal courts, see chapter 2.

60. Fletcher calls it "unite and rule," contesting the theme of divide and rule. Fletcher, *British Imperialism and 'The Tribal Question,'* 173; for a different perspective, see Falah, *The Role of the British Administration*, 2–4.

61. Ben-David and Kressel, "The Bedouin Market," 5.

62. Al-ʿAref, *Tārīx Bir al-Sabaᶜ wa-Qabāᶜiluha* (appendix). Other maps are available in Ben-David, "HaBedu'im BaNegev," 85; Ben-David, *HaBedu'im BeIsrael*, 85; Braslavy, *HaYad'ata Et HaAretz* (appendix); Bailey, "Negev in the Nineteenth Century," 74; Shimoni, *Arviye Eretz Israel*, (appendix).

63. Al-ʿAref, *Shivtey HaBedu'im BeMehoz Be'er Sheva* (appendix).

64. Muhsam, *Bedouin of the Negev*, 24, noted that "the wary observer might be inclined to agree with the only conclusion ʿAref al-ʿAref thought himself entitled to draw from his 1931 enumeration [of the Bedouin], namely, that 'Allah alone knows the truth'"; Marx, *Bedouin of the Negev*, 12; Frantzman, Levin, and Kark, "Counting Nomads," 552.

65. Goadby and Doukhan, *Land Law of Palestine*, 29–32; Albeck and Fleisher, *Diney Mekarke'in BeIsrael*, 36; Sandberg, *Hesder Zkhuyot BeMekarke'in*; *Official Gazette* 258, June 1, 1928, 260.

66. See CA 4220/12 *al-ʿUgbi v. State of Israel* (2015).

67. Doukhan, *Diney Karka'ot BeMedinat Israel*, 47–53; CA 4220/12 *al-ʿUgbi v. State of Israel*.

68. Ibid.

69. Goadby and Doukhan, *Land Law of Palestine*, 44.

70. The Mewat Land Ordinance, 1921, *Official Gazette* 38, March 1, 1921; see also Goadby and Doukhan, *Land Law of Palestine*, 46.

71. Al-ʿAref, *Bedouin Love, Law and Legend*, 180.

72. Meir, "Contemporary State Discourse and Historical Pastoral Spatiality," 837; Kressel, Ben-David, and Abu-Rabi'a, "*Changes in Land Usage*," 32; CA 4220/12 *al-ʿUgbi v. State of Israel*.

73. Sandberg, *Hesder Zkhuyot BeMekarke'in*, 27; Yahel, "Land Disputes between the Negev Bedouin and Israel," 11.

74. See CA 288/43 *Kattan v. Kattan*, P.L.R 1944 (2) 408. In this court debate, the judges refused to give legal standing to a land transaction that was not registered according to the law.

75. Gavish and Kark, "Cadastral Mapping of Palestine 1928–1958," 39.

76. Kark, *Toldot HaHityashvut HaHalutsit HaYehudit BaNegev*, 41, 44, 93–95; Zivan, *Yaḥasey Yehudim VeBedu'im*, 54–73.

77. Gal-Peer, "HaNokhehut HaYehudit BeBe'er Sheva: 1900–1948," 31–36. For further reading on the Jewish community in Be'er Sheva, see Bar-Zvi, "MeZikhronot Reshoney HaYehudim BeBe'er Sheva"; Gal-Peer, "HaNokhehut HaYehudit BeBe'er Sheva Lifney Kum Hamedina."

78. Gal-Peer, "HaNokhehut HaYehudit BeBe'er Sheva: 1900–1948," 41.

79. Suwaed, "Yahasey Bedu'im-Yehudim," 255.

80. For further information on the Jewish community in Be'er Sheva, see Gal-Peer, "Ha-Nokhahut HaYehudit BeBe'er Sheva Lifney Kum Hamedina," 95.

81. The plan designated a total of 17 percent of the land for Jews in the Eastern Galilee, the Jezreel Valley, and the coastal strip from Haifa to Tel Aviv, and for the Arabs in Judea and Samaria, the Western Galilee, and the coastal plain—a total of 40 percent of the land. The Negev and Jerusalem were destined to be left under direct British rule. Morrison Grady Plan, S25, file 10031, ISA.

82. Kark, *Toldot HaHityashvut HaHalutsit HaYehudit BaNegev*, 96–97, 147.

83. Suwaed, "Yahasey Bedu'im-Yehudim," 259; Braslavy, *HaYad'ata Et HaAretz*, 35.

84. On February 7, 1947, three additional settlements were established: Tze'elim, and Alumim. On August 28, 1947, Gevim was established, and on November 19, 1947, Halutza and Afikim (both south of Tze'elim); the latter two were abandoned after the War of Independence.

85. Kark, *Toldot HaHityashvut HaHalutsit HaYehudit BaNegev*, 149, indicated 2,464 people, but 500 more from the northern kibbutzim should be added.

86. For further details on the development of the mukhtar system, see Ueno, "In Pursuit of Laicized Urban Administration."

87. Porat, *HaMukhtarin HaIvriyim BaNegev*; Efrat, *Shkhenim BeShea'rey HaNegev*; Baer, *HaMukhtar Hakafri BeErets Israel*.

88. For further details on the Jewish mukhtars, see Porat, *HaMukhtarin HaIvriyim BaNegev*.

89. Blas, *Mey Meriva VeMa'as*, 140–43; Weitz, *Yomani VeIgrotay LaBanim*, 119–20; Brezner, *HaNegev BeHityashvut VeBeMilhama*, 118; Kark, *Toldot HaHityashvut HaHalutsit HaYehudit BaNegev*, 140–43; Gvati, *Mea Shnot Hityashvut*, 335.

90. Blas, *Mey Meriva VeMa's*, 143; Brezner, *HaNegev BeHityashvut VeBeMilhama*; Kark, *Toldot HaHityashvut HaHalutsit HaYehudit BaNegev*, 144; Suwaed, "Yahasey Bedu'im-Yehudim," 254; Zivan, *Yaḥasey Yehudim VeBedu'im*, 60–61.

91. Gellner, *Nations and Nationalism*.

92. Weiner, *Rule of the Clan*, 4.

93. Locke, *Two Treatises of Government*, 146.

94. Maine, *Ancient Law*. John Stuart Mill's democracy puts the rule in the hands of the people through their elected representatives in free, fair, and frequent elections (Mill, *Considerations on Representative Government*).

95. Popper, *Open Society and Its Enemies*.

96. Barak, "Shilton HaHok VeElyonut HaHuka," 388.

97. For additional information on historical geography methodologies, see Rubin, "Geografia Historit BeIsrael"; Donkin, "A Servant of Two Masters?"; Holdsworth, "Historical Geography"; Baker, *Geography and History*; Darby, "Historical Geography"; Ben-Arieh, "Erets

Israel KeNosse Lemehkar Geografi-Histori"; Ben-Arieh, Aharonson, and Lavski, *Erets Bere'i Avara*; Baker, *Ideology and Landscape in Historical Perspective*.

98. Such as Marx, *Bedouin of the Negev*.

99. For the study of the Bedouin in that region, see Mintzker, "HaJanabib."

100. For the use of oral history, see Peled, *Words Like Daggers*; Peled, "Palestinian Oral History as a Source for Understanding the Past"; Abu-Lughod, *Veiled Sentiments*; Kurpershoek, *Oral Poetry and Narratives from Central Arabia*.

1. Bedouin in the War of Independence, 1947–49

1. Gelber, *Komemiyut VeNakba*; Morris, *1948*; Golani and Manna, *Two Sides of the Coin*; Al-'Aref, *Al-Nakbah*; Kadish, *Milhemet Ha'Atsma'ut*; Milstein, *Milhemet Ha'Atsma'ut*; Yahel, "Mediniyut Hanhagat HaYishuv HaYehudi." Some of the thesis findings were published in Yahel and Kark, "Israel's Negev Bedouin."

2. Zivan, *Yahasey Yehudim VeBedu'im*; Suwaed, "HaBedu'im BeMilhemet Ha'Atsma'ut"; Porat, "Mediniyut Hapituah VeShe'elat HaBedu'im BaNegev BiShenoteha HaRishonot Shel HaMedinah."

3. For further information on the Jewish settlement during the Yishuv period, see the introductory chapter.

4. Gelber, *Nitsaney HaHavatselet*, 350.

5. For detailed discussion, see Shemesh, "Mashber HaManhigut HaPalestinit," 318–23.

6. "Aluka" intelligent reports, September 8 and 21, 1947, RG 105, file 194, HA. For detailed information about the various confederations and tribes in the Negev, see the introductory chapter.

7. See, for example, the detailed list of acts of sabotage in the "security log for the line" in November 1947, prepared by A. Cohen Henfling, December 2, 1947, CZA, Record Group (RG) KKL5, file 16614; Gilad, *Pirkey Palmah*, 149; Ofer and Ofer, *HaGedud HaRishon*, 205.

8. Intelligence report, undated, describing events on October 1947, RG 105, file 194, HA; for more information about the origin of fellahin-Bedouin, see the introductory chapter. Efrat, *Sipurim Min HaSakayim*, 118–19; Kouzli, "Mediniyut HaMimsad HaIsraeli," 116–18; Ze'ev Taub, personal interview, April 30, 2009, Shoval; Ya'akov Shemesh and Zeharia Sade, personal interviews, both on February 12, 2009, Revivim; Freih Salim al-A'sam, personal interview, Tel Sheva, May 15, 2017; 'Ali Abu Ghanem, personal interview, August 28, 2020, Tel Sheva.

9. Y. Weitz, January 10, 1948, noted the following about the Negev: "This region is at the forefront of our concerns today. . . . All our haters and first of all our gentlemanly allies look up to a weak spot for our deprivation from it. They do not want to agree with the allocation of the Negev to Jews. This wasteland that suddenly had renaissance, the British and the effendis do not want to give it up. . . . And so the Negev and the Arab connected here to set us a trap. The 'Tommy' who is now walking in the Negev alludes to Muhammad towards the thin and loose huts and tells him: let's blow them and they fly will away." CZA, RG A2, file 4612; Asia, *Moked HaSikhsukh*, 41, 47; Suwaed, "Yahasey Bedu'im-Yehudim," 290–91. The British financed the Arab Legion in Jordan, headed by Sir John Bagot Glubb, until 1956.

10. Intelligence review on Sheikh al-Huzayyil, March 13, 1947; intelligence report, October 26, 1947; two intelligence reports by "Aluka," November 13 and 23, 1947, all in RG 105, file 194, HA. This contradicts Suwaed's argument that "for the first time, at least in the Negev, a new reality in which the tribes ignored the tribal considerations and united for a common purpose and that is the war in the Jewish community." Suwaed, "Yahasey Bedu'im-Yehudim," 254.

11. "Aluka" intelligent reports, September 8, 21 and 22, 1947, RG 105, file 194, HA.

12. Suwaed, "Yahasey Bedu'im-Yehudim," 258.

13. 'Abu Hshim Intelligence report on "Gathering of Sheikhs in Be'er Sheva" that took place on November 25, 1947, December 1, 1947, RG 105, file 194, HA.

14. There is a debate between historians about the reasoning. While Uri Milstein notes that they reached this decision at a time when it seemed feasible to drive a small number of Jews out of the Negev (Milstein, *Milhemet Ha'Atsma'ut*, 225), Suwaed argues that the call for independence was due to the Bedouin's recognition of what the Jewish settlers would contribute to the development and economy of the region (Suwaed, "Yahasey Bedu'im-Yehudim," 257).

15. Sinanoglou, *Partitioning Palestine*, 170–71.

16. UN General Assembly A/RES/181(II) of November 29, 1947, UNA.

17. Kark, *Toldot HaHityashvut HaHalutsit HaYehudit BaNegev*, 92.

18. Morris, *1948*; Gelber, *Ḳomemiyut VeNakba*.

19. Negev Bloc Committee to D. Ben-Gurion, December 9, 1947, CZA, RG KKL5, file 16614.

20. D. Ben-Gurion, December 11 and 26, 1947, BGD, BGA.

21. Brezner, *HaNegev BeHityashvut VeBeMilhama*.

22. D. Ben-Gurion, December 17, 1947, BGD, BGA; Adan, *Ad Degel HaDyo*, 99–102; Gilad and Megged, *Sefer HaPalmah*, 60–67.

23. Sarig, "Hativat HaPalmah BaNegev," 2.

24. D. Ben-Gurion, December 14, 1947, BGD, BGA; Brezner, *HaNegev BeHityashvut VeBeMilhama*, 228ff.

25. Tene Intelligence (Gevuli), "Evacuation of the Negev Settlements," December 7, 1947, RG 115, file 27, HA; Negev Bloc Committee to D. Ben-Gurion, December 9, 1947, RG KKL5, file 16614, CZA. Report on a series of meetings held between January 8 and 15, 1948, unnamed person gives details of the meetings with Brigadier Nelson as well as a Tene intelligence report following a meeting with the Gaza district governor, January 19, 1948, both documents, RG 115, file 27, HA.

26. D. Ben-Gurion, December 14 and 20, 1947, BGD, BGA; Y. Weitz, December 20, 1947, and February 2, 1948, both in RG A2, file 4612, CZA; Brezner, *HaNegev BeHityashvut VeBeMilhama*, 132–37, 226–28; Gvati, *Mea Shnot Hityashvut*, 13.

27. D. Ben-Gurion, December 18, 1947, BGD, BGA; Danin, *Tsiyoni BeKhol Tnay*, 210; Y. Weitz, December 24, 1947, RG A2, file 4612, CZA; Minutes of Negev Committee, December 21, 1947, A246 file 30 (26), CZA.

28. D. Ben-Gurion, December 26, 1947, BGD, BGA; Brezner, *HaNegev BeHityashvut VeBeMilhama*, 138.

29. Unsigned leaflet to the Arabs of the Gaza District and Beersheba [Be'er Sheva], December 19, 1947 [in Arabic]; Intelligence information, January 25, 1948, refers to the positive influence of the leaflets calling for peace with the moderate sheikhs and specifying the names of the active Bedouin sheikhs: Freih al-Musaddar, 'Ali Abu Madun, Hasan al-Efranji, Hasan Abu Jaber, and 'Abdallah Abu Sittah, RG 105, files 32 and 194, HA.

30. Tene Intelligence, February 5–9, 1948, as well as additional undated intelligence items, all in RG 105, file 32, HA; Milstein, *Milḥemet Ha'Atsma'ut*, 172.

31. Unsigned intelligence item, February 4, 1948, RG 105, file 32, HA.

32. Tene Intelligence, from January 20 and 26, 1948, RG 105, file 32, HA.

33. Ben-Gurion, *BaMa'araha*, 278.

34. Y. Weitz, March 1, 1948, RG A2, file 4612, CZA.

35. "Report on the events in the Negev," unnamed, March 7, 1948, RG 105, file 194, HA. Personal interviews: Freih Salim al-A'sam, May 15, 2017, Tel Sheva; Ya'akov Shemesh and Zechariah Sadeh, February 12, 2009, Revivim; Benni Meitiv, July 5 and 29, 2004, Ashkelon; Hiram Danin, September 25, 2003, Jerusalem; Dodik Shoshani, July 10, 2008, Lahav. Suwaed, "Yahasey Bedu'im-Yehudim," 256.

36. Intelligence item, "Purification and repentance," undated, probably September 1947, RG, 105 file 21, HA; A. S. to E. D. [Danin], December 23, 1947, S25-3560, CZA. In another intelligence report by RA, "On the Events in the Negev," from March 7, 1948 (also dated March 22,

1948), it was indicated that "certain Bedouin dignitaries sought to clean up their past crimes—their ties regarding land issues with Jews. Sheikhs in Be'er Sheva and the surrounding area even gave money for this purpose," RG S25, file 3569, CZA.

37. Intelligence item, undated [after February 18, 1948] and Intelligence item, February 23, 1948, both in RG 105, file 32, HA.

38. Tene Intelligence (Na'im), March 2, 1948, RG 105, file 32, HA. From the report, it is unclear if the right well was blown up. Mention of blowing up a well is also found in a Tene intelligence report, March 25, 1948, RG 105, file 32, HA.

39. Attacks on Arab vehicles are described in Tene intelligence reports, March 2 and 10, 1948, RG 105, file 32, HA.

40. Y. Weitz, March 27, 1948, RG A2, file 4612, CZA.

41. Report from the District Commissioner Gaza to Chief Secretary, February 16, 1948, Public Record Office (PRO), London, CO 537/3853.

42. Y. Weitz, March 11, 1948, RG A2, file 4612, CZA; Benni Meitiv, personal interview, July 29, 2004, Ashkelon.

43. "Bedouins in the State of Israel," Intelligence Review, appended to the letter by P. Amir, Negev military governor, to the head of the Southern Command and others, January 24, 1948, 473-72/1970, IDFA; Keren, *Nayeh BaMidbar*, 65; Adan, *Ad Degel HaDyo*, 99–102; Cohen, Cohen, and Mendelson, *Ḥaṭivat HaNegev*, 46. Regular reports by Israel Lebertovsky to the Mekorot Directorate, events occurring around the water pipeline, March 9, 1948, RG KKL5, file 16615, CZA; Minutes of the Negev Committee, March 19 and 31, 1948, 30(26), file A246, CZA; Y. Weitz, April 17, 1948, RG A2, file 4612, CZA; Al-'Aref, *Al-Nakbah*, 724; Meitiv, *Sippuro Shel Gevul*, 117.

44. Tene Intelligence, February 25, 1948, RG 105, file 194, HA.

45. Abu-Rabi'a, *Bedouin Century*, 125.

46. Intelligence item, February 18, 1948, RG 105, file 194, HA.

47. Tene Intelligence, March 10, 1948, RG 105, file 98, HA. Tene Intelligence, April 8, 1948, considered the infiltration of outsiders in the region as a factor requiring military action, RG 105, file 194, HA.

48. Tene Intelligence, "Meeting of the Tarabin Sheikhs in al-'Imarah," April 13, 1948; Tene Intelligence, "Organization and Action in the Tarabin Confederation," March 26, 1948, both in RG 105, file 194, HA. The involvement of the Germans in the war is a topic not yet explored. Rickenbacher, "Arab States," 143–45.

49. Tene Intelligence, Organization and Activity in the Tarabin Confederation, March 26, 1948, RG 105, file 194, HA; Tene Intelligence, "Allotment to the Bedouin," April 8, 1948, RG 104, file 194, HA.

50. Tene Intelligence, March 22, 1948, RG 105, file 194, HA.

51. Y. Weitz, February 26 and March 20, 1948, RG S25, file 3569, CZA; D. Ben-Gurion, February 13, 1948, BGA, BGD; Asia, *Moked HaSikhsukh*, 42. Another argument that was raised against the Jewish holdings in the Negev was the potential of finding oil there, which would compensate the Arabs and appeal to US oil investors.

52. Gelber, *Ḳomemiyut VeNakba*, 152–53; Brezner, *HaNegev BeHityashvut VeBeMilhama*, 228.

53. Intelligence report by RA, "On the Events in the Negev," March 7, 1948 (also dated March 22, 1948), RG S25, file 3569, CZA; D. Ben-Gurion, January 9 and February 19, 1948, BGD, BGA; Report by Lebertovsky to Mekorot Directorate, "Events surrounding the water pipeline, March 16–23. 1948," March 23, 1948, RG KKL5, file 16615, CZA; Y. Weitz, "The Negev These Days," around March 1948, RG KKL5, file 16615, CZA.

54. Tene Intelligence, March 17, 1948, RG 105, file 98, HA; Israel Lebertovsky to the Mekorot Directorate, "Events occurring around the water pipeline from March 9–17, 1948," RG KKL5, file 16615, CZA; Tene Intelligence, "Bedouin Gangs in the Negev," March 18, 1948, RG 45, bin 22, file 11, YTA; Hagana spokesman, March 22, 1948, file 35–481/1949, IDFA.

55. Cohen, Cohen, and Mendelson, *Ḥaṭivat HaNegev*, 75. When the Arab armies invaded, the Jubarat became heavily involved. Calm is also mentioned in Tene Intelligence, April 7, 1948, RG 27, file 115, HA.

56. Intelligence report by RA, "On the events in the Negev, March 7, 1948" (also dated March 22, 1948), RG S25, file 3569, CZA; Israel Lebertovsky to Mekorot Directorate, "Events surrounding the water pipeline, for the months of March, April, May 1958," RG KKL5, file 16615, CZA; Tene Intelligence, April 11, 1948, RG 12–14, bin 22, file11, YTA; Intelligence review "The Bedouins in the State of Israel," appended to the letter of P. Amir, Negev military governor, to the Commander of the Southern Command and others, January 24, 1957, file 1970/473-72, IDFA.

57. Tene Intelligence, April 12, 1948, RG 105, file 98, HA.

58. Tene Intelligence, April 18, 1948, RG 105, file 98, HA.

59. Tene Intelligence, April 13, 1948, 45, bin 22, file 11, YTA; April 18, 1948, RG 105, file 98, HA.

60. Tene Intelligence, "Meeting with the Sheikhs in Gaza," April 9, 1948, RG 105, file 194, HA, stated that many of the sheikhs did not attend and that the participants were Hasan al-Efranji, Ibrahim a-Sane', Ibrahim Abu 'Abdun, Salam al-Breiqi, Ibrahim al-'Ugbi, and 'Id Abu Rabi'ah.

61. Tene intelligence, "Actions among the al-'Atawnah tribe," April 8, 1948, RG 105, file 194, HA.

62. Tene Intelligence, "Preparation for Peace," April 13, 1948, 45, Bin 22, file 11, YTA.

63. Cohen, *Truman and Israel*, 209.

64. Tene Intelligence, May 10 and 12, 1948, RG 105, file 98, HA.

65. Al-'Aref, *Al-Nakbah*, 720–21.

66. Ibid., 738.

67. Setting mines near Sheikh al-Huzayyil as revenge for his connections with the Jews. Tene Intelligence, May 9, 1948, RG 45, bin 22, file 11, YTA.

68. Mordecai Artzieli, "The Bedouin Sheikh Abu Mu'ammar Received the War of Independence Medal," *Haaretz*, February 27, 1963; Efrat, *Sipurim Min HaSaḳayim*, 118–19; Kouzli, "Mediniyut HaMimsad HaIsraeli," 116–18; Ze'ev Taub, personal interview, April 30, 2009, Shoval; Ya'akov Shemesh and Zechariah Sadeh personal interviews, February 12, 2009, Revivim; Freih Salim al-A'sam, May 15, 2017, Tel Sheva.

69. Tene Intelligence, May 15, 1948, RG 105, file 98, HA. Muhsam, *Beduin of the Negev*, 115. Moshe Shemesh, personal interview, February 12, 2009, Revivim; Yossi Tzur, personal interview, April 30, 2009, Shoval.

70. Report by Lebertovsky to Mekorot Directorate regarding events surrounding the water pipeline, from March 24–27, 1948 and May 4, 1948, RG KKL5, file 16615, CZA; Tene Intelligence, April 24, 1948, RG 105, file 98, HA.

71. Tene Intelligence, May 10, 1948, RG 105, file 98, HA.

72. Eilat, "Revivim BaNegev," 133, 135; Danin, *Tsiyoni BeKhol Tnay*, 223; Gelber, *Ḳomemiyut VeNakba*, 68–69; Brezner, *HaNegev BeHityashvut VeBeMilhama*, 170; Morris, *Birth*; Ze'ev Taub, personal interview, August 2, 2009, Shoval; Yosef Reichel, personal interview, August 2, 2009, Shoval.

73. Headquarters Front D/Intelligence, "Meeting of Intelligence Officers, November 16, 1948," file 17–1041/1949, IDFA.

74. Uriyah Da'at, "Report of a visit to the Negev on September 12–17, 1948," RG 105, file 94, HA: "The 'Alamat tribes [Jubarat Confederation], who are in contact with Egyptians, moved and are moving eastward to Khuweilfah and Kohlah near Bir (Khuweilfah)"; Ze'ev Taub, personal interview, April 30, 2009, Shoval; Bailey, "Reshimot Al HaUkhlusiya."

75. Meitiv, *HaZor'im BaMidbar*, 58; Meitiv, *Sippuro Shel Gevul*, 119. There were a few exceptions, indicated in the report of an Egyptian patrol commander from the Revivim and

Halutza area in the southern region on May 25, which indicated the "al-Tarabini tribe are allied with the Jews." Apparently, part of the material captured in June 1948 at 'Asluj and translated into Hebrew from Arabic, RG 105, file 124, HA.

76. Tene Intelligence, April 18, 1948, RG 105, file 98, HA.

77. Havakook, *Aḵavot Bahol*, 24–27; Suwaed, "Yahasey Bedu'im-Yehudim," 295; Ya'akov Shemesh and Zekharya Sadeh, personal interview, February 12, 2009, Revivim.

78. Uriah (Da'at), "Report of a visit to the Negev on September 12–17, 1948," September 20, 1948, RG 105, file 194, HA; Efrat, "Arviye HaEzor," 49.

79. Sheikh Sliman al-'Ugbi to the military governor, December 8, 1950, as part of his reply to the claims voiced against him by members of his tribe, file 281–834/1953, IDFA.

80. Ben-David, *Meriva BaNegev*, 44. According to "A Survey of the Bedouins," unnamed author and undated, RG 102, file 13927/20, ISA, the Abu Rgayyig Sheikh cooperated with the Jews and was a guard around Nevatim.

81. Third Battalion Intelligence to Headquarters of the Yiftah Corps Intelligence, "Reconnaissance Report," September 27, 1948, file 1225–922/1975, IDFA; Tene Intelligence, June 17, 1948, RG 105, file 124, HA; Tene Intelligence, May 20, 1948, RG 105, file 98, HA; Gelber, *Nitsaney HaHavatselet*, 421; Wallach, *Atlas Karta LeToldot Erets Israel*, 12.

82. A description of joint Egyptian and Bedouin actions in Egyptian documents apparently seized in June of 1948 at 'Asluj and translated into Hebrew, RG 105, file 124, HA.

83. Tene Intelligence, "Review of the Situation in the Negev toward the Ceasefire," June 17, 1948, RG 105, file 124, HA.

84. Letter of Mukhtars from Dorot, Nir Am, and Ruhama to Prime Minister, August 4, 1948, Kibbutz Dorot Archive; Cohen, Cohen, and Mendelson, *Ḥaṭivat HaNegev*, 155.

85. Tene Intelligence, "Review of the Situation in the Negev toward the Ceasefire," June 17, 1948, RG 105, file 124, HA.

86. Al-Sharif, "HaAhim HaMuslemim BeMilhemet Palestine," 101; Sergey [code name] Tene Intelligence, June 29, 1948; Sergey Intelligence, "Summation Report about the Enemy in the South," July 6, 1948, both in RG 105, file 124a, HA.

87. D. Ben-Gurion, June 29, 1948, BGD, BGA; Bernadotte, *To Jerusalem*, 129–33.

88. Information from the Research Division, July 19, 1948, RG 105, file 98, HA.

89. Tene Intelligence, July 13, 1948, actions of the Abu M'eileg gang and its ties with the Muslim Brotherhood, RG 105, file 98, HA; Israel Lebertovsky to the Mekorot Directorate, "The events surrounding the period June 29 to July 27," RG KKL5, file 16615, CZA.

90. "The Bedouins in the State of Israel," an intelligence survey, appended to the letter by P. Amir, the Negev military governor, to the commander of the Southern Command and others, January 24, 1957, file 473–72/1970, IDFA; Sheikh Sliman al-'Ugbi to the military governor, December 8, 1950, replying to accusations by his tribe members, file 281–834/1953, IDFA.

91. Uriah (Da'at), "Report on a visit in the Negev, September 12–17, 48," dated September 20, 1948, RG 105, file 194, HA.

92. The blowing up of the Jewish Khalsa well and the killing of the Jewish mukhtar are described in an intelligence report from Battalion 1 to the Yiftah Intelligence, daily reports of September 1948, file1227-9222/1975, IDFA. The explosion of the wells of Abu Yihya and a-Sufi on September 24 and 25, 1948, is described in a daily battalion report to Yiftah Intelligence on October 4, 1948, file 1227–922/1975, IDFA; Report by Lebertovsky to Mekorot Directorate, "Events of the period of September 14–October 12, 1948," undated, RG KKL5, file 16615, CZA.

93. Two operational orders from Yiftah Operations to the First Battalion and others, undated (apparently September 29, 1948), "Operational Orders," file 1227–922/1975, IDFA.

94. Report of Negev Brigade operations office, October 1948, file 1227–922/1975, IDFA; Israel Lebertovsky to the Mekorot Directorate, reports for the months of September and October 1948, RG KKL5, file 16615, CZA.

95. Yiftah Operations to the First Battalion, undated (apparently in September), "Operations Order No. 4," Yiftah daily intelligence report from September 29, 1948; Reports on actions for the period October 2–6, 1948, file 1227–922/1975, IDFA; Letter by Ya'akov Shimoni, October 10, 1948, file 2564/10, ISA, indicating that carrying out "sweeps" was against formal policy.

96. Minutes of the Provisional Government, October 6, 1948, ISA.

97. Collection of daily items (by unnamed) intelligence officer, from the Yiftah/Palmah Brigade, October 2, 3, 4, 7, and 8, 1948, file 1216–922/1975, IDFA; "The Bedouins in the State of Israel," Intelligence review appended to the letter by P. Amir, Negev military governor, to the Commander of the Southern Command and others, January 24, 1957, file 473–72/1970, IDFA, reporting that Bedouin participated in the attack on Gush Etzion.

98. Brezner, *HaNegev BeHityashvut VeBeMilhama*, 309–14.

99. It was named after Yoav, code name of Yitzhak Dubno, the senior officer in charge of defending Kibbutz Negba, who had been killed on May 21, 1948 during an Egyptian air raid on the kibbutz.

100. The Yiftah Brigade, October 19 and 21, 1948, file 1216–922/1975, IDFA; Report on the capture of Be'er Sheva in the Yiftah Brigade Intellectual Journal, October 21, 1948, file 1216–922/1975, IDFA; M. Hanegbi to Gen. Avner, October 31, 1948, file 233–121/1950, IDFA; Cohen, *LeOr HaYom*, 184–85; Brezner, *HaNegev BeHityashvut VeBeMilhama*, 321; The order for Operation Yoav, October 1948, file 1225–922/1975, IDFA; Cohen, *LeOr HaYom*, 168–69; History Branch, *Toldot Milhemet Ha'Atsma'ut*, 99; Wallach and Lissak, *Aṭlas Karṭa LeToldot Medinat Israel*, 54.

101. Minutes of the meetings of the Negev Committee, April 27, 1948, RG A246, file 30 (26), CZA.

102. Ben-Bassat and Ben-Artzi, "The Collision of Empires as Seen from Istanbul," 26, 28; Ben-David and Kressel, "The Bedouin Market," 3–6; Braslavy, *HaYad'ata Et HaAretz*, 236.

103. M. B. Karai, the Kirya to E. Elath, London, October 6, 1950, file G-2592/18, ISA; D. Shaltiel to Chief of Staff, "The Military Administration," March 8, 1949, file 439–1308/1950, IDFA.

104. M. Hanegbi to General Avner, October 31, 1948, file 233–121/1950, IDFA.

105. D. Ben-Gurion, October 30, 1948, BGD, BGA.

106. "Minutes—Meeting of the Provisional Government," October 31, 1948, ISA.

107. Among them, 'Id Ibn Hdheirah, Gharem Abu Ghaylun, 'Abd Abu Rgayyig, [Farhan] Abu Yihya, and from Abu Rabi'ah, Jarawin and other tribes.

108. According to the report, Sheikh a-Sane' did not arrive due to illness; M. Hanegbi to Gen. E. Avner, November 5, 1948, file G-2564/10, ISA; Report from Y. Berdichevsky to G. Machnes, November 4, 1948, file G-297/59, ISA.

109. Report by M. Hanegbi to Gen. E. Avner, November 5, 1948, file G-2564/10, ISA; Gen. Avner to Foreign Ministry, November 8, 1948, file G-2564/10, ISA.

110. Report by Y. Berdichevsky to G. Machnes, November 4, 1948, file G-297/59, ISA. Berdichevsky's report referred also to a side conversation with Sheikh al-Huzayyil that took place after the meeting in which the latter "expressed the opinion that the Bedouin should be well-treated and that arrangements should be made easier." He also noted that David Kron had advised Sheikh al-Huzayyil to suggest that the sheikhs should "distance themselves entirely from the area" and promised him and his tribe of about a thousand people sufficient land in Wadi a-Shari'ah. He also advised him to sell the lands arguing that they might get nothing for them later.

111. Report by M. Hanegbi to Gen. E. Avner, November 5, 1948, file G-2564/10, ISA. See also documentation of a similar meeting in Gelber, *Komemiyut VeNakba*, 356.

112. Y. Berdichevsky to G. Machnes, November 4, 1948, file G-297/59, ISA.

113. "To withdraw those of their forces which have advanced beyond the positions held on 14 October, the Acting Mediator being authorized to establish provisional lines beyond which no movement of troops shall take place." United Nation Security Council Resolution 61, November 4, 1948, S/RES/61, UNA.

114. Named after the biblical character, Abraham's nephew, who settled in Sodom near the Dead Sea and escaped before the city was destroyed for its sins.

115. Summary of information of the S' [Southern] Front Headquarters/Intelligence, November 24, 1948, file 17–1041/1949, IDFA; History Branch, *Toldot Milhemet Ha'Atsma'ut*, 336; Wallach and Lissak, *Atlas Karta LeToldot Medinat Israel*, 117; Oren, "Be'er Sheva BaMa'arakhot HaNegev," 148.

116. D. Ben-Gurion, November 24, 1948, BGD, BGA; Asia, *Moked HaSikhsukh*, 75.

117. Operations officer of the Negev Brigade to Battalions 7 and 9, November 3, 1948, file 21–6287/1948, IDFA; Kouzli, "Mediniyut HaMimsad HaIsraeli," 44; Al-'Aref, *Al-Nakbah*, 745.

118. Y. Berdichevsky to G. Machnes, general director of the Ministry of Minority Affairs, November 10, 1948, file G-302/109, ISA.

119. M. Hanegbi to Gen. E. Avner, "Weekly Activity Report, November 9–15, 1948," November 18, 1948, file 841–721/1972, IDFA.

120. Ibid. For further details, see Yahel and Kark, "Israel's Negev Bedouin."

121. M. Hanegbi to Gen. E. Avner, "Weekly Activity Report, November 9–15, 1948," November 18, 1948, file 841–721/1972, IDFA.

122. Ibid.

123. Headquarters of Front D/Intelligence, "Meeting of Intelligence Officers, November 16, 1948," unsigned, file 17–1041/1949, IDFA.

124. Y. Weitz, November 18, 1948, RG A2, file 4612, CZA; M. Hanegbi to Gen. E. Avner, "Weekly Activity Report, November 9–15, 1948," November 18, 1948, file 841–721/1972, IDFA. See also M. Hanegbi interviewed by Aviva Limon, July 31, 1989, TA.

125. Y. Weitz, November 19, 1948, RG A2, file 4612, CZA. Ten sheikhs from the Tiyaha and Tarabin confederations were mentioned by name: from the Tiyaha, Salman al-Huzayyil, Harb Abu Rgayyig, Hajj Ibrahim a-Sane', Hasan ['Id] Abu 'Abdun, Salmam [Muhammad] al-A'sam, and 'Awwad Abu Rgayyig. From the Tarabin-Jarawin, Farhan Abu Yihya, Salamah Abu Ghalyun, Hlayyel Abu 'Omrah, and Sliman 'Id a-Sane,' among others of those tribes.

126. "Report on the Meeting of the Bedouin Sheikhs Held on November 18, 1948," a different unnamed handwritten note sent on November 3, 1948, file 380–384/1953, IDFA; handwritten in "War Journal of Military Administration Unit in the Headquarters of the Occupied Territories," signed S. Ag., on November 30, 1948, file 841–721/1972, IDFA; "The Bedouin Tribes in the Negev Request to be Accepted Under the Auspices of the State of Israel," *Davar*, November 19, 1948, 1; IDR reporter in the Negev, "The Bedouin Tribes in the Negev are Asking for Israel's Auspices," *Al Hamishmar*, November 19, 1948, 6.

127. These included al-'Ugbi [private name unclear], two sheikhs of Abu Rgayyig, and Ibrahim a-Sane' and Hasan Abu 'Abdallah.

128. Appeal by the sheikhs to the military governor on November 18, 1948, file G-2567/10, ISA [in Arabic]. Translation by the Middle East Department of the appeal by the sheikhs to the military governor, on November 28, 1948, appended to Shimon's letter, HaKirya, to the general director, the adviser for Arab matters, and the director of the Political Department, November 29, 1948, file G-3749/1, ISA.

129. D. Ben-Gurion, November 19, 1948: "Yesterday in Be'er Sheva a gathering of Bedouins took place—the Ministry of Minority Affairs did not know about it," BGD, BGA.

130. Y. Weitz, November 18, 1948, RG A2, file 4612, CZA.

131. Y. Weitz, November 19, 1948, RG A2, file 4612, CZA.

132. Y. S. [Shimoni], November 23, 1948, file G-3749/1, ISA.

133. Ibid.

134. [Y.] Shimoni, to the General Director, Adviser to Arab Affairs and Director of the Political Department, November 29, 1948, file G-3749/1, ISA.

135. Application of 'Awdah Mansur to the military administration in the Be'er Sheva region [Arabic] appended to a letter concerning "The Application of the Azazyat Tribe" from the Research Branch of the Prime Minister, December 5, 1948, file G-2567/10, ISA.

136. Political Department to [Y.] Shimoni, November 30, 1948, file G-2567/10, ISA.

137. Distribution of the Bedouin according to the findings of this study and the deployment of the military forces according to Wallach and Lissak, *Atlas Karta LeToldot Medinat Israel*, 62–63; History Branch, *Toldot Milhemet Ha'Atsma'ut*, 337–45; Oren, "Be'er Sheva BeMa'arakhot HaNegev," 148.

138. Negev Brigade Commander to the 7th Battalion commander and others, "Attitude of the Army to the Bedouins Residing in the Vicinity," November 25, 1948, file 380–834/1953, IDFA.

139. D. Ben-Gurion, October 30, 1948, BGD, BGA; Y. Weitz, November 25, 1948, RG A2, file 4612, CZA. See also Cohen-Shani, *Paris Campaign*, 52.

140. He was a member of the intelligence service and became the first head of the Mossad.

141. D. Ben-Gurion, November 25, 1948, BGD, BGA; Y. Dori, chief of staff, and E. Danin were also invited, November 23, 1948, RG A246, file 36, CZA.

142. D. Ben-Gurion, November 25, 1948, BGD, BGA; Y. Weitz, November 25, 1948, RG A2, file 4612, CZA.

143. Y. Weitz, November 25, 1948, RG A2, file 4612, CZA.

144. D. Ben-Gurion, November 25, 1948, BGD, BGA.

145. Ibid.

146. Y. Weitz, November 25, 1948, RG A2, file 4612, CZA.

147. D. Ben-Gurion, November 25, 1948, BGD, BGA.

148. Ibid.

149. Y. Weitz, November 25, 1948, RG A2, file 4612, CZA. He was invited.

150. D. Ben-Gurion, November 25, 1948, BGD, BGA.

151. "Minutes—Meeting of the Provisional Government," September 12, 1948, ISA, statements of M. Shertok and D. Ben-Gurion; see also Gelber, *Komemiyut VeNakba*, 279; Karsh, *Fibruk*, 72; Morris, *Birth*; Oren, "MeHatsa'at HaTransfer," 82. Oren refers to Israel's willingness to absorb one hundred thousand refugees as part of the Lausanne Conference, which failed.

152. Lif was born in Moscow, where he studied engineering and became a Zionist. He moved to Mandatory Palestine in 1924, where he became a pioneer of mapping and photogrammetry and worked for the Zionist Institutions. Later, he was a member of the Jewish delegation to the discussions on the 1947 Partition Plan and in 1949 took part in the Lausanne Conference and the Armistice talks held in Rhodes.

153. Danin was born in Jafa to a Jewish family that has Iraqi roots in Baghdad. He was an Arab speaker, and during the 1936–39 Revolt he headed the Arab Intelligent section of the Haganah. He was a consultant on issues relating to the Arab question before and after the establishment of Israel.

154. "Committee of Three for Refugee Affairs," in Danin, *Tsiyoni BeKhol Tnay*, 304, 310; see also a version in Ben-Gurion, *Yoman HaMilhama*, 776; Gelber, *Komemiyut VeNakba*, 308. According to Ben-Gurion, the final report on the returning refugees was completed on December 3, 1948; Ben-Gurion, *Yoman HaMilhama*, 863.

155. "Minutes—Meeting of the Provisional Government," November 28, 1948, ISA.

156. Report by Y. Allon to Y. Weitz, Y. Yadin, and the Negev military governor, December 1, 1948, RG A246, file 36, CZA; Y. Yadin to Chief of Staff, December 3, 1948, A246-747, CZA.

157. "Minutes—Meeting of the Committee Appointed by the Government," December 3, 1948, file G-308/141, ISA.

158. Report by Y. Allon to Y. Weitz, Y. Yadin, and the Negev military governor, December 1, 1948, RG A246, file 36, CZA.

159. Report by Y. Allon, December 1, 1948. "No-man's-land" is the area that was captured by the IDF in the northeastern Negev that was intended to be in the Arab State, according to the Partition Plan.

160. D. Ben-Gurion, January 10, 1949, BGD, BGA.

161. Marx, "Bedu'ey HaNegev," 91. The three tribes lost pastureland in the east but retained most of the land for sowing as well as three wells: Arara, Tel Malhata, and Mashash.

162. Sheikh al-As'am was closely connected with the leadership of the Yishuv regarding every aspect of land acquisition. This matter is extensively detailed in Ben-David, *Meriva BaNegev*, 43–44.

163. Bailey, "Reshimot Al HaUkhlusiya HeBedu'it," 50.

164. Report by Y. Allon to Y. Weitz, Y. Yadin, and the Negev military governor, December 1, 1948, RG A246, file 36, CZA.

165. For further discussion on the role of land rights within Israeli policy during the war, see Yahel and Kark, "Israel's Negev Bedouin," 33–34, versus Porat, "Mediniyut Hapituah," 410.

166. Y. Weitz, November 30, 1948, RG A2, file 4612, CZA.

167. On one of the copies of a letter by Yadin to the chief of staff, two handwritten notes were added on December 9, 1948, for the chief of staff by Nehemiah, "B. G. [Ben-Gurion] does not approve the agreement" and on December 24, 1948, note to Yigael [the name of the writer cannot be identified]: "What did you finally conclude on this?"; Y. Yadin to the Chief of Staff, December 3, 1948, file 233–121/1950, IDFA.

168. Y. Yadin to the Chief of Staff, December 3, 1948, file 233–121/1950, IDFA.

169. Minutes, "A Meeting of the Committee Appended to the [Military] Administration," December 3, 1948, and "Decisions of the Committee Appended to the [Military] Administration," December 29, 1948, both in file G-308/141, ISA. See also Gelber, *Ḳomemiyut VeNakba*, 357.

170. Y. Berdichevsky to G. Machnes, December 8, 1948, file G-302/109, ISA. In his letter he also referred to plans for Bedouin settlement, which will be discussed in the next chapter.

171. Named after Assaf Sheknai, who had fallen a year earlier while heading a platoon that secured the water pipeline in the area of the operation.

172. History Branch, *Toldot Milhemet Ha'Atsma'ut*, 337; D. Ben-Gurion, December 6, 1948, BGD, BGA.

173. D. Ben-Gurion, December 6, 1948, BGD, BGA; "Minutes—Meeting of the Provisional Government," December 8, 1948, ISA.

174. Headquarters of the S' [Southern] Front/Intelligence, "Summary of Information no. 81," December 9–10, 1948, RG A246, file 36, CZA.

175. Intelligence officer to the military administration in Be'er Sheva and vicinity, December 15, 1948, and a handwritten reply, apparently from the Negev military administration, no explicit date, both in file 380–834/1953, IDFA.

176. "Minutes of a Meeting of the Provisional Government," December 15, 1948, ISA; D. Ben-Gurion, December 22, 1948, BGD, BGA; Y. Allon, "Order of the Day before the Horev Campaign," December 22, 1948, file 434–1046/1970, IDFA.

177. History Branch, *Toldot Milhemet Ha'Atsma'ut*, 341.

178. Asia, *Moḳed HaSikhsukh*, 78.

179. "Minutes—Meeting of the Provisional Government," December 19, 1948, ISA; Asia, *Moḳed HaSikhsukh*, 82.

180. D. Ben-Gurion, December 29, 1948, BGA, BGD; United Nations Security Council, Resolution 66, December 29, 1948, S/RES/66, UNA; Gelber, *Ḳomemiyut VeNakba*, 342.

181. "Minutes—Meeting of the Provisional Government," January 5, 1949, 6, ISA; History Branch, *Toldot Milhemet Ha'Atsma'ut*, 358, 360; Gelber, *Ḳomemiyut VeNakba*, 338.

182. D. Ben-Gurion, January 10, 1949, BGD, BGA. As noted, on November 25, 1948, Ben-Gurion recounted a discussion on this topic in his diary, and his position was that the return of the Bedouin would not constitute a detriment to security.

183. "Decisions Taken at a Meeting," file G-308/141, ISA.

184. Y. Berdichevsky to G. Machnes, director general of the Ministry of Minority Affairs, "Weekly Report, January 16–22, 1949," January 23, 1949, and an earlier "Weekly Report" by Y. Berdichevsky, January 9, 1949, both in file G-302/109, ISA. This too coincides with statements by Ze'ev Taub, mukhtar of Kibbutz Shoval, according to which he was asked to verify the identity of members of the al-Huzayyil tribe and those under their protection who were in Dhahiriyya prior to their return to Israel in 1949. Ze'ev Taub, personal interview, April 20, 2009, Shoval. According to Shaul Sade on May 6, 2009, personal interview, Sde Teiman. When he arrived together with the founders of Kibbutz Beit Kama on April 15, 1949, members of al-Huzayyil were in the area.

185. The original text was submitted to the Security Council on February 22, 1949, S/1264, UNA; Gelber, *Ḳomemiyut VeNakba*, 336.

186. Some of the area captured in Operation Uvda were returned to the Jordanian as part of the Armistice Agreement in exchange for areas elsewhere.

187. Z. Lif to the Ministry of Foreign Affairs, July 25, 1949, file HZ-2402/20, ISA.

188. M. B. Karai to E. Elath, London, October 6, 1950, file G-2592/18, ISA; D. Shaltiel to Chief of Staff, "The Military Administration," March 8, 1949, file 439–1308/1950, IDFA.

189. Y. Berdichevsky reported that "many requests are coming in from the governor on behalf of sheikhs of various tribes requesting to be accepted under the aegis of Israel." Y. Berdichevsky to G. Machnes, February 20, 1949, file G-297/59, ISA.

190. M. B. Karai to Ambassador E. Elath, London, October 6, 1950, file G-2592/18, ISA.

191. Reviews on the topic of minorities and their treatment between March and June 1949, file G-307/37, ISA.

192. M. B. Karai to Ambassador E. Elath, London, October 6, 1950, file G-2592/18, ISA; see also Report from Lieutenant Colonel E. Mor, Commander of the Military Administration in the Occupied Territories to the Minister of Defense and the Ministry of Foreign Affairs, May 9, 1950, file HZ-2402/20, ISA.

193. M. B. Karai to Ambassador E. Elath, London, October 6, 1950, file G-2592/18, ISA.

194. Al-'Aref, *Al-Nakbah*, 747.

195. Michael Hanegbi interview with Aviva Limon, July 31, 1989, TA.

2. Creation of the Military Regime

1. Reches, "Yesodot HaMediniyut"; Benziman and Mansour, *Dayarey Mishne*; Stendel, *Arviye Israel*; Lustick, *Arabs in the Jewish State*; Ozacky-Lazar, "Hitgabshut Yahasey HaGomlin."

2. Among the most relevant studies of the Bedouin during the time frame of the current chapter are Mintzker, "HaJanabib"; Marx, *Bedouin of the Negev*; Porat, *HaBedu'im BaNegev*; Zivan, *Yaḥasey Yehudim VeBedu'im*.

3. Ozacky-Lazar, "HaMimshal HaTseva'i KeManganon Shlita"; Degani, "Both Arab and Israeli"; Jiryis, *Arabs in Israel*; Benziman and Mansour, *Dayarey Mishne*; Robinson, *Citizen Strangers*; Cohen, *Good Arabs*; Ozacky-Lazar, "Hitgabshut Yahasey HaGomlin"; Bauml, *Tsel Kahol Lavan*; Bauml, "HaMimshal HaTseva'i VeTahalikh Bitulo"; Hitman and Moskowitz, "HaYelhu Shnayim Yahdav."

4. Fletcher, *British Imperialism and 'The Tribal Question,'* 10.

5. Hofnung, *Democracy, Law and National Security*, 152–53; Ozacky-Lazar, "Hitgabshut Yahasey HaGomlin," 50–51; Lustick, *Arabs in the Jewish State*, 136.

6. Michael Hanegbi was the governor until 1952, when he was replaced by Bazil Herman (1952–53), Joshua Verbin (1953–56), Pinhas Amir (1956–63), and the last governor, Sasson Bar-Zvi (1963–66). Various archival documents and personal interview, Pinhas Amir, Ramat-Hasharon, July 28, 2013; Mintzker, "HaJanabib," 165.
7. Kachensky, "Ma'barot," 85.
8. Morris, *Israel's Border Wars*, 34–35.
9. For further discussion of the legal basis, see Hofnung, *Democracy, Law and National Security*; Rubinstein and Medina, *HaMishpat HaHukati*.
10. Morris, *Israel's Border Wars*, 28–172; Ozacky-Lazar, "HaMimshal HaTseva'i," 106; Cohen, *Good Arabs*, 65–94; Degani, "Both Arab and Israeli," 22.
11. Pinhas Amir and Beni Lubotkin, who served in the military administration since 1953 including two positions of governor in the north and in the center. Personal interviews, Ramat-Hasharon, July 28, 2013.
12. "Procedure for Operating the Military Administration," February 24, 1954, file 57-626/10, IDFA.
13. Y. Palmon to the Foreign Minister, "Requests of Arabs to Ministers and Government Ministries," March 17, 1950, file HZ-2402/19, ISA.
14. Mintzker, "HaJanabib," 164.
15. The Ministry of Minorities, which was previously involved in Bedouin issues, was dismantled in June 1949.
16. Morris, *Israel's Border Wars*, 84–92.
17. Talmon, "HaHityashvut HaHakla'it," 147.
18. See chapter 1; Yahel, "Hatsa'ot LeYishuv Bedui'ey HaNegev," 18–19.
19. He was replaced by M. Hanegbi, who held both positions in July 1949; "Hanegbi—Moshel Migdal Gad [al Majdal, later Ashkelon]," *Davar*, July 21, 1949, 6. Israel did not allow Arabs to stay in Migdal Gad, and most left to Egypt; in 1950, the Military Administration there ceased. See Morris, *1948 and After*, 323–47.
20. Y. Weitz, January 27, 1949, RG A2, file 4612, CZA. There are further discussions on the matter such as on March 31 and July 26, 1949.
21. Porat, "Trumat HaTfisa HaGeografit-Yeshuvit."
22. In Minutes of the Meeting of the Secondary Coordination Committee, January 25, 1950, ISA G-2564, Hanegbi provided more details: 2,000 near Kibbutz Shoval (mostly members of al-Huzayyil tribes); 8,000 northeast of Be'er Sheva (members of Tiyaha tribes including the Dhullam subconfederation); 5,000 west of Be'er Sheva (members of Tarabin tribes); and 1,500 between Bir-'Asluj and Be'er Sheva (members of 'Azazmah tribes). Also, in M. Hanegbi, "General Remarks for Details to Clarify the Bedouin Problem in the Negev," March 6, 1950, file G-6840, ISA. Hanegbi indicated that there are changes in the Bedouin numbers: according to the last count, which exact date he did not mention, Bedouin numbered 18,500 people, but their sheikhs indicated a total number of 17,040 in July 1949.
23. Protocol, "Meeting—Committee for Refugee Affairs, September 1, 1949," file KKL5/17149, CZA.
24. Ibid.
25. For further details on land types according to legislation, including the Miri type, see the introduction.
26. Protocol, "Meeting, Committee for Refugee Affairs, September 1, 1949," file KKL5/17149, CZA. He explained his plan also in his diary from March 31, 1949.
27. Y. Weitz, June 4, 1949, RG A2, file 4612, CZA.
28. Protocol, "Meeting, Committee for Refugee Affairs, September 1, 1949," file KKL5/17149, CZA.
29. Ibid.

30. Protocol, "Session No. 6, the Committee for Refugee Affairs of October 12, 1949"; Protocol, "Session 7, the Committee for Refugee Affairs of October 19, 1949," both in file 721–843/1972, CZA.

31. In the archival materials, there is a report of about sixty families of the al-'Atawnah tribe of the Tiyaha who received lands in the eastern Negev and not in the western areas most of them inhabited before the war. Avraham Shemesh to the military administration in the Negev, "Weekly Report," n.d. [from the content the week of December 8, 1949], file 721–843/1972, CZA.

32. H. Ben-Adi, "A Good Year for Israeli Bedouin," *Maariv*, January 24, 1950, 2.

33. See discussion ahead.

34. Z. Lif to Custodian of Absentee Property, December 11, 1949, file HZ-2402/20, ISA.

35. M. Hanegbi, "General Remarks for Details to Clarify the Bedouin Problem in the Negev," March 6, 1950, G-6840, ISA.

36. Y. Weitz, December 12, 1949, RG A2, file 4612, CZA.

37. For example, a letter of the Negev Military Administration indicated a lack of mobility due to a shortage of cars. October 26, 1952, file 405-20/1954, IDFA.

38. Minutes of the meeting of the Secondary Coordination Committee, January 25, 1950, file G-2564, ISA.

39. Report, June 21, 1950, file L-2176/21, ISA. In the late 1950s, another one was added.

40. Y. Weitz, May 9, 1950, file RG A2, file 4612, CZA.

41. Minutes of the meeting of Negev Military Administration officers, August 20, 1951, file 834-133/1953, IDFA.

42. Knesset Minutes, February 2, 1952, KA. See also Riftin, *BaMishmeret*, 112–14.

43. M. Hanegbi to Agam/Operations, "Bedouin Transfer in the Negev," November 14, 1951, file 54-848/1959, IDFA.

44. M. Hanegbi, "General Security Report No. 12, which summarizes March 1951," April, 1951; M. Hanegbi, "General Security Report No. 13, which summarizes April 1951," May 14, 1951; Attached to Hanegbi letter to the armistice officer unsigned, "List of Bedouin Expulsion," May, 1951, all in file L-2176/21, ISA; M. Mualem Office of the Registrar of Minorities in the Negev Region to Dr. Gil, Central Bureau of Statistics, "The Negev Bedouin Tribes and the Numbers of People," November 19, 1951; Negev Military Administration to the Military Administration, October [?], 1951, both in file GL-17102/37, ISA.

45. Hanegbi explained a few months earlier in the Negev Military Administration meeting that at first Ibrahim a-Sane' accepted the move upon compensation but later changed his mind. Meeting minutes, November 8, 1951, IDFA, Dan Gazit personal archive.

46. Chief of Staff of the Truce Supervision Organization to the Secretary-General, "A Report on the Decision Made during the Period November 1, 1951, to October 30, 1952, by the Mixed Armistice Commission," November 3, 1951, S/2833 November 4, 1952, UNA.

47. Knesset Minutes, December 8, 1954, 282–83, KA; H. Ben-Adi, "Land reform of dispossession," November 24, 1954, file 4-610/1960, IDFA.

48. Applications to the Governor of the Military Administration Negev, file 382-834/1953, IDFA.

49. S. Vadish, Memorandum, June 25, 1951, file 834-133/1953, IDFA; B. Herman to Military Administration, August 18, 1952, file G-17006/13, ISA; Mintzker, "HaJanabib," 161. The number of tribes changed between eighteen and twenty-one during the period.

50. Minutes of the meeting of the Secondary Coordination Committee, January 25, 1950, file G-2564, ISA.

51. Marx, *HaḤevrah HaBedu'it BaNegev*, 41.

52. Ibid., 40.

53. This was the case of a letter by distinguished elders from al-'Ugbi to the military governor against Sheikh Sliman al-'Ugbi, November 13, 1951, file 281-834/1953, IDFA; Porat, *HaBedu'im BaNegev*, 153.

54. Statements of Sheikh al-Huzayyil and Sheikh al-'Ugbi in E. Talmi, "The Bedouin in the Negev Declare Their Loyalty to Israel," *Davar*, May 3, 1950, 1.

55. During the mandate period, the sheikhs were granted formal powers and were expected to fill specific responsibilities. See, for example, the roles of the sheikhs in Prevention of Crime (Tribal and Village Areas) Ordinance, 1924–1925, *Legislation of Palestine 1, 1918–1925*, at 386 (Norman Bentwich, compiler, 1926).

56. Marx, *HaḤevrah HaBedu'it BaNegev*, 40–44; Ben-David, *HaBedu'im BeIsrael*, 418; Mintzker, "HaJanabib," 161.

57. Negev Military Governor to three sheikhs of the Dhullam, October 11, 1951, file 834/380-1953, IDFA.

58. Ben-David, *HaBedu'im BeIsrael*, 418.

59. Bentwich, "Legal System of Palestine," 37.

60. "Minutes of a headquarters meeting," May 21, 1951, file 834–133/1953, IDFA; Mintzker, "HaJanabib," 161.

61. M. Hanegbi to South Headquarters, "The Situation of the Bedouin in Israel," February 22, 1952, file 20–405/1954, IDFA.

62. In a booklet published by the General Staff/Intelligent Division, "Bedouin of the Negev in the State of Israel," in a series titled Booklet for Knowing the Middle East no. 4, from November 1954, it was written that "from a purely legal perspective, the authorization [of the tribal court] may not be sufficiently established, in any case there was no Magistrate's Court in Be'er Sheva until 1953, and the tribal court filled the space to some extent and is still in operation"; 30, file 135–535/2004, IDFA.

63. For further discussion on the issue, see the correspondence in ISA GL-17098/35; Al-sraiha, "Deconstruction and Reconstruction."

64. Minutes of the meeting of the Secondary Coordination Committee, January 25, 1950, file G-2564, ISA. For further details, see Mintzker, "HaJanabib."

65. Hutchison, *Violent Truce*, 63, 73–75; Morris, *Israel's Border Wars*, 64.

66. Our reporter, "There is a necessity to change the organizational status of the Bedouin in the Negev," *Davar*, June 9, 1953, 4.

67. See also Porat, *HaBedu'im BaNegev*. Porat argued that the *Davar* article, which unreservedly supported the positions of the government and the military administration, indicates a great deal of false innocence and an attempt to hide the government's responsibility for the power of the sheikh.

68. The article referred to a letter that was sent by Sheikh al-Huzayyil and others to the president of the State of Israel on February 24, 1953, file G-6840, ISA, in which they called for rescue due to a severe drought during the winter of 1952–53 and a Knesset motion that followed of MK Moshe Aram from Mapam. The Knesset appointed a subcommittee to discuss the Bedouin issues. This committee found that the Bedouin issues were not as dire as they argued. Review of Chairman N. Het of the Protocol of the Knesset Interior Committee, June 30, 1953, KA; see also Yahel and Kark, "Land and Settlement."

69. Y. Ya'akobi, "Sheikh Exploits His Tribe," *Davar*, November 10, 1953, 2.

70. Recorder by Sasson Bar-Zvi from Sliman Ibn 'Edesan of the 'Azazmah. Sasson Bar-Zvi Collection, Booklet 6, 36–39.

71. Subcommittee (of the Economic Committee) for Absentees Properties, June 15, 1954, KA.

72. The aim of the Land Acquisition Law (Validation of Acts and Compensation), 5713–1953, was to validate the taking of lands, mainly from Arabs, that occurred during the war and shortly thereafter. The law validated the taking of lands for development, settlements, and security reasons while granting land and monitorial compensations.

73. Shatner explained that the authority would implement a lenient policy. Recorded from statements by Shatner, "Acquisition Law," end 1954, file G-2264/6, ISA.

74. General Staff/Intelligent Division, "Bedouin of the Negev in the State of Israel," 32, file 135-535/2004, IDFA.

75. M. Sharet Diary, March 21, 1955, The Moshe Sharett Heritage Society.

76. M. Shatner, "Nomination of committee to the Negev," August 16, 1954, file 4-610/1960, IDFA.

77. Announcement signed by M. Shatner, director, Development Authority [n.d.], file GL-13907, ISA; E. Rivlis, "The Bedouin of the Negev also want to Live," *Al Hamishmar*, October 24, 1955, 3.

78. Whether the letter was sent is not clear. Summary of a meeting on the problems of the land survey; J. Verbin to Y. Shani (in handwriting it noted that at the request of Shani, the letter was not sent), both October 25, 1954; J. Verbin to Ministry of Defense, October 26, 1954, all in file 4-610/1960, IDFA.

79. Minutes, "Planning Exemplary Arab Village among the Bedouin," November 16, 1954, file 4-610/1960, IDFA.

80. Minutes of a Meeting, January 20, 1955; Summary of a Meeting, both IDFA 4-610/1960.

81. This is far less than the 3,220 claims to almost 800,000 dunams that were submitted two decades later. See Yahel, "Lifnim MeShurat HaDin."

82. A summary report of the implementation of the Land Acquisition Law in the Negev, handwritten: "Submitted by Zuckerman at a Meeting of the Committee for the Implementation of the Land Acquisition Law, August 30, 1955," file 4-610/1960, IDFA.

83. Ibid.

84. A summary report of the implementation of the Land Acquisition Law in the Negev, handwritten: "Submitted by Zuckerman at a Meeting of the Committee for the Implementation of the Land Acquisition Law, August 30, 1955," file 4-610/1960, IDFA.

85. J. Verbin to the PM Adviser for Arab Affairs, October 5, 1955, file 4-610/1960, IDFA.

86. Sverdlov to Military Administration, April 15, 1956, file 478-72/1970, IDFA; Y. Ya'akobi, "They Sowed—but Will Not Harvest," *Davar*, August 5, 1956, 3; Personal interview with Elyahu Shayek, June 23, 2015, Be'er Sheva.

87. A summary of a meeting, September 23, 1955, file 4-610/1960, IDFA.

88. Protocol, March 8, 1956, file 4-610/1960, IDFA; Cohen to the Village Department, "The Transfer of Eliyahu Shayek," file 47-490/1956, IDFA; Personal interview with Eliyahu Shayek, June 23, 2015, Be'er Sheva.

89. M. H., "Review for Correction," *Al Hamishmar*, December 2, 1955, 1; M. D., "Establishment of a Government Committee to Review the Military Administration," *Davar*, December 1, 1955, 1; "On the Agenda: The Establishment of the Committee to Review the Military Administration," *Kol Ha'am*, December 8, 1955, 1, 4; "Committee to Review the Military Administration," *The Jerusalem Post*, December 7, 1955, 1; *Al-Ittihad*, December 2, 1955, 1; Editorial, *Herut*, December 4, 1955, 2.

90. Over the years, others were asked to examine the issue, but with less public involvement.
Ozacky-Lazar, "HaMimshal HaTseva'i"; Degani, "Both Arab and Israeli"; Bauml, "Ha-Mimshal HaTseva'i VeTahalikh Bitulo."

91. J. Verbin, Committee Protocol, January 25, 1956, file G-2263/4, ISA.

92. M. Amit, Committee Protocol, January 25, 1956, file G-2263/4, ISA.

93. Kafkafi, *Milhemet Breira*, 21, 42; Shamir, "Collapse of Project Alpha," 93–94.

94. Morris, *Israel's Border Wars*, 239. There were many border incidents with Egypt over Nitzana. The Armistice Agreement with Egypt included a demilitarized zone in Nitzana. Both states tried to annex the area and solicited local Bedouin groups, such as the Sarahin, to bully the other side. For further discussion, see Sicron, "HaEzor HaMeforaz."

95. J. Verbin to the Police, South District, December 1, 1955; "The Negev Bedouin," December 30, 1955, both in file 50-782/1958, IDFA.

96. "Review on the Negev Bedouin," January 12, 1956, file 478-72/1970, IDFA.
97. Ibid.
98. Report of the Committee for the Examination of the Affairs of the Military Administration, February 24, 1956, GL-13904/9, ISA; Salomon, *BeDarki Sheli*, 285.
99. Knesset Minutes, May 28, 1956, KA; Y. Ya'akobi, "The Desert Is Pushed Southward," *Davar*, July 27, 1956, 2.
100. Sheikh Salamah Sager al-Huzayyil to the Minister of Agriculture, May 17, 1956, file GL-17003/4, ISA; Knesset Minutes, May 28 and June 8, 1956, KA.
101. Minutes of a meeting in the Negev Military Administration, October 8, 1956, file 21-86/1960, IDFA.
102. Ibid.
103. Marx, "Bedu'ey HaNegev," 94–95. Marx studied the Bedouin community as part of his military administration at the Hebrew University in Jerusalem and his role as an employee in the Office of the PM Adviser on Arab Affairs. Marx continued his research on the Bedouin in his PhD and later founded the anthropology discipline in Tel Aviv.
104. Y. Ya'akobi, "The Desert Is Pushed Southward," *Davar*, July 27, 1956, 2.
105. S. Bar-Zvi to Military Administration, July 30, 1956, file GL-13923/2, ISA. He signed as the deputy governor and noted that the letter was also on behalf of the governor.
106. S. Bar-Zvi, "Shlita BeShivtey HaBedu'im BaNegev," 28; a similar opinion was expressed by Pinhas Amir, personal interview, July 28, 2013, Ramat-Hasharon.
107. For examples, see the case of a-Nasasrah in chapter 4.
108. The Israeli invasion was after Egypt blocked the passage of Israeli ships in the Straits of Tiran. In addition, Britain and France, for their own reasons including Egypt nationalization of British and French rights over the Suez Canal, put pressure on Israel to invade Sinai. For further reading on the Sinai Campaign, see Troen and Shemesh, *The Suez-Sinai Crisis*; Golani, *Israel in Search of a War*; Henkin, *The 1956 Suez War and the New World Order in the Middle East*.

3. Bedouin Exit from the Negev, 1957–60

1. Ozacky-Lazar, "Hitgabshut Yahasey HaGomlin," 13–14; Bauml, *Tsel Kahol Lavan*, 112–13, 169; Kousli, "Mediniyut HaMimsad HaIsraeli," 24.
2. These included a massive influx of Arab workers in the Israeli labor market; the publication of a government plan for compensation and rehabilitation of internal refugees; land legislation that enabled the takeover of Arab lands; the opening of the Histadrut, Israel's federation of labor, to Arab members; the modernization of Arab cultivation methods; the establishment of a division for Arab education at the Ministry of Education; and the inclusion of Arab local authorities in the Local Government Center. Bauml refers likewise to the establishment of the Rosen Committee for the Examination of Military Governance and Facilitation and the establishment of the Mapai Committee on Arab Affairs in late 1957. Bauml, *Tsel Kahol Lavan*, 14.
3. Bedouin issues of these years are the focus of several studies: The historical geographer Hanina Porat emphasizes the contribution of left-wing Arab parties in the advance of their concerns; Ze'ev Zivan, in *Yaḥasey Yehudim VeBedu'im*, studied Jewish-Bedouin relations in the Negev and surveys the leading role played by the military administration in these relations during the 1950s compared to the 1940s, when relations with the Bedouin were in the hands of the Jewish Yishuv; in *Bedouin of the Negev*, Emanuel Marx draws insights from his professional role as an employee in the Office of the PM Adviser and from his in-depth academic research; in "Mediniyut HaMimsad HaIsraeli," the historian Sa'id Kousli discusses policy matters regarding the Negev and Galilee Bedouin; and Yair Bauml, in *Tsel Kahol Lavan*, elaborates on the military administration general policy toward the Arabs, with sections specifically on the Negev Bedouin. A highly relevant study was conducted by Amit Tubi and Eran

Feitelson in "Drought and Cooperation" and "Changing Drought Vulnerabilities," which focus on the implication of the drought from the perspectives of climate change and the social vulnerability of nomadic communities. They also discuss the interactions between herders and settled communities.

4. It was headed by Kadish Luz between 1955 and 1957.

5. He was replaced by G. Yoseftal (1961–62) and Y. Almogi, who also was minister of housing (1962–65), both from Mapai.

6. See Marx, *Bedouin of the Negev*, 73–88.

7. See chapter 2.

8. Sheikhs 'Ali [Salman] Abu Grenat, Musa [Hasan] al-'Atawnah, Hammad [Khalil] Abu Rabi'ah, Muhammad [Mheisen] Abu Jwe'ed, 'Awwad Abu Rgayyig, and Hasan Abu Rabi'ah to the Ministry of Agriculture and the Development Authority, February 4, 1957, file GL-17003/5, ISA.

9. S. Svardalov, E. Shayik, and M. Yon, Report on Leases in the Negev in the season of 1956/7, March 1957, file GL-17003/5, ISA.

10. P. Amir to the PM Adviser, April 28, 1957, file 478–72/1970, IDFA.

11. M. Berger to the Ministry of the Interior, February 20, 1957, file 47-490/1956, IDFA.

12. P. Amir to Military Administration, March 3, 1957, file 47-490/1956, IDFA.

13. Ibid. One such concern was the case of Sheikh Sliman a-Sane', who was judged and acquitted, and then new evidence of his links to Egyptian intelligence were captured in Gaza. Parliamentary Question by Y. Khamis and D. Ben-Gurion's Answer, Knesset Minutes, April 9, 1957, KA.

14. E. Marx, "Proposal for Negev Bedouin Settlement," May 27, 1957, file, 478–72/1970, IDFA; personal interview with Emanuel Marx, December 17, 2018, Ramat-Hasharon; Yahel, "Rural or Urban?," 611–612.

15. P. Amir to Military Administration, June 27, 1957, and K. Luz to the PM Adviser, July 30, 1957, file 478–72/1970, IDFA.

16. S. Bar-Zvi's correspondence with Military Administration, September 16, 1957, file 478–72/1970, IDFA.

17. The head of the committee was the PM Adviser, and its members were the head of the Israeli Security Agency's Arab Bureau and the Special Task Force of the Police and Commander of the Military Administration. Bauml, *Tsel Kahol Lavan*, 29, fn. 5, 342; Bauml, "Ekronot Mediniyut HaAflaya," 392.

18. B. Lubotkin on Behalf of the Military Administration Operations Division to Negev Military Administration, October 6, 1957, file 478–72/1970, IDFA.

19. P. Amir to Military Administration, October 20, 1957, 47-490/1956, IDFA.

20. B. Lubotkin on Behalf of the Military Administration Operations Division, to the Negev Military Administration, October 24, 1957, file 47-490/1956, IDFA.

21. This follows Ottoman legislation and court decisions on Miri lands. For further details on the criteria for land rights, see the introduction.

22. Selection from the protocol of a meeting of the Committee for Land Settlement in the Galilee, February 11, 1958; M. Levin to the director of the Ministry of Justice, July 6, 1958; both in ISA 5742/C. For extensive information on land settlement, see Sandberg, *Hesder Zkhuyot BeMekarke'in*, 339–46.

23. Sheikh al-'Atawnah et al. to Minister of Justice, April 21, 1958, and Memo of August 6, 1958, file G-3520-5733, ISA.

24. B. Lubotkin to the PM Adviser, May 4, 1958, file GL-17003/5, ISA.

25. Y. Kukia to the head of the Development Authority, July 17, 1958, file G-5742, ISA.

26. A. Efrat, "Report on Activity in the Bedouin Area in the Negev," May 29, 1958, file 39–590/1961, IDFA.

27. P. Amir Comments on Efrat's letter, June 1958, file 39–590/1961, IDFA.

28. Parliamentary Question by Y. Khamis, answered by Ministry of Agriculture, Knesset Minutes, June 25, 1958, KA.

29. A. Harsina to Military Administration, July 21, 1958. This was a second version of his previous plan from 1956 that was not promoted. A. Harsina to the General Staff, IDF, "Permanent Settlement for the Bedouin, Sayig Area and Decision on Security Settlement in That Area," June 24, 1956, both in file 478-72/1970, IDFA; Porat, *HaBedu'im BaNegev*, 113-23.

30. A. Harsina to Military Administration, July 21, 1958, file 478-72/1970, IDFA.

31. Ibid. See the final outline map of Harsina's recommendation in chapter 4.

32. Y. Kukia to Y. Elster of the Surveying Division and Others, July 31, 1958, file G-5742/2, ISA.

33. Protocol of a meeting of the Subcommittee for Land Settlement in the Negev, August 18, 1958, file GL-17003/5, ISA.

34. The idea of legislating a special law was discussed further over the ensuing years.

35. Protocol of a meeting of the Subcommittee for Land Settlement in the Negev, August 18, 1958, file GL-17003/5, ISA.

36. "The Committee for Land Settlement in the Negev," unsigned and undated, files G-5742/2 and GL-17003/5, ISA.

37. *Palestine Gazette*, Supplement No. 1 (1943), 44.

38. "A Bedouin Sheikh at a Press Conference—We Want Permanent Settlement," *Herut*, December 28, 1958, 3.

39. D. Ben-Gurion's statement of government decisions regarding the military administration, August 5, 1959, KA; for further reading on the Rosen Committee, see Ozacky-Lazar, "Security and Israel's Arab Minority," 347-69; Bauml, *Tsel Kahol Lavan*, 229.

40. D. Ben-Gurion's statement of government decisions regarding the military administration, August 5, 1959, KA; Bauml, *Tsel Kahol Lavan*, 229.

41. Government Decision 611, August 4, 1959.

42. Summary of the discussion of the Supreme Committee for Land Settlements in the Negev, December 7, 1959, file KKL5/25568, CZA. They also decided to promote the registration of land in the southern region and to initiate a survey of the eastern Negev.

43. Section from an oral poem recorded by Sasson Bar-Zvi from Ali al-Kurshan of the Jahalin and from Awwad a-Jallad from Tel Sheva, Sasson Bar-Zvi Collection, Booklet 4, 52-54.

44. Tubi and Feitelson, "Drought and Cooperation," 31; Tubi and Feitelson, "Changing Drought Vulnerabilities," 477; Degen, "Traditional Livestock Production," 128; Degen and El-Meccawi, "Livestock Production among Urban Negev Bedouin," 327; Bizikova et al., "Review of Key Initiatives," 837; Bose, "Climate Adaptation," 576.

45. Salzman, *When Nomads Settle*, 11.

46. P. Amir to the Military Administration, February 18, 1958, file 44-611/1960, IDFA.

47. Degen, "Traditional Livestock Production," 133; Levin, Kark, and Galilee, "Maps and the Settlement," 14; Tubi and Feitelson, "Drought and Cooperation," 31; Tubi and Feitelson, "Changing Drought Vulnerabilities," 480.

48. Tubi and Feitelson, "Drought and Cooperation," 32.

49. Recommendations of the Committee to Determine Boundaries for Dryland Cultivation of Negev Bedouin, 1962. The report was sent by H. Molcho, head of the committee, to M. Dayan on June 5, 1962, file G-3506/7, ISA; Degen, "Traditional Livestock Production," 119. However, in other documents the amount appears as about seventy thousand sheep and goats: see B. Lubotkin to the Negev Military Administration, August 19, 1958, and the reply of P. Amir to the General Staff of the Military Administration, August 1958, file 44-611/1960, IDFA.

50. Tubi and Feitelson, "Drought and Cooperation," 38.

51. Records of Ministry of Agriculture, files G-3506/3, G-2419 and G-3505/5, ISA.

52. Degen, "Traditional Livestock Production," 133.

53. Ninety percent of their claims were approved, and they received the sum of one million liras allocated among the claimants. See list in file G-3506/3, ISA.

54. Knesset Minutes, January 14 and 19, 1959, KA; Y. Porat of the Ministry of Commerce and Industry to the Director of the Food Division, January 30, 1959; A. Efrat, January 25, 1959, both in file 43–611/1960, IDFA.

55. Summary of a Meeting on the Arrangement of Emergency Work for the Bedouin, February 8, 1959, file 43–611/1960, IDFA.

56. P. Amir to the Military Administration, February 9, 1958, file 478–72/1970, IDFA.

57. P. Amir to the Commander-in-Chief of the Southern Command, "Overview of the Bedouin Problems in the Period June 10 to July 20, 1958," July 21, 1958, file 478–72/1970, IDFA.

58. A report for that year estimated that 320,000 dunams used by 2,500 Bedouin families were damaged by the drought; "Estimation of Drought and Nature Damages for 1959," July 13, 1959; S. Zamir, Development Officer to the Department of Agricultural Development, Ministry of Agriculture, "Summary of Drought Compensation for the Bedouin," October 5, 1959, both in file G-3506/6, ISA; Kouzli, "Mediniyut HaMimsad HaIsraeli," 60; Zivan, *Yaḥasey Yehudim VeBedu'im*, 136.

59. Meeting of the Sheikhs with the Drought Committee for Bedouin Affairs, May 26, 1960, file 114–590/1961, IDFA.

60. Tubi and Feitelson, "Changing Drought Vulnerabilities." The data provided in the 1962 report of the Ministry of Agriculture indicated only a small decrease.

61. M. Dayan to the Eco, July 5, 1960; G. Ya'akobi to the Government Secretariat, July 11, 1960, file G-6405/5, ISA.

62. Recommendations of the Committee for the Determination of Boundaries for Dry-Land Cultivation of the Negev Bedouin. 1962. The report indicated between two thousand permanent wage earners and up to three thousand seasonal. It was sent by H. Molcho, head of the committee, to M. Dayan on June 5, 1962, file G-3506/7, ISA. Marx indicated smaller numbers: four hundred permanent and up to one thousand seasonal wage employees; Marx, "HaBedu'im BeShnot HaShishim," 640–41. See also Degen, "Traditional Livestock Production," 123; Kouzli, "Mediniyut HaMimsad HaIsraeli," 59; Tubi and Feitelson, "Drought and Cooperation," 34.

63. Tubi and Feitelson, "Drought and Cooperation," 36–37, 39; Records of the Bedouin Drought, 1958, in the Ministry of Agriculture files, file G-3533/7, ISA; Zivan, *Yaḥasey Yehudim*, 142.

64. Bauml, *Tsel Kahol Lavan*, 132; Zarhi and Achiezra, *Economic Conditions of the Arab Minority*, 23.

65. See Tzur, "HaKooperativ HaBedu'i HaRishon," 12–18; Porat, *HaBedu'im BaNegev*, 112; Zivan, *Yaḥasey Yehudim VeBedu'im*, 136.

66. Appeal submitted by A. Hellman from Be'er Sheva Economic Office to the Ministry of Agriculture, January 19, 1958; Y. Cohen from the Histadrut to P. Amir, May 27, 1958; Y. Cohen to R. Aloni, June 25, 1958, all in file 44–611/1960, IDFA.

67. Knesset Minutes, January 27, 1960, KA; Draft Answer to Parliamentary Question, January 26, 1960, file G-6276/7, ISA.

68. Al-Salam was disassembled. There were differences and disagreements among its members. See Tzur, "HaKooperativ HaBedu'i HaRishon," 29; Porat, *HaBedu'im BaNegev*, 112. The New Negev existed later but remained a small-scale operation.

69. Tubi and Feitelson, "Drought and Cooperation," 33.

70. Knesset Minutes, February 9, March 25, and April 4, 1960, all in KA.

71. R. Aloni to Ministry of Agriculture, February 1960, file G-17003/5, ISA.

72. Tubi and Feitelson, "Changing Drought Vulnerabilities," 485.

73. Dayan, *Yoman Ma'rekhet Sinai*, 177; Teveth, *Moshe Dayan*, 323; Bar-On, *Moshe Dayan*, 101; For Dayan's role in promoting the Sinai Campaign, see Golani, "Dayan Movil LeMilhama," 117–35.

74. R. Aloni to Ministry of Agriculture, February 8, 1960, file G-17003/5, ISA.
75. Government Decision 266, March 20, 1960.
76. Ministry of Agriculture to the PM and the PM to the Cabinet Secretary, both May 24, 1960, file G-5405/5, ISA.
77. Ibid.
78. S. Divon, PM Adviser to PM Office, May 26, 1960, file G-3369/5, ISA.
79. Government Decision 355, May 29, 1960, Cabinet Minister to Minister of Agriculture, May 30, 1960, both in file G-6405/5, ISA.
80. Decision of the Ministerial Committee for Economic Affairs, Eco/94, authorized as Government Decision 389, "Transition of Bedouin to Mixed Cities," June 12, 1960, ISA G-6405/5.
81. M. Dayan to Chairman of the Ministerial Committee, July 5, 1960; G. Ya'akobi to Cabinet Secretariat, July 11, 1960, both in file G-6405/5, ISA.
82. P. Amir to Operation Division, Military Administration, "Monthly Security Report of June 1–30, 1960," July 1, 1960, file 34–146/1961, IDFA; personal interview with Pinhas Amir, July 28, 2013, Ramat-Hasharon.
83. P. Amir to the Head of the Southern Command, July 3, 1960, file 475–72/1970, IDFA.
84. P. Amir to Operation Division, Military Administration, Monthly Security Report of June 1–30, 1960, July 1, 1960, file 34–146/1961, IDFA.
85. He divided them between seven hundred and eight hundred families already in Ramleh, Lod, and Rehovot, and about two hundred near Be'er Sheva. M. Dayan to the Ministerial Committee for Economic Affairs, July 5, 1960; G. Ya'akobi to the Government Secretariat, July 11, 1960, both in file G-6405/5 ISA.
86. R. Aloni to Military Administration, August 28, 1960, ISA G-3369/5.
87. Muhammad Ibrahim Elbaz to the Ministry of Agriculture and the Military Administration, "Request to Move to the Lod Region," July 21, 1960; R. Aloni to Ministry of Agriculture, August 8, 1960; Ministry of Agriculture to Muhammad Ibrahim Elbaz, Abu Rgayeg, August 11, 1960, all in file G-3369/5, ISA; *Davar* reporter in the Negev, "80 Negev Bedouin Families Want to Move to the Center of the State," *Davar*, August 12, 1960, 10.
88. Government Decision 531 (following Eco Decision 143), August 14, 1960, file G-6405/5, ISA.
89. Ministry of Labor to Ministry of Agriculture, August 23, 1960; G. Ya'akobi to S. Soroker, Budget Division, Treasury, November 22, 1960, all in file G-3369/5, ISA.
90. R. Aloni to the Ministry of Agriculture, November 13, 1960, file G-336/5, ISA.
91. M. Dayan to Minister of Development, November 21, 1960; Minister of Development, M. Bentov to M. Dayan, November 29, 1960; M. Dayan to PM, December 5, 1960, all in file G-3369/5, ISA; M. Dayan to the Cabinet Secretary, December 5, 1960, file G-6405/5, ISA.
92. "They Deny the Establishment of an Exemplary Bedouin Village," *Davar*, October 12, 1960, 7; M. Bentov to M. Dayan, November 29, 1960, file G-3369/5, ISA; Porat, *HaBedu'im BaNegev*, 160–61; Shoked, "Housing Others," 308; Yahel, "Rural or Urban?," 613.
93. Y. Pressman to the head of the Operations Command, October 1960, file G-3369/5, ISA.
94. "They Deny the Establishment of an Exemplary Bedouin Village," *Davar*, October 12, 1960, 7.
95. M. Dayan to Minister of Development, November 21, 1960; M. Dayan to PM, December 5, 1960, both in file G-3369/5, ISA. See Yahel, "Rural or Urban?," 613. In the late 1980s, the town of Hurah was established in Khirbat Hurah.
96. Personal interview with Pinhas Amir, July 28, 2013, Ramat-Hasharon; personal interview with Elyahy Shayek, June 23, 2015, Be'er Sheva; *Haner*, July–August 1960, 28–29; Porat, *HaBedu'im BaNegev*, 158; Kouzli, "Mediniyut HaMimsad HaIsraeli," 73.

97. *Davar* reporter in the Negev, "The Bedouins Built Buildings Without Permission," *Davar*, September 19, 1960, 4; "Bedouins Establish Buildings in the Negev," *Haner*, September–October 1960, 31; Knesset Minutes, November 14, 1960, KA.

98. Sheikh al-'Atawnah, "What Do the Bedouin Want?," *New Outlook*, September 15, 1960, 4; Porat, *HaBedu'im BaNegev*, 157; P. Amir to IDF Headquarter, "Monthly Security Report, February 1–28, 1961," March 7, 1961, file 31–568/1964, IDFA.

99. Reports from 1964 and 1965 show funding and construction of twenty-five apartments in the Jawarish neighborhood for the absorption of Bedouin from the Negev and the preparation of one hundred lots for independent construction. Minister of Finance, "Proposal for the Government Decision," "Deciding upon Building Localities for Negev Bedouin," March 2, 1964, file 474–72/1970, IDFA; Adv. B. Leibe to Ministry of Agriculture, April 27, 1964; Summary "Settlement of the Bedouin in Ramleh," December 29, 1964; Ciechanover, Legal Adviser, Ministry of Agriculture to Adv. B. Leibe, February 3, 1965; Declaration by Muhammad Ibrahim Elbaz et al., July 27, 1964; Text of Declaration of Renunciation, Adv. Glickstadt to the PM Adviser, July 2, 1965, all in file GL-43215/9, ISA; S. Bar-Zvi to Operation Division, Military Administration, November 8, 1965, file 187–72/1970, IDFA.

100. P. Amir to Military Administration, December 14, 1959; Summary, Remarks of Subcommittee Meeting of the Localities Committee, January 26, 1960, both in file 482–72/1970, IDFA. An example of military administration involvement in tribal affiliation is found in a discussion that took place on December 14, 1959, within the Localities Committee dealing with the formal list of tribes that would be registered. The military administration promoted a decision in which eighteen tribes would be formally registered. In the meeting, it was decided that the Bedouin of Sager al-Huzayyil, who exited the al-Huzayyil tribe a few years earlier and gained a separate tribal status, were "returned" to al-Huzayyil while members of al-Gawa'in kept their separate status.

101. Knesset Minutes, June 28, 1960, KA. Another example is MK H. Rubin's parliamentary question against military administration involvement in welfare issues, which were not part of their task, to which Peres answered that the military administration was needed to help other agencies.

102. "The Registration of Drought Damage among the Bedouins Has Begun," *Haner*, May–June 1960, 28.

103. Comptroller Report, 296.

4. The Decline of the Military Administration, 1961–66

1. Arad was one of the oldest cities that was mentioned in the Bible (Bamidbar 21:1), and archeological excavation conducted in Tel-Arad, located nearby, found remnants from five thousand years ago. In 1921, the British regime gave permission for soldiers discharged from the Jewish Legion to establish a settlement there, but the initiative failed, and the settlement was abandoned. For further reading on Arad, see Shadar, "Arad"; Vilnay, "Arad"; Eliav, "Ir Ola Min HaMidbar," 161–72.

2. P. Amir to IDF Headquarter, "Monthly Security Report, February 1–28, 1961," March 7, 1961, file 31–568/1964, IDFA.

3. Members of the a-Sane' tribe had claims on lands in the Lagiyyah area located in B1. In 1952, the tribe was asked to relocate to the Arad area. The tribe decided to move to Jordan instead. However, Jordan refused to let the tribe in and involved the UN. With no other option, the tribe accepted the Arad location. For further discussion about this episode, see chapter 2. When the lands in Arad were needed, the tribe conditioned its approval to move again upon returning to Lagiyyah.

4. Based on Harsina proposal of 1958; see chapter 3.

5. Minutes of the Committee, March 22, 1961, file A246/840, CZA.

6. In 1960, the Israel Land Administration was formed and took over the responsibility of managing the Development Authority's lands. Basic law: Israel lands; and Israel Land

Administration Law, 5720–1960. The Israel Land Administration included two divisions: Land Ownership and Registration, headed by Moshe Levin, which was previously part of the Development Authority, and the Land Use Division, which was previously in the Ministry of Agriculture. "The 'Israel Land' Standard was Completed," *Davar*, January 24, 1961, 4. Sandberg, *Land Law and Policy in Israel*, 29.

7. Minutes of the Committee, March 22, 1961, file A246/840, CZA.
8. Ibid.
9. Ibid.
10. Ibid.
11. Central Bureau of Statistics, 1961.
12. Y. Vardimon to Deputy Minister of the Interior, May 22, 1961, file G-2746/3, ISA.
13. P. Amir to the Planning Division, Ministry of the Interior, May 1, 1961, file G-2746/3, ISA.
14. E. Riblis, "Joy in the Bedouin Tents in the Negev When the First Building Permit was Received," *Al Hamishmar*, October 17, 1961, 4.
15. Y. Vardimon to the head of the minority department in Ministry of the Interior, November 2, 1961, file G-2746/3, ISA.
16. Y. Allon to the Cabinet Secretary, December 19, 1961, file G-6405/5, ISA.
17. N. Touitou, "The Bedouins Built Clay Buildings and Continue to Live in Tents," *Yedioth Ahronoth*, December 25, 1961, file G-2746/3, ISA.
18. Y. Vardimon to CEO, Ministry of the Interior, December 31, 1961, file G-2746/3, ISA.
19. A. Harsina to the Deputy Chief of Staff, "The Bedouin in the Negev—a Review," January 12, 1962, file 154-72/1970, IDFA.
20. A. Harsina to the Deputy Chief of Staff, "The Bedouin in the Negev—Proposal for Permanent Sites," January 25, 1962, file 154-72/1970, IDFA.
21. The Minister of Labor, Motion for Government Resolution, January 24, 1962, file 154-72/1970, IDFA.
22. "The Problem of the Concentration and Settlement of the Bedouin in the Negev: Government Motion," in Booklet of the Department for Settlement and Territorial Defense/Operation Division, "The Bedouin of the Negev," February 1962, file 154-72/1970, IDFA.
23. P. Amir to the Head of Southern Command, February 12, 1962, file 154-72/1970, IDFA.
24. Personal interview with Pinhas Amir and Binyamin Lubotkin, July 28, 2013, Ramat-Hasharon.
25. Vardimon to Office of the Minister of the Interior, March 6, 1962, file G-2746/3, ISA.
26. Vardimon to CEO Ministry of the Interior, April 9, 1962, file G-2746/3, ISA. Up to September 1962, the court ruled in twenty-one cases, convicting the defendants and imposing fines and demolition orders.
27. On January 24, 1962, the government decided to postpone the continuation of the discussion. Eliav resigned from his position as director of the Arad Region and did not take part in the committee. Y. Weitz to Cabinet Secretary, September 20, 1962, file G-6405/5, ISA.
28. Government resolution 363, March 25, 1962; Y. Allon to the Cabinet Secretary, asking to correct the decision by adding a member of the PM office to the Interministerial Committee, March 27, 1962; Cabinet Secretary to the Prime Minister, March 28, 1962, all in file G-6405/5, ISA.
29. Yahel and Kark, "Land and Settlement," 14–17.
30. K. Katz, the Government Secretary, to Y. Weitz, April 27, 1962, file G-6405/5, ISA. The list also includes another member of the Ministry of Defense, A Grosman, head of Assets and Services; Y. Gil, director of the Craft and Cooperation Division in the Ministry of Trade and Industry; Deputy Superintendent H. Tavori, the Ministry of Police; Y. Habushi, the Ministry of Labor; and Y. Tamir, the Ministry of Housing.

31. Committee Chair, "Recommendations: The Interministerial Committee for Locating Residential Sites for the Bedouin Population in the Negev," September 14, 1962; it was submitted to the government secretariat on September 18, 1962, file G-6405/5, ISA. See also Porat, *HaBedu'im BaNegev*, 159; Kousli, "Mediniyut HaMimsad HaIsraeli," 75–76.

32. Committee Chair, "Recommendations."

33. See secret map titled "Proposal—Examining Locations for Construction Areas for the Bedouin Population in the Negev," file GL-17092/1, ISA.

34. Recommendations of the Interministerial Committee, September 14, 1962, file G-6405/5, ISA.

35. Although not specifically mentioned, the recommendations were given after legal precedents had been decided, concerning land in the northern part of the country, in which land had been classified as Mewat because of its distance from a settlement and lack of registration before 1921. One of the rulings dealt specifically with Bedouin tent encampments. CA [Civil Appeal] 518/61 *State of Israel vs. Badran*, PD 16 (3) 1717; CA 342/61 *State of Israel vs. Hasin Suwaed*, PD 15 (4) 2470; CA 25/62 *State of Israel vs. Diab*, PD 17 (2) 1485.

36. A map was attached to the recommendation in which land was divided into areas according to cultivation, 1962, file GL-17092/1, ISA.

37. Y. U [Uzai], Acting Cabinet Secretary, Memo, November 28, 1962, file G-6405/5, ISA.

38. Government Resolution 106, December 2, 1962; Acting Cabinet Secretary to the Ministry of Finance, December 3, 1962, both in file G-6405/5, ISA.

39. Knesset Minutes, July 17, 1963, KA; Y. Allon to the Secretary of the Ministers Committee for Economic Affairs, August 28, 1963, file G-6405/5, ISA.

40. J. Verbin to Head of Operation, IDF, December 26, 1965, file 187–72/1970, IDFA.

41. M. Dayan, June 5, 1962, file 3506/7, ISA.

42. Composition of the Tribal Committees for 1961/1962, file 3506/7, ISA.

43. H. Molcho to M. Dayan, Recommendations of the Committee for Determining the Boundary of the Cultivated Bedouin Area, 1962, file 3506/7, ISA.

44. Ibid.

45. Minutes, Meeting, October 18, 1962, file GL-17003/5, ISA.

46. M. Artzieli, "The Bedouin in the Negev: The Drought Caused Death to Half of Our Herds; The Government Deprives Us," *Haaretz*, January 8, 1963, file GL-17003/5, ISA.

47. Tubi and Feitelson, "Drought and Cooperation," 36. For more information on the drought, see chapter 3.

48. Z. Inbar, on Behalf of Head of Operation Division, IDF, "Summary of Governors Meeting," March 28, 1963, file 2–565/1965, IDFA.

49. S. Bar-Zvi to Police and Others, "Meeting of Regional Committee," April 25, 1963, file 3–565/1965, IDFA.

50. Sastiel, Police Commander of the Southern District, to Negev Military Administration, May 3, 1963, file 17–564/1965, IDFA; Tubi and Feitelson, "Drought and Cooperation," 36.

51. Minister of Interior to Cabinet Secretary, May 20, 1963, file G-6405/5, ISA.

52. Government Resolution 476, "Prevention of Damage Caused by Bedouin Herds," June 9, 1963, file G-6405/5, ISA.

53. *Haaretz* reporter, "M. Dayan on the Land Policy and the Bedouin Problem," *Haaretz*, July 31, 1963, file GL-17003/5, ISA. He also referred to his policy to halt the drought compensation and more.

54. Government Resolution 634, August 6, 1963. Corrected version, August 28, 1963, both in file G-6405/5, ISA.

55. Sheikh al-Huzayyil to the PM, August 8, 1963, file GL-17003/5 ISA. The letter was signed by two additional sheikhs, Hasan and Hammad [Khalil] Abu Rabi'ah. Adv. Gilon wrote a letter on behalf of al-Huzayyil, November 26, 1963, and answered by the PM Adviser on December 6, 1963, file GL-7447/25, ISA.

56. A. Yoeli, "Bedouin Sheikhs Claiming Recognition on Desert Lands," *Haboker*, October 17, 1963, 4. In the interview, Sheikh Hammad [Khalil] Abu Rabi'ah explained that they were not against the establishment of Arad, whose lands were of Bedouin that left Israel, but additional lands that were distant from Arad and were used by them and recently taken without consultation with them.

57. L. Eshkol, Knesset Minutes, October 22 and 23, 1963, KA; Bauml, *Tsel Kahol Lavan*, 238. Bauml indicated that the same policy was already started under D. Ben-Gurion, although not declared as such.

58. Bauml, *Tsel Kahol Lavan*, 231–38.

59. T. Simon, on Behalf of the Negev Military Administration to Agencies, "Summary of Representatives Meeting from December 12, 1963," December 13, 1963, file 160–254/1968, IDFA.

60. S. Bar-Zvi to Military Administration, December 12, 1963, and March 17, 1964, both in file 31–564/1965, IDFA; Y. Vardimon to Head of Minority Department, Ministry of the Interior, May 15, 1964, file G-3103/19, ISA.

61. Y. Allon to the secretary of the Ministers Committee for Economic Affairs, August 28, 1963, file G-6405/5, ISA.

62. Decision of the Ministers Committee for Economic Affairs, Eco/50, January 12, 1964, Authorized as a Government Decision 225, January 19, 1964; Porat, *HaBedu'im BaNegev*, 164.

63. S. Bar-Zvi to Commander Southern Command, January 15, 1964 (mistakenly written as 1963), file 474–72/1970, IDFA.

64. Ministry of Finance, proposal for Government Decision "Determining Locations for Construction for the Bedouin in the Negev," March 2, 1964, file 474–72/1970, IDFA.

65. It was also different from the version of the proposal supposedly agreed to by D. Ben-Gurion as PM, the minister of finance, and the Ministry of Agriculture, which mentioned three to five localities. "Construction Locating Program for the Bedouin of the Negev, Background and Principles," without author name, August 11, 1963, file GL-6405/5, ISA.

66. S. Brigrikh to the PM and the ministers, April 20, 1964, file G-6405/5, ISA; Decision of the Ministers Committee for Economic Affairs, Eco/92, Authorized as a Government Decision 418, April 26, 1964; A. Layish to the Director Generals of the Ministries, May 21, 1964, file G-6405/5, ISA.

67. "A Secret Plan for the Bedouin 'Settlement,'" *Al Hamishmar*, February 21, 1964, 1; MK Y. Hamis, Knesset Minutes, March 23, April 8, and May 20, 1964, file 474–72/1970, IDFA.

68. "Determining Construction Sites for Construction for the Bedouin in the Negev—Proposal for Decision," appended to Weitz's letter to the secretary of the Ministers Committee for Economic Affairs, July 26, 1964, file G-6405/5, ISA.

69. Objections to Proposal for Decision on Determining Construction Sites for the Negev Bedouin, July 31, 1964, file G-6405/5, ISA.

70. Proposal for decision on determining construction sites for the Negev Bedouin, July 31, 1964, file G-6405/5, ISA.

71. Decision of the Ministers Committee for Economic Affairs, Eco/154, Authorized as a Government Decision 658, August 23, 1964. See also Kousli, "Mediniyut HaMimsad HaIsraeli," 78.

72. T. Toubi to the PM, December 10, 1964, file G-6276/7, ISA.

73. A. Layish, December 20, 1964, file G-6276/7, ISA.

74. Planning Team, Bedouin Settlement in the Negev—Interim Memorandum (December 1965), file GL-7447/12, ISA.

75. Decision of the Ministers Committee for Economic Affairs, Eco/144, September 12, 1965, file G-6405/5, ISA.

76. The Supreme Committee would become a prominent body for promoting Bedouin settlements after the abolishment of the military administration; see chapter 5.

77. Planning Team, Bedouin Settlement in the Negev—Interim Memorandum (December 1965), file GL-7447/12, ISA.

78. The expropriation was published in *Yalkut HaPirsumim*, 1271, April 21, 1966.

79. G. Wigart, "Again 'A Plan' for Bedouin Settlement," *Al Hamishmar*, December 8, 1965, 4.

80. Ibid.

81. Minutes of a Tour and Discussion on Bedouin Settlement with the Head of the Southern District, January 19, 1966, file L-6/263, ISA.

82. Ibid.

83. The request was on behalf of a-Nasasrah and the al-'Amur families. The tribal affiliation was registered as address in Bedouin ID. Adv. Eliyahu Saadon advocated their issue among the authorities as well as taking their demands to the Supreme Court (SCJ 54/63). See Oz et al., "Between Two Hegemonies," 112–23.

84. Hasan Salem a-Nasasrah and Others to the Southern District Officer, September 17, 1964, file 55-410/1960, IDFA.

85. S. Bar-Zvi to the Military Administration, September 24, 1964, file 55-410/1966, IDFA. The letter was signed by representatives of al-'Amur, Abu Ayash, and others.

86. S. Bar-Zvi to Military Administration, May 21, 1965, December 6, 1965 (date of acceptance), both in file 187-72/1970, IDFA.

87. Sliman Mustafa a-Nasasrah to the PM Adviser, September 9, 1966; J. Ginat to the PM Adviser, September 4, 1966; Central Committee Decision, September 26, 1966, all in file GL-17003/1, ISA. A-Nasasrah formally received a full separate status with independent sheikh position in May 1967. "Three new Sheikhs were Appointed for the Bedouin Tribes in the Negev," *Lamerhav*, May 4, 1967, 4.

88. Abu Rafik, March 5, 1965, file 187-72/1970, IDFA; Porat, *HaBedu'im BaNegev*, 163.

89. Bauml, *Tsel Kahol Lavan*, 240, explained that D. Ben-Gurion, who was traditionally against this step, was now in the opposition; the new personnel in the Central Committee, except for J. Verbin as the military governor, approved it, as well as Issar Harel.

90. L. Eshkol, Knesset Minutes, January 12, 1966, KA.

91. "Summary of Meeting from January 4, 1966, in Issar Harel's Office," file 54-254/1968, IDFA. See also H. Gvati, Knesset Minutes, March 22, 1966, KA.

92. S. Bar-Zvi to the Military Administration, February 11 and March 21, 1966; I. Abu Rgayyig, *al-Marzad*, March 18, 1966, translated by Bar-Zvi, all in file 187-72/1970, IDFA.

93. S. Bar-Zvi to the Military Administration, May 19, 1966, file 277-72/1970, IDFA.

94. A Memorandum of a Telephone Report by S. Bar-Zvi, June 29, 1966; translation from *al-Marzad*, July 15, 1966, both in file 117-72/1970, IDFA; Kousli, "Mediniyut HaMimsad HaIsraeli," 83.

95. S. Bar-Zvi to Operation Military Administration, June 29, 1966, file 187-72/1970, IDFA.

96. S. Bar-Zvi to Military Administration, June 29, 1966, file 187-72/1970, IDFA. He referred to statements by 'Awdah Abu Mu'ammar and Hasan Abu Rabi'ah.

97. A. Harsina to Operation IDF, July 4, 1966, file 187-72/1970, IDFA; Details from a Telephone Report by S. Bar-Zvi, June 29, 1966; A Memorandum of a Telephone Report by S. Bar-Zvi, June 29, 1966; translation from *al-Marzad*, July 15, 1966; B. Gur-Aryeh to Operation IDF, July 3, 1966, all in file 117-72/1970, IDFA.

98. S. Bar-Zvi to Operation, Military Administration, July 5, 1966, file 187-72/1970, IDFA.

99. MH Tadmor to Negev Military Administration, "Central Committee," July 8, 1966, file 187-72/1970, IDFA.

100. S. Bar-Zvi to Operation Military Administration, July 11, 1966, file 187-72/1970, IDFA. He proposed to expropriate all B2, to start with collecting land claims from one tribe or one

area, to register leased lands, to extend the publicity of information, and to build houses and allocate lands instead of only prosecuting offenders.

101. Porat, *HaBedu'im BaNegev*, 169, referred to a letter from July 1, 1966, with the same continent and argued that Bar-Zvi's position had influenced the IDF. But there is no reference for that. Central parts of Bar-Zvi proposal—that is, the expropriation of B1 and land registration—were not promoted. The other sections were repetitions of previous plans.

102. Y. Tzemah to Operation Military Administration, July 28, 1966, file 187-72/1970, IDFA; S. Mikunis, Knesset Minutes, July 13, 1966, KA.

103. A. Harsina to Operation IDF, July 4, 1966, file 187-72/1970, IDFA.

104. L. Eshkol, Knesset Minutes, November 8, 1966, KA.

105. M. Tadmor, Military Administration to Negev Military Governor, August 25, 1966, file 66-254/1968, IDFA; P. Mazeh, Police Headquarter to the PM Adviser, January 19, 1967, file 13909/1, ISA.

5. New Institutions—Old Alliances: 1967-71

1. Correspondence in Israel comptroller files, undated, file GL-11706/19, ISA.
2. Comptroller Report, 296.
3. Numerous documentations in file GL-17005/4, ISA; Bauml, *Tsel Kahol Lavan*, 243. There was also the Israeli Security Agency.
4. A. Dekel, head of operation and planning department in the police to the police units, "Organizing Ordinance: Increasing Activity in Minority Areas," January 1, 1966; "The Chief of Police to the Ministry of Defense, the Military Administration," May 11, 1966, all in file GL-17005/4, ISA. The Arad police station received thirty out of total one hundred policemen that were added statewide.
5. Bauml, *Tsel Kahol Lavan*, 245.
6. Adviser to the PM, April 9, 1967, in Bauml, *Tsel Kahol Lavan*, 245.
7. Although the military administration was over, the Defense (Emergency) Regulations enacted in 1945 by the British Mandate remained in force and were the legal basis for the limitation of rights and freedoms. These regulations are still valid today. IDF Military Advocate General, "Defense (Emergency) Regulation, 1945: Legislation Amendments," March 1966, file GL-17005/4, ISA; Bauml, *Tsel Kahol Lavan*, 243.
8. Y. Beniel, on Behalf of Operation Officer Southern Command, "Assistant Military Commander, Southern Command—Means and Personnel," December 9, 1969, file 113-18/1974, IDFA.
9. Ibid.; Kouzli, "Mediniyut HaMimsad HaIsraeli," 192-93.
10. J. Ginat moved to Kibbutz Urim in 1957, where he became the coordinator of the Negev region in the Arab Department of the Histadrut. He also gained academic knowledge in his studies of archaeology, anthropology, and Middle Eastern studies. He later received a PhD from the University of Utah on the status of Arab women in rural society in Israel and became an academic scholar along with the continuation of his professional activities. U. Mor studied Orientalism at the Hebrew University of Jerusalem and joined the Office of the PM Adviser for Arab Affairs in 1966 in various positions. In 1977, he moved to work in the Ministry of Religions, mainly in Christian affairs, and in 1987 became the director of the Christian Section and also an adviser to the commander of IDF forces in southern Lebanon. He had written a booklet about the Bedouin and a book about the relations between Israel and the Lebanese sects, which was censored.
11. This was already chaired by Toledano, including Aloni, deputy CEO of the Israel Land Authority, and heads of divisions in the Ministries of Housing and the Interior, the commander of the Southern Command in the police, and the assistant military commander. See chapter 4.
12. Other members were local representatives of security agencies such as the police southern district, the Israeli Security Agency, the IDF-Southern Command, and the assistant

military commander. As we shall see, during the period under discussion, this committee became highly influential and accompanied additional members such as the district officer of the Ministry of the Interior and others.

13. Members included the Israel Land Authority and the Ministry of Agriculture.

14. It had already been several years that the Bedouin did not need to get permits for leaving northward, but they did need permits for pasture lands.

15. P. Mazeh, Police Headquarter to the PM Adviser, January 19, 1967, file GL-13909/1, ISA; *Haaretz*, February 19, 1967.

16. J. Ginat, "Review," n.d., attached to a letter from March 20, 1967, files GL-13909/1 and GL-17003/2, ISA.

17. "General Review," unsigned, 1967, file GL-13909/1, ISA. It indicated also that the Bedouin of the ʿAzazmah stayed in the Negev.

18. November 1966, February 9 and 23, and March 9, 1967, file GL-17003/2, ISA.

19. Central Committee Summary, "The Bedouin Tents between the Jewish Settlements," February 9, 1967, file GL-17003/2, ISA.

20. Head of the Spatial Security Branch to the Head of Operation Division, March 8, 1967; Moshe Tadmor to Headquarters of Central Command and Headquarters of Southern Command, April 1967, both in file 277-72/1970, IDFA.

21. J. Ginat, "Review," n.d., attached to a letter from March 20, 1967, files GL-13909/1 and GL-17003/2, ISA.

22. See their requests in chapter 4.

23. "Nomination of Three New Sheikhs for the Bedouin Tribes in the Negev," *Lamerhav*, May 4, 1967, 4.

24. Disputes over leadership in Abu Rgayyig was not new. In 1955, their old sheikh had been contested by his nephew, Ibrahim Abu Rgayyig, when the latter asked to immigrate from Israel. Ibrahim Abu Rgayyig was considered a troublemaker by the authorities. In 1955, S. Bar-Zvi referred to his anti-Israel attitude.

25. J. Ginat, "Review," n.d., attached to a letter from March 20, 1967, files GL-13909/1 and GL-17003/2, ISA.

26. The options were Ibrahim Abu Rgayyig versus his uncle Hasan Abu Rgayyig. "Nomination of Three New Sheikhs for the Bedouin Tribes in the Negev," *Lamerhav*, May 4, 1967, 4.

27. According to Bauml, *Tsel Kahol Lavan*, 245, the limitation on the Arabs ended in October 1967, but it seems that he does not refer to the Bedouin.

28. East Jerusalem and the Golan Hights were later annexed to Israel, and their populations were offered Israeli citizenship, but the rest of the captured territories became under military rule. For a full list of the legislation, see the IDF website: https://www.idf.il.

29. Z. Mars to J. Ginat, "Demolition of 6 Structures in the al-Huzayyil Tribe," March 14, 1969, file GL-17093/7, ISA.

30. Amiran, Shinar, and Ben-David, "Yishuvey HaBedu'im BeBik'at Be'er Sheva," 654.

31. In September 1967, the Central Committee refused Ginat's request to grant Bedouin three months' permit instead of a daily one, while deciding that for longer permits Bedouin should demonstrate a permanent residence in the Negev. J. Ginat to the PM Adviser, September 14, 1967, and Decision of Central Committee, September 19, 1967, both in file GL-17003/2, ISA.

32. Decision of Central Committee, April 17, 1968, file GL-17003/2, ISA.

33. Winkler, *Meahorey HaMisparim*, 143; personal interview with Gideon Kressel, December 22, 2015, Sde-Boker; personal interview with Shlomo Tsizer, December 20, 2015, Be'er Sheva.

34. Booklet, "Report on the Bedouin in the Negev," attached to J. Ginat, Letter to the PM Adviser, November 17, 1968, file GL-17091/22, ISA. According to the census, between 1967

and 1976 the Bedouin population reached about forty thousand. See Winckler, *Meahorey HaMisparim*, 143.

35. Z. Mars to J. Ginat, "Demolition of 6 Structures in the al-Huzayyil Tribe," March 14, 1969, file GL-17093/7, ISA; Amiran, Shinar, and Ben-David, "Yishuvey HaBedu'im BeBik'at Be'er Sheva," 657.

36. And three thousand in 1973. Z. Mars to J. Ginat, "Demolition of 6 Structures in the al-Huzayyil Tribe," March 14, 1969, file GL-17093/7, ISA; Amiran, Shinar, and Ben-David, "Yishuvey HaBedu'im BeBik'at Be'er Sheva," 657.

37. Yahel and Kark, "Land and Settlement," 17.

38. Y. Vardimon, January 10, 1969, file GL-17093/7, ISA.

39. Supreme Bedouin Committee, January 4, 1970, file GL-17097/4, ISA. The relations between Israel and al-Huzayyil and their effect on the establishment of Rahat is beyond the scope of the current book.

40. U. Mor to Deputy to the PM Adviser, December 13, 1968, file GL-17093/6, ISA.

41. See chapter 1.

42. Nissim Kazzaz became a representative of the military administration of the Galilee in 1958 and in 1962 moved to be representative in the Negev. In September 1968, he became the assistant military commander in the Southern Command until he was replaced in 1970 by Lieutenant Colonel Yosi Cohen; Kazzaz, *Seyfa VeSafra*, 182.

43. Kazzaz, *Seyfa VeSafra*, 182; See also U. Mor to Deputy PM Adviser, June 15, 1969, file GL-17003/2, ISA.

44. Decision of the Ministers Committee for Economic Affairs, Eco/154, authorized as Government Decision 658, August 23, 1964. See chapter 4.

45. Lehanover to Amiad, "Bedouin Settlement in the Negev," May 9, 1966, file G-43215/9, ISA.

46. An interview of Michael Jacobson with Arieh Peled, in Jacobson, "Sivuv BeTel Sheva."

47. Yahel, "Rural or Urban?," 615.

48. Lewando-Gundt, "Tel-Sheva," 666; Frenkel-Horner, "Planning for Bedouin," 168–70.

49. Submitted on March 10, 1967, and approved on November 20, 1967, by the District Committee for Planning and Construction, Plan 137/03/7.

50. Lewando-Gundt, "Tel-Sheva," 667; Frenkel-Horner, "Planning for Bedouin," 169; Y. Gilat, "The Negev Bedouin Move to Permanent Settlement," *Al Hamishmar*, June 13, 1969, 8.

51. Summary of a Meeting, March 10, 1967, file GL-17093-5, ISA.

52. Summary, March 25 and 30, 1968, file GL-17093/6, ISA.

53. Booklet, "Report on the Bedouin in the Negev," attached to J. Ginat's Letter to the PM Adviser, November 17, 1968, file GL-17091/22, ISA.

54. M. Ad, "The Tenants of the Bedouin Village are Demanding—Register their Ownership in the Land Registrar," *Davar*, January 7, 1969, 8; they also repeated the claim that Bedouin should get ownership titles on their houses instead of the usual long leases and argued that the prices were higher than promised.

55. *Lamerhav* reporter in the Negev, "Bedouin Refused to Settle in Village Built for Them Near Be'er Sheva," *Lamerhav*, November 8, 1968, 11. Long leases were the standard format of public land allocation in Israel.

56. The PM Adviser, January 8, 1969, file GL-17031/19, ISA.

57. M. Bentov to chair of the Ministerial Committee on Economic Affairs, April 22, 1968.

58. The PM Adviser, Report, February 12, 1969, file GL-17002/2, ISA; the first to pay deposits were families of Ibn-Barri, Muhammad Abu Taha, Farhan al-Baz, and Nayif Abu Rgayyig, file GL-17093/6, ISA.

59. The PM Adviser, January 8, 1969, file GL-17093/19, ISA.

60. J. Ginat, "Summary of a Meeting of the Bedouin Committee," February 11, 1969, file GL-17093/7, ISA.

61. J. Ginat, "Summary of the Meeting of the Bedouin Settlement Committee [High Bedouin Committee] Dated June 17, 1969," June 23, 1969, file GL-17093/7, ISA.

62. M. Bentov, June 4, 1969, file 0721.09.001, TA; *Davar* reporter in the Negev, "Inaugurated First Town for the Bedouin—Tel Sheva," *Davar*, June 5, 1969, 8; Y. Gilat, "The Negev Bedouin Move to Permanent Settlement," *Al Hamishmar*, June 13, 1969, 8.

63. G. Shlomo, "Bedouin Wonder: Permanent Settlement," *Maariv*, June 15, 1969, 16; *Davar* reporter in the Negev, "Inaugurated First Town for the Bedouin—Tel Sheva," *Davar*, June 5, 1969, 8.

64. Razi Abu Taha, Ahmad Abu Taha, Ibrahim Abu Taha, and Muhammad Abu Taha, "Complaint to the Negev District Police, Be'er Sheva," October 20, 1969, file GL-17031/19, ISA.

65. Z. Mars to J. Ginat, "Demolition of 6 Structures in the al-Huzayyil Tribe," March 14, 1969, file GL-17093/7, ISA.

66. Reuven Aloni stated in the speech he delivered at the official inauguration ceremony of Tel Sheva that each Bedouin would obtain a written document on the matter. Y. Gilat, "The Negev Bedouin Move to Permanent Settlement," *Al Hamishmar*, June 13, 1969, 8.

67. The recommendation of the Interministerial Committee headed by Weitz in 1962. See chapter 4.

68. About three thousand claims were submitted. According to the legal process, the registration office collected the claims and was supposed to forward those under dispute to the courts. Land (Settlement of Title) Ordinance of 1928, *Official Gazette*, 260, May 30, 1928. It was amended by Land (Settlement of Title) Ordinance (New Version), 5729–1969, *Diney Medinat Israel (Nosah Hadash)* 13, 292; Sandberg, *Hesder Zhuyot BeMekarke'in*, 205–332; Albeck and Fleisher, *Diney Mekarke'in BeIsrael*, 275–316; Yahel, "Lifnim MeShurat HaDin," 92.

69. Land Settlement Cases 1/69 and 3/69-17/69 (Be'er Sheva District Court) *The State of Israel vs. al-Hawashlah et al.* It was not indicated in the archival documents why this group of cases was selected to be dealt with first. The reason may be connected to the fact that the al-Hawashlah families were the remnant of a separate tribe whose majority left Israel during the War of Independence in 1948. They were affiliated by the authorities with the Abu Rgayyig although they were located far away. In the 1950s, there was a dispute between them and the Abu Rgayyig that led to blood revenge. Over the years, they sought to establish a separate tribe but were refused. Given their problematic position within the Bedouin society, it was not expected that their issue would gain sweeping support from others.

70. Elyahu Shayek, personal interview, June 23, 2015, Be'er Sheva. As the al-Hawashlah cases were being heard in the district court, the legal adviser to the government, Meir Shamgar, held discussions regarding alternative ways to settle the land disputes; meanwhile, it was ordered not to submit additional cases to the court. M. Shamgar, Summary of Discussion on Land Settlement in the Negev, April 13, 1970, Ministry of Justice.

71. Ruling was given on March 13, 1974, in the Land Settlement Cases 1/69 and 3/69-17/69 (Be'er Seva District Court), *The State of Israel vs. al-Hawashlah et al.*, and only in 1984 in the Supreme Court CA218/74 *al-Hawashlah et al. vs. the State of Israel*, PD 38(3)141.

72. Z. Mars to S. Toledano, "The Problem of the Bedouin in the Negev," May 11, 1969, file GL-17003/2, ISA.

73. Statement to Y. Allon, n.d. unsigned [Arabic]. Translation August 3, 1969, file GL-17002/2, ISA.

74. A Booklet of the PM Adviser, "Settlement of the Negev Bedouin Land Problem," March 15, 1970, date was added in handwriting, file GL-17094/2, ISA.

75. Ibid.

76. S. Toledano to Z. Mars, "Settlement Sites for the Bedouin in the Negev," June 26, 1969, file GL-17003/2, ISA.

77. Z. Mars to S. Toledano, "Settlement Sites for the Bedouin in the Negev," September 29, 1969, file GL-17003/2, ISA. It included local representatives from the PM Adviser, the Israeli Land Administration, and the Ministries of the Interior and Housing.

78. Ibid.

79. Amos Yarkoni was born in the village of Naʻurah in the Galilee as ʻAbd al-Majid Khadher al-Mazarib. During the War of Independence, he enlisted to the IDF and changed his name to Amos Yarkoni. He was the first commander of Shaked Battalion in the Southern Command. He retired from the army in 1969; he worked in the Ministry of Housing and lived with his family in Be'er Sheva. After his death, the Be'er Sheva municipality named a street after him.

80. The Outline Plan Team for the Southern District of the Ministry of the Interior, "Minutes of Meeting 1 on Bedouin Topic," June 17, 1970, file GL-17093/12, ISA.

81. Indicated in the Protocol of the High Bedouin Committee, November 18, 1971, file GL-17093/12, ISA.

82. U. Mor to A. Ben-Yaacov, Report on "A Meeting of the Negev Regional Committee" convened on January 10, 1971, February 3, 1971, file GL-17093/10, ISA.

83. Sheikh Abu Muʻammar to Toledano, January 4, 1971, and from January 5 and 26, 1971, all in file GL-17093/9, ISA.

84. U. Mor to A. Ben-Yaacov, Report on "A Meeting of the Negev Regional Committee" convened on January 10, 1971, February 3, 1971, file GL-17093/10, ISA.

85. A. Yarkoni to Ministry of the Interior, January 26, 1971, file GL-17093/10, ISA. The Ministry of Housing was in charge of settling Tel Sheva.

86. U. Mor to A. Yarkoni, February 8, 1971, file GL-17093/10, ISA.

87. "Proposed program of the Ministry of Housing for the Bedouin in the financial year 1971/2," January 17, 1971, file GL-17093/10, ISA.

88. "Memorandum of a Meeting of the Committee for Bedouin Sites Which Convened on February 11, 1971, in the District Officer's Office," February 11, 1971, file GL-17093/10, ISA.

89. S. Toledano, March 19, 1971, file GL-17093/10, ISA.

90. S. Peleg to S. Toledano, April 21, 1971, GL-17093/10, ISA.

91. Minutes, Operational Committee (Members of the Supreme Bedouin Committee), August 1, 1971, file GL-17093/11, ISA.

92. Minutes, Supreme Bedouin Committee, August 31, 1971, file GL-17093/11, ISA; Minutes of Populating Committee, November 1, 1971, file GL-17093/12, ISA.

93. Minutes, Negev Regional Committee, December 8, 1971, file GL-17093/12, ISA.

94. Shiekh Abu Muʻammar to S. Toledano, undated, accepted on December 13, 1971, file GL-17093/13, ISA.

95. S. Toledano to Shiekh Abu Muʻammar, handwriting drafts, January 2, 1972, file GL-17093/13, ISA. He agreed that the returns would be discussed upon the relocation.

96. Lewando-Gundt, "Tel-Sheva," 667.

Conclusion

1. There is a historical irony in that attempt since the assimilation approach was adopted by European states regarding the Jews during the emancipation, and Zionism was based on the understanding that this system has deficiencies.

2. Hemsley, "Consent, Democracy and the Future of Liberalism," 254.

3. Weiner, *Rule of the Clan*, 4.

4. Rabi, *Tribes and States*, 4.

5. A. Layish, deputy PM adviser for Arab Affairs to the PM Adviser, December 20, 1964, file G-6276/7, ISA.

6. Rabi, *Tribes and States*, 4.

BIBLIOGRAPHY

Archives including Digital Archives

Ben Assa Archive
Ben-Gurion Archive (BGA)
British National Archives (BNA)
Central Zionist Archives (CZA)
Dan Gazit Archive
Hagana History Archive (HA)
Historical Jewish Press
Israel Defense Forces and Defense Establishment Archives (IDFA)
Israel State Archives (ISA)
Kibbutz Dorot Archive
Knesset Archive (KA)
Library of Congress
The Moshe Sharett Heritage Society
National Photo Collection Israel
Pinhas Amir Archive
Toviyahu Archive of the Negev (TA)
United Nations Archives and Records Management Section (UNA)
Yad Ben-Zvi Archive
Yad Tabenkin Archive

Newspapers

Al Hamishmar
Davar
Haaretz
Haboker
Haner
Herut
al-Ittihad
Kol Ha'am
Lamerhav
Maariv

al-Marzad
The Jerusalem Post
Yedioth Ahronoth

Books and Articles

Abu-Lughod, Lila. *Do Muslim Women Need Saving?* Cambridge, MA: Harvard University Press, 2013.
———. *Veiled Sentiments: Honor and Poetry: Honor and Poetry in a Bedouin Society.* Berkeley: University of California Press, 2016.
Abu-Rabi'a, Aref. *A Bedouin Century: Education and Development among the Negev Tribes in the 20th Century.* New York: Berghahn, 2001.
———. "The Bedouin Refugees in the Negev." *Refugee* 14, no. 6 (1994): 15–17.
———. "A Century of Education: Bedouin Contestation with Formal Education in Israel." In *Nomadic Societies in the Middle East and North Africa: Entering the 21st Century,* edited by Dawn Chatty, 865–82. Leiden: Brill, 2006.
———. "Negev Bedouin: Displacement, Forced Settlement and Conservation." In *Conservation and Mobile Indigenous Peoples, Displacement, Forced Settlement, and Sustainable Development,* edited by Dawn Chatty and Marcus Colchester, 202–11. Oxford: Berghahn, 2002.
Abu-Rabia, Rawia. "The Law on the Books Versus the Law in Action: Muslim Women in Polygamous Marriages under the Jewish State." *Social Politics: International Studies in Gender, State and Society* 29, no. 2 (2022): 634–57.
———. "Redefining Polygamy among the Palestinian Bedouins in Israel: Colonialism, Patriarchy, and Resistance." *American University Journal of Gender, Social Policy and the Law* 19, no. 2 (2011): 459–93.
Abu-Rabia-Queder, Sarab. "The Paradox of Professional Marginality among Arab-Bedouin Women." *Sociology* 51, no. 5 (2017): 1084–100.
Adan (Bren), Avraham. *Ad Degel HaDyo* (The Ink Flag). Tel Aviv: Ministry of Defense, 1984.
Al-'Aref, 'Aref. *Al-Nakbah: Nakbat Bayt al-muqaddas wa-al-Firdaws al-mafqūd: 1947–1949* (Al-Nakba: The Nakba of Jerusalem and the Lost Paradise, 1947–1949). Vol. 3. Sidon: Modern Press, 1956–61 [Arabic].
———. *Bedouin Love, Law and Legend: Dealing Exclusively with the Badu of Beersheba.* Jerusalem: Cosmos, 1944.
———. *Tārīx Bir al-Sabaʿ wa-Qabāʿiluha* (The History of Beersheba and Its Tribes). Jerusalem: Maṭbaʿat Bayt al-Maqdis, 1934 [Arabic].
———. *Shivtey HaBedu'im BeMehoz Be'er Sheva.* Translated by Menahem Kapelyuk. Tel Aviv: Bustenai, 1937 [Hebrew].
Al-Krenawi, Alean, Vered Slonim-Nevo, and John R. Graham. "Polygyny and Its Impact on the Psychosocial Well-Being of Husbands." *Journal of Comparative Family Studies* 37, no. 2 (2006): 173–89.
Al-Sharif, Kamil Isma'il. "HaAhim HaMuslemim BeMilhemet Palestine" ("The Muslim Brotherhood in the Palestine War"). In *Enemies' Eyes,* translated by Shmuel Sabag. Branch of Military History. Tel Aviv: Ma'arakhot, 1955 [Hebrew].
Albeck, Plia, and Ran Fleisher. *Diney Mekarke'in BeIsrael* (Land Laws in Israel). Jerusalem: The authors, 2005 [Hebrew].
Alon, Yoav. "Tribal Shaykhs and the Limits of British Imperial Rule in Transjordan, 1920–1946." *Journal of Imperial and Commonwealth History* 32, no. 1 (2004): 69–92.
Alsraiha, Kassim. "Deconstruction and Reconstruction: The Case of the Naqab's Tribal Courts in the Shadow of the Israeli Military Government." *Arab World Geographer* 22, nos. 1–2 (2019): 186–205.

Amiran, David, Amnon Shinar, and Joseph Ben-David, "Yishuvey HaBedu'im BeBik'at Be'er Sheva" ("Bedouin Settlements in the Be'er-Sheba Valley"). In *Eretz HaNegev: Adam VeMidbar* (The Land of the Negev: Man and Desert), edited by Avshalom Shmueli and Yehuda Gradus, 653–65. Tel Aviv: Ministry of Defense Publishing, 1979 [Hebrew].

Ashkenazi, Tuvia. *HaBedu'im* (The Bedouin). Jerusalem: Rubin Mass Publication, 1957 [Hebrew].

Asia, Ilan. *Moḳed HaSikhsukh: HaMa'avaḳ Al HaNegev 1947–1956* (Core of the Conflict—the Struggle for the Negev 1947–1956). Jerusalem: Yad Ben-Zvi and The Ben-Gurion Research Center, 1994 [Hebrew].

Baer, Gabriel. *HaMukhtar Hakafri BeEretz Israel: Toldot Ma'mado VeTafkidav* (The Village Mukhtar in Eretz Israel: History of His Status and Role). Jerusalem: Magnes, 1979 [Hebrew].

———. *Population and Society in the Arab East*. London: Praeger, 1964.

Bailey, Clinton (Yitzhak). *Bedouin Law from Sinai and the Negev: Justice without Government*. New Haven, CT: Yale University Press, 2009.

———. "Dating the Arrival of the Bedouin Tribes in Sinai and the Negev." *Journal of the Economic and Social History of the Orient* 28 (1980): 20–49.

———. "The Negev in the Nineteenth Century: Reconstructing History from Bedouin Oral Tradition." *Asian and African Studies* 14 (1980): 35–80.

———. "A Reply to F. Stewart's 'Notes on the Arrival of the Bedouin Tribes in Sinai.'" *Journal of Economic and Social History of the Orient* 34 (1991): 110–15.

———. "Reshimot Al HaUkhlusiya HeBedu'it BeRtsu'at Gaza—Mifkad 1981" ("Lists of the Bedouin population in the Gaza Strip—1981 Census"). *Reshimot BeNose HaBedu'im* 12 (1982): 45–53 [Hebrew].

———. "Review: [untitled]." *Journal of the American Oriental Society* 109, no. 4 (1989): 714–15.

Baker, Alan H. *Geography and History—Bridging the Divide*. Cambridge: Cambridge University Press, 2003.

———. *Ideology and Landscape in Historical Perspective*. Edited by Alan H. Baker and Gideon Bigger. Cambridge: Cambridge University Press, 1992.

Bar, Gabriel. *Arviye HaMizrah HaTikhon: Ukhlusiya VeHevra* (Arabs in the Middle East: Population and Society). Tel Aviv: Hakibbutz Hameuhad, 1960 [Hebrew].

Barak, Aharon. "Shilton HaHok VeElyonut HaHuka" ("The Rule of Law and the Supremacy of the Constitution"). *Mishpat Umimshal* 5 (2000): 375–99 [Hebrew].

Bar-On, Mordechai. *Moshe Dayan: Israel's Controversial Hero*. New Haven: Yale University Press, 2012.

Bar-Zvi, Sasson. "Me'afyenim Shel Haye HaBedu'im BaNegev BeTerem Hitnahalut" ("Characteristics of Pre-settlement Bedouin Life in the Negev"). In *Eretz HaNegev: Adam VeMidbar* (The Land of the Negev: Man and Desert), Vol. 2, edited by Avshalom Shmueli and Yehuda Gradus, 621–30. Tel Aviv: Ministry of Defense, 1979 [Hebrew].

———. "MeZikhronot Rishoney HaYehudim BeBe'er Sheva" ("From the Memories of the First Jews in Beer Sheva"). In *Sefer Be'er Sheva* (The Book of Be'er Sheva), edited by Yehuda Gradus and Yair Stern, 101–10. Jerusalem: Keter, 1979 [Hebrew].

———. "Shlita BeShivtey HaBedu'im BaNegev" ("Controlling the Negev Bedouin Tribes"). *Reshimot BeNose HaBedu'im* 4 (1973): 26–32 [Hebrew].

Bar-Zvi, Sasson, and Joseph Ben-David. "Bedu'ey HaNegev Bishnot HaShloshim VeHaArba'im Shel Hame'a HaEsrim KeHevra Navadit LeMehza" ("Negev Bedouin in the '30s and '40s of the Twentieth Century, as a Semi-Nomadic Society"). *Studies in the Geography of Israel* 10 (1978): 107–36 [Hebrew].

Bauml, Yair. "Ekronot Mediniyut HaAflaya Klapey Ha'rvim BeIsrael: 1948–1968" ("Principles of the Policy of Discrimination Towards the Arabs in Israel: 1948–1968"). *Iyunim BiTkumat Israel* 61 (2006): 391–413 [Hebrew].

———. "HaMimshal HaTseva'i VeTahalikh Bitulo, 1948–1966" ("The Military Administration and the Process of Its Abolition"). *Hamizrah HaHadash* 43 (2002): 133–56 [Hebrew].

———. *Tsel Kahol Lavan: Mediniyut HaMimsad HaIsraeli VePeulotav BeKerev HaEzrahim Ha'Arvim BeIsrael: HaShanim HaMe'atzvot, 1958–1968* (Blue and White Shadow: The Israeli Establishment's Policy and Actions among its Arab Citizens—the Formative Years, 1589–1968). Haifa: Pardes, 2007 [Hebrew].

Ben-Arieh, Yehoshua. "Eretz Israel KeNosse Lemehkar Geografi-Histori" ("Eretz Israel as a Topic for Historical-Geography Study"). *Riv'on LeMehkar Hevrati* 9–10 (1974): 5–26 [Hebrew].

Ben-Arieh, Yehoshua, Ran Aharonson, and Hagit Lavski. *Eretz Bere'i Avara: Mehkarim BeGeografia Historit shel Israel* (A Land Reflected in its Past, Studies in the Historical Geography of Israel). Jerusalem: Magnes and Yad Ben-Zvi, 2000 [Hebrew].

Ben-Arieh, Yehoshua, and Shaul Sapir. "Reshita Shel Be'er Sheva BeShilhey HaTekufa HaOtomanit" ("The Beginning of Be'er Sheva at the End of the Ottoman Period"). In *Sefer Be'er-Sheva* (The Book of Be'er Sheva), edited by Yehuda Gradus and Yair Stern, 55–68. Jerusalem: Keter, 1979 [Hebrew].

Ben-Bassat, Yuval, and Yossi Ben-Artzi. "The Collision of Empires as Seen from Istanbul: The Border of British-Controlled Egypt and Ottoman Palestine as Reflected in Ottoman Maps." *Journal of Historical Geography* 50 (2015): 25–36.

Ben-David, Joseph. "HaBedu'im BaNegev: 1900–1960" ("The Bedouin in the Negev: 1900–1960"). In *Yishuv HaNegev: 1900–1960 (The Settlement of the Negev 1900–1960)*, edited by Mordechai Naor, 81–89. Jerusalem: Ben Zvi Institute, 1985 [Hebrew].

———. *HaBedu'im BeIsrael: Hebeṭim Hevratiyim VeKarkaʻiyim* (The Bedouin in Israel—Land Conflicts and Social Issues). Jerusalem: Land Policy and Land Use Research Institute, 2004 [Hebrew].

———. *Meriva BaNegev: Bedu'im, Yehudim, Adamot* (Dispute in the Negev: Bedouin, Jews, Lands). Ra'anana: Research Center for Arab Society in Israel, 1996 [Hebrew].

———. "The Negev Bedouin: From Nomadism to Agriculture." In *The Land That Became Israel—Studies in Historical Geography*, edited by Ruth Kark, 181–95. New Haven, CT: Yale University Press and Magnes, 1989.

Ben-David, Joseph, and Gideon M. Kressel. "The Bedouin Market: The Axis Around Which Beer-Sheva Developed in the British Mandatory Period." *Nomadic Peoples* 39 (1996): 3–27.

Ben-Gurion, David. *BaMa'arakha* (In Battle). Tel Aviv: Am-Oved, 1957 [Hebrew].

———. *Yoman HaMilhama* (The War Diary). Edited by Gershon Rivlin and Oren Elhanan. Tel Aviv: Ministry of Defense, 1982 [Hebrew].

Bentwich, Norman. "The Legal System of Palestine under the Mandate." *Middle East Journal* 2, no. 1 (1948): 33–46.

Benziman, Uzi, and Atallah Mansour. *Dayarey Mishne: Arviye Israel: Ma'amadam VeHaMediniyut Klapeihem* (Secondary Tenants: Israeli Arabs and Policies Regarding Them). Jerusalem: Keter, 1992 [Hebrew].

Bernadotte, Folke. *To Jerusalem*. Translated by Joan Bulman. London: Hodder and Stoughton, 1951.

Bitzan, John. "When Lawrence of Arabia Met David Ben-Gurion: A History of Israeli 'Arabist' Expertise in the Negev 1943–1966." MA thesis, Ben-Gurion University of the Negev, 2006.

Bizikova, Livia, Jo-Ellen Parry, Julie Karami, and Daniella Echeverria. "Review of Key Initiatives and Approaches to Adaptation Planning at the National Level in Semi-Arid Areas." *Regional Environmental Change* 15, no. 5 (2015): 837–50.

Blas, Simha. *Mey Meriva VeMa'as* (Water Conflicts and Activities). Ramat-Gan: Masada, 1973 [Hebrew].

Bose, Purabi. "Climate Adaptation: Marginal Populations in the Vulnerable Regions." *Climate and Development* 9, no. 6 (2017): 575–78.

Braslavy, Joseph. *HaYad'ata Et HaAretz: Eretz HaNegev* (Know the land: The Negev). Tel Aviv: Hakibbutz Hameuhad, 1950 [Hebrew].

Brezner, Amiad. *HaNegev BeHityashvut VeBeMilhama: HaMa'vak Al HaNegev, 1941–1948* (The Negev in settlement and war: The struggle over the Negev, 1941–1948). Tel Aviv: Ministry of Defense, 1994 [Hebrew].

Chatty, Dawn, ed. *Nomadic Societies in the Middle East and North Africa: Entering the 21st Century*. Leiden: Brill, 2006.

Cohen, Ardon, Michael (Miki) Cohen, and Amos Mendelson. *Ḥaṭivat HaNegev BeMilḥemet Ha'Atṣma'ut* (The Negev Brigade in the War of Independence). Tel Aviv: published by the authors, 2011 [Hebrew].

Cohen, Hillel. *Good Arabs: The Israeli Security Agencies and the Israeli Arabs, 1948–1967*. Berkeley: University of California Press, 2010.

Cohen, Michael J. *Truman and Israel*. Berkeley: University of California Press, 1990.

Cohen, Yeruham. *LeOr HaYom UvaMaḥshakh* (By Light and in Darkness). Tel Aviv: Amikam, 1969 [Hebrew].

Cohen-Hattab, Kobi. *Nekudot HaMishtara HaBritiyot BaNegev: 1917–1948* (The British police stations in the Negev: 1917–1948). Jerusalem: Reichman Publication Series, the Hebrew University of Jerusalem, 1996 [Hebrew].

Cohen-Shani, Shmuel. *Paris Campaign: Intelligence and Secret Diplomacy*. Tel Aviv: Ramot, 1994.

Danin, Ezra. *Tsiyoni BeKhol Tnay* (Unconditional Zionist). Jerusalem: Kiddum, 1987 [Hebrew].

Danin, Hiram. "Rekhishat Karka'ot VeRishuman BeEretz Israel" (Land Purchase and Registration in Eretz Israel). Unpublished paper [Hebrew].

Darby, Henry C. "Historical Geography." In *Approaches to History: A Symposium*, edited by H. P. R Finberg, 127–56. Toronto: Toronto University Press, 1962.

Davis, Seth. "Tribalism and Democracy." *William and Mary Law Review* 62 (2020): 431–86.

Dayan, Moshe. *Yoman Ma'rakhet Sinai* (The Sinai Campaign Diary). Tel-Aviv: Am HaSefer, 1965.

Degani, Arnon Y. "Both Arab and Israeli: The Subordinate Integration of Palestinian Citizens into Israeli Society, 1948–1967." PhD diss., University of California, 2018.

Degen, Allan. "Traditional Livestock Production among the Bedouin in the Negev Desert." In *International Handbook of Research on Indigenous Entrepreneurship*, edited by Leo-Paul D. and Robert B. Anderson, 115–36. Cheltham: Edward Elgar, 2007.

Degen, Allan, and Shaher El-Meccawi. "Livestock Production among Urban Negev Bedouin." *Outlook on Agriculture* 38, no. 4 (2009): 327–35.

Dekel, Tomer. "Critique and Progress: Production of Knowledge and the Planning of Bedouin Settlements in Israel." *Journal of Planning Education and Research* 44, no. 1 (2021): 387–402.

Dinero, Steve C. "Women's Roles, Polygyny and Cultural Transformation in Negev Bedouin Townships: A Gendered Landscape of National Resistance to Post-Colonial Conquest and Control." In *Nomadic Societies in the Middle East and North Africa: Entering the 21st Century*, edited by Dawn Chatty, 883–915. Leiden: Brill 2006.

Donkin, Robert A. "A Servant of Two Masters?" *Journal of Historical Geography* 23, no. 3 (1997): 247–66.

Doughty, Charles M. *Travels in Arabia Deserta*. Cambridge: Cambridge University Press, 1888. Reprint, New York: Heritage, 1953.

Doukhan, Moshe. *Diney Karka'ot BeMedinat Israel* (Land Laws in the State of Israel). Jerusalem: Ahva, 1953 [Hebrew].

Efrat, Aryeh. "Arviye HaEzor Bizman HaMilhama" ("The Arabs of the Area during War Time"). In *First Year of the War*, 49. Dorot: Hakibbutz Hameuhad, 1989 [Hebrew].

———. *Shkhenim BeShea'rey HaNegev* (Neighbors in the Gates of the Negev). Jerusalem: Kahana, 1982 [Hebrew].

———. *Sipurim Min HaSaḳayim* (Stories from the Saddlebag). Tel Aviv: Ministry of Defense, 1992 [Hebrew].

Eilat, Avraham. "Revivim BaNegev" ("Revivim in the Negev"). In *The Book of the Negev: Sketches, Stories and Songs*, edited by Efraim Talmi and Menahem Talmi, 133–35. Tel Aviv: Amihai, 1953 [Hebrew].

Ekeh, Peter P. "Social Anthropology and Two Contrasting Use of Tribalism in Africa." *Comparative Studies in Society and History* 32, no. 4 (1990): 660–700.

Eliav, Lova. "Ir Ola Min HaMidbar: Yamim Rishonim B'Arad" ("A City Rising from the Desert—First Days in Arad"). *Idan* 6 (1990): 161–72 [Hebrew].

Epstein, Eliahu. "Bedouin of the Negeb." *Palestine Exploration Quarterly* 71, no. 2 (1939): 59–73.

———. *HaBedu'im: Hayehem VeMinhageihem* (The Bedouin: Their Life and Traditions). Tel Aviv: Shtibel, 1933 [Hebrew].

Falah, Ghazi. "The Development of the 'Planned Bedouin Settlement' in Israel 1964–1982: Evaluation and Characteristics." *Geoforum* 14, no. 3 (1983): 311–23.

———. "Israeli State Policy towards Bedouin Sedentarization in the Negev." *Journal of Palestine Studies* 18, no. 2 (1989): 71–91.

———. "Israelization of Palestine Human Geography." *Progress in Human Geography* 4 (1989): 535–50.

———. *The Role of the British Administration in the Sedentarization of the Bedouin Tribes in Northern Palestine 1918–1948*. University of Durham, Center for Middle Eastern and Islamic Studies, Occasional Papers, no. 17., 1983.

Fenster, Tovi. "Ethnicity and Citizen Identity in Planning and Development for Minority Groups." *Political Geography* 15 (1996): 405–18.

Fletcher, Robert S. *British Imperialism and 'The Tribal Question': Desert Administration and Nomadic Societies in the Middle East, 1919–1936*. New York: Oxford University Press, 2015.

Frantzman, Seth J., Yahel Havatzelet, and Ruth Kark. "Contested Indigeneity: The Development of an Indigenous Discourse on the Bedouin of the Negev, Israel." *Israel Studies* 17, no. 1 (2012): 78–104.

Frantzman, Seth J., and Ruth Kark. "Bedouin Settlement in Late Ottoman and British Mandatory Palestine: Influence on the Cultural and Environmental Landscape, 1870—1948." *New Middle Eastern Studies* 1 (2011): 1–22.

Frantzman, Seth J., Noam Levin, and Ruth Kark. "Counting Nomads: British Census Attempts and Tent Counts of the Negev Bedouin 1917 to 1948." *Population Space and Place* 20, no. 6 (2014): 552–68.

Frenkel-Horner, Deborah. F. "Planning for Bedouin: The Case of Tel-Sheva." *Third World Planning Review* 4, no. 2 (1982): 159–76.

Fukayama, Francis. "Against Identity Politics: The New Tribalism and the Crises of Democracy." *Foreign Affairs* 97, no. 5 (2018): 90–114.

Gal-Peer, Ilan. "HaNokhahut HaYehudit BeBe'er Sheva Lifney Kum HaMedina" ("The Jewish Presence in Be'er Sheva before the Establishment of the State"). In *Sefer Be'er-Sheva* (The Book of Be'er Sheva), edited by Yehuda Gradus and Yair Stern, 83–100. Jerusalem: Keter 1979 [Hebrew].

———. "HaNokhahut HaYehudit BeBe'er Sheva: 1900–1948." (The Jewish presence in Be'er Sheva: 1900–1948). In *Yishuv HaNegev: 1900–1960* (The Settlement of the Negev 1900–1960), edited by Mordechai Naor, 30–48. Jerusalem: Ben Zvi Institute, 1985 [Hebrew].

Gavish, Dov, and Ruth Kark. "The Cadastral Mapping of Palestine 1928–1958." *Geographical Journal* 159, no. 1 (1993): 70–80.

Gelber, Yoav. *Komemiyut VeNakba: Israel, HaPalestinayim VeMedinot Arav, 1948* (Independence and Nakba: Israel, the Palestinians, and the Arab Countries 1948). Or-Yehudah: Zmora-Bitan, Dvir, 2004 [Hebrew].

———. *Nitsaney HaHavatselet: HaModi'in BeMilḥemet Ha'atsma'ut, 1948–1949* (A Budding Fleur-de-lis: Israeli Intelligence Services during the War of Independence: 1948–1949). Tel Aviv: Ministry of Defense, 2000 [Hebrew].

Gellner, Ernest. *Nations and Nationalism*. Malden, MA: Blackwell, 2006.

Gilad, Zrubavel. *Pirkey Palmaḥ* (Palmah Episodes). Ein Harod: Hakibbutz Hameuhad, 1950 [Hebrew].

Gilad, Zrubavel, and Matti Megged. *Sefer HaPalmaḥ* (The Book of the Palmah). Tel-Aviv: Hakibbutz Hameuhad, 1953 [Hebrew].

Goadby, Frederic, and Moses Doukhan. *The Land Law of Palestine*. Tel Aviv: Shoshany, 1935.

Golani, Motti. "Dayan Movil LeMilhama" ("Dayan Leads to War"). *Iyunim BiTkumat Israel* 4 (1994): 117–35 [Hebrew].

———. *Israel in Search of a War: The Sinai Campaign, 1955–1956*. Brighton: Sussex Academic Press, 1998.

Golani, Motti, and Adel Manna. *Two Sides of the Coin: Independence and Nakba 1948*. Dordrecht: Republic of Letters, 2011.

Gvati, Haim. *Mea Shnot Hityashvut* (A Hundred Years of Settlement). Vol. 2. Tel Aviv: Hakibbutz Hameuhad, 1981 [Hebrew].

Havakook, Ya'acov. *Akavot Bahol: Gashashim Bedu'im BeSherut Tsahal* (Footprints in the Sand—the Bedouin Trackers of the Israel Defense Forces). Tel Aviv: Ministry of Defense, 1998 [Hebrew].

Hemsley, Elizabeth. "Consent, Democracy and the Future of Liberalism." *Review of Austrian Economics* 33 (2020): 253–70.

Henkin, Yagil. *The 1956 Suez War and the New World Order in the Middle East: Exodus in Reverse*, Lanham: Lexington Books, 2015.

History Branch of General Headquarters. *Toldot Milhemet Ha'Atsma'ut* (History of the War of Independence). Tel Aviv: Ma'arakhot, 1959 [Hebrew].

Hitman, Gadi, and Libby Moskowitz. "HaYelhu Shnayim Yahdav Bilty Im Noadu: Mifleget Herut VeMapam VeEmdatan BeYahas LeMimshal HaTseva'i" ("Will Two Walk Together Unless They Are Agreed? The Herut and Mapam Parties and Their Position in Relation to the Military Government"). *Hosen Leumi, Politika VeHevra* 1, no. 1 (2019): 35–58 [Hebrew].

Hofnung, Menachem. *Democracy, Law and National Security in Israel*. Aldershot: Dartmouth, 1996.

Holdsworth, Derek. "Historical Geography: New Ways of Imagining and Seeing the Past." *Process in Human Geography* 27, no. 4 (2003): 486–93.

Huss, Efrat. "Tziyurim KeTriger LeNeratiev Shel Metzuka Hevratit BeKerev Nashim Bedu'iyot Mudarot" ("Paintings as a Trigger for a Narrative of Social Distress among Excluded Bedouin Women"). In *Litzor Mehkar, Lahkor Yetzira* (Create Research, Explore Creation), edited by Efrat Huss, Lea Kasan, and Einav Segev, 203–20. Be'er Sheva: Ben-Gurion University of the Negev, 2012 [Hebrew].

Hutchison, Elmo, H. *Violent Truce: A Military Observer Looks at the Arab-Israeli Conflict 1951–1955*. New York: Devin-Adair, 1955.

Ibn Khaldun, 'Abd al-Rahman. *The Muqaddimah: An Introduction to History*. Vol. I. Translated by Franz Rosenthal. Princeton, NJ: Princeton University Press, 1958.

Jacobson, Michael. "Sivuv BeTel Sheva: HaIr HaRiShona SheHekima Israel LaBedu'im" ("A Tour of Tel Sheva—the First City That Israel Established for the Bedouins"). Halon Ahory (Back Window). Accessed July 15, 2023. https://michaelarch.wordpress.com/2014/06/12/%d7%a1%d7%99%d7%91%d7%95%d7%91-%d7%91%d7%aa%d7%9c-%d7%a9%d7%91%d7%a2-%d7%94%d7%a2%d7%99%d7%a8-%d7%94%d7%a8%d7%90%d7%a9%d7%95%d7%a0%d7%94-%d7%a9%d7%94%d7%a7%d7%99%d7%9e%d7%94-%d7%99%d7%a9%d7%a8%d7%90/.

Jiryis, Sabri. *The Arabs in Israel*. New York: Monthly Review, 1976.

Kachensky, Miriam. "Ma'barot" ("Immigrant Transit Camps"). In *Olim VeMa'barot: 1948–1952* (Immigrants and Immigrant Transit Camps: 1948–1952), edited by Mordechai Naor, 69–86. Jerusalem: Yad Ben-Zvi, 1986 [Hebrew].

Kadish, Alon. *Milhemet Ha'atsma'ut Tashah–Tashat: Diyun Mehudash* (The War of Independence, 1948–1949: A Re-examination). Tel Aviv: Ministry of Defense, 2004 [Hebrew].

Kafkafi, Eyal. *Milhemet Breira: HaDereh LeSinai VeHazara: 1956–1957* (War of Choice: The Road to Sinai and Back). Tel Aviv: Yad-Tabenkin, 1994 [Hebrew].

Kark, Ruth. *Toldot HaHityashvut HaHalutsit HaYehudit BaNegev: 1880–1948* (The History of the Pioneering Jewish Settlement in the Negev: 1880–1948). Lahav: Joe Alon Center, 1974 [Hebrew].

Karsh, Ephraim. *Fibruk HaHisṭoryah HaYiśre'elit: "HaHistoriyonim HahHadashim"* (Fabricating Israeli History of Israel: "The New Historians"). Tel Aviv: Hakibbutz Hameuhad, 1999 [Hebrew].

Kazzaz, Nissim. *Seyfa VeSafra: Zihronotav Shel Na'ar Yehudi* (End and a Story—Memories of a Jewish Boy). Jerusalem: Reuven Mas, 2010 [Hebrew].

Kedar, Alexander, Ahmad Amara, and Oren Yiftachel. *Emptied Lands: A Legal Geography of Bedouin Rights in the Negev*. Stanford, CA: Stanford University Press, 2018.

Keren, Zvi. *Naṿeh BaMidbar: Sipuro Shel Ish Ḥatzerim* (Oasis: The Story of a Man from Hatzerim). Hatzerim: Hatzerim Publishing, 1974 [Hebrew].

Khazanov, Anatoly. *Nomads and the Outside World*. Madison: University of Wisconsin Press, 1994.

Khazanov, Anatoly. "Nomads in the History of the Sedentary World." In *Nomads in the Sedentary World*, edited by Anatoly Khazanov and Andre Wink, 1–23. London: Routledge, 2001.

Khoury, Philip S., and Joseph Kostiner. *Tribes and State Formation in the Middle East*. Berkeley: University of California Press, 1990.

Kouzli, Sa'id. "Medinat Israel VeHaBedu'im BaNegev (1948–1963): Mediniyut VeMetziut BeSugiyat HaKaraka, HaHityashvut VeHaGiyus HaTseva'i" ("Israel and the Bedouin: Policy Regarding Land, Settlement and Army Recruitment"). PhD diss., University of Haifa, 2014 [Hebrew].

———. "Mediniyut HaMimsad HaIsraeli Klapey HaBedu'im: 1948–1963" ("The Israeli Establishment Policy Toward the Bedouin 1948–1963"). MA thesis, University of Haifa, 2007 [Hebrew].

Krakover, Shaul. "Demographic Examination of the Bedouin Settlement Program and Its Linkage to Their Claims on Lands." *Studies in the Geography of Israel* 16 (2002): 220–46 [Hebrew].
Kressel, Gideon M. *Pratiy'ut LeUmat Shivtiyut: Dinamika Shel Kehilat Bedu'im BeTahalikh Hitayrut* (Privacy vs. Tribalism: Dynamics of the Bedouin Community during the Urbanization Process). Tel Aviv: Hakibbutz Hameuhad, 1977 [Hebrew].
Kressel, Gideon M., and Reuven Aharoni. *Egyptian Émigrés in the Levant of the 19th and 20th Centuries*. Jerusalem: Jerusalem Center for Public Affairs, 2013.
Kressel, Gideon M., Joseph Ben-David, and Khalil Abu-Rabi'a. "Changes in Land Usage by the Negev Bedouin since the Mid-19th Century." *Nomadic Peoples* 28 (1991): 28–55.
Kurpershoek, Marcel P. *Oral Poetry and Narratives from Central Arabia*. Leiden, NY: Koln, 1994.
Levin, Noam, Ruth Kark, and Emir Galilee. "Maps and the Settlement of Southern Palestine, 1799–1948: An Historical/GIS Analysis." *Journal of Historical Geography* 36, no. 1 (2010): 1–18.
Lewando-Gundt, Gillian. "Tel-Sheva: Kfar Bedu'i Metukhnan" ("Tel Sheva: A Planned Bedouin Village"). In *Eretz HaNegev: Adam VeMidbar* (The Negev: Man and Desert), edited by Avshalom Shmueli and Yehuda Gradus, 666–72. Tel Aviv: Ministry of Defense, 1979 [Hebrew].
Locke, John. *Two Treatises of Government*. A New Edition, Corrected. Vol. V. London: Printed for Thomas Tegg, 1823. Prepared by Rod Hay for the McMaster University Archive of the History of Economic Thought, 1690. https://www.yorku.ca/comninel/courses/3025pdf/Locke.pdf.
Lustick, Ian S. *Arabs in the Jewish State: Israel's Control of a National Minority*. Austin: University of Texas Press, 1980.
Luz, Nimrod. "Yetsirata Shel Be'er Sheva HaModernit: Proyekt Imperiali Ottomani" ("The Creation of Modern Beersheba: An Imperial Ottoman Project"). In *Be'er Sheva: Metropolin BeHithavut* (Be'er Sheva—a Metropolis in the Making), edited by Yehuda Gardus and Esther Meir-Glitzenstein, 177–94. Be'er Sheva: Be'er Sheva University and Be'er Sheva Center for Regional Development, 2008 [Hebrew].
Maine, Henry. *Ancient Law: Its Connections with the Early History of Society, and its Relation to Modern Ideas*. London: John Nurry, 1861.
Marx, Emanuel, and Avinoam Meir. "Land, Town Planning: The Negev Bedouin and the State of Israel." *Geography Research Forum* 25 (2005): 43–61.
Marx, Emanuel. *Bedouin of the Negev*. Manchester: Manchester University Press, 1967.
———. "Bedu'ey HaNegev" ("Bedouins of the Negev"). *Hamizrah Hahdash* 7, no. 2 (1956): 89–98 [Hebrew].
———. "HaBedu'im BeShnot HaShishim" ("The Negev Bedouin in the 1960s"). In *Eretz HaNegev: Adam VeMidbar* (The Land of the Negev: Man and Desert), edited by Avshalom Shmueli and Yehuda Gradus, 631–51. Tel Aviv: Ministry of Defense, 1979 [Hebrew].
———. *HaHevrah HaBedu'it BaNegev* (Bedouin Society of the Negev). Tel Aviv: Reshafim, 1974 [Hebrew].
———. "HaMivne HaHevrati Shel Bedu'ey HaNegev" ("The Social Structure of the Negev Bedouins"). *Hamizrah Hahdash* 8, no. 1 (1957): 393–409 [Hebrew].
———. "The Political Economy of Middle Eastern and North African Pastoral Nomads." In *Nomadic Societies in the Middle East and North Africa: Entering the 21st Century*, edited by Dawn Chatty, 78–97. Leiden: Brill, 2006.
———. "The Tribe as a Unit of Subsistence: Nomadic Pastoralism in the Middle East." *American Anthropologist* 79 (1977): 343–63.Meir, Avinoam. *As Nomadism Ends: The Israeli Bedouin of the Negev*. Boulder, CO: Westview, 1997.

———. "Demographic Transition among the Negev Bedouin in Israel and Its Planning Implications." *Socio-Economic Planning Sciences* 18, no. 6 (1984): 399–409.

———. *HaMetah Beyn Bedu'ey HaNegev LaMedina: Mediniyut VeMetsiut* (The Tension between the Negev Bedouin and the State: Policy and Reality). Jerusalem: Floersheimer Institute, 1999 [Hebrew].

———. "Contemporary State Discourse and Historical Pastoral Spatiality: Contradictions in the Land Conflict between the Israeli Bedouin and the State." *Ethnic and Racial Studies* 32, no. 5 (2009): 823–843.

Meitiv, Benny. *HaZor'im BaMidbar* (The Sowers in the Desert). Merhavya: Hapoalim and Hakibbutz Haartzi, 1972 [Hebrew].

———. *Sippuro Shel Gevul* (Story of a Frontier). Tel Aviv: Ministry of Defense, 1986 [Hebrew].

Mill, John Stuart. *Considerations on Representative Government*. London: Parker, Son, and Bourn, West Strand, 1861.

Milstein, Uri. *Milḥemet Ha'Atsma'ut: HaHodesh HaRishon* (The War of Independence: The First Month). Tel Aviv: Zmora Bitan, 1989 [Hebrew].

Mintzker, Uri. "HaJanabib BaHar HaGavoa BaNegev: Shevet, Teritoria VeKvutsa Mukeret" ("The Janabib in the Negev Highland: Tribe, Territory and Recognized Group"). PhD diss., Ben-Gurion University of the Negev, 2013 [Hebrew].

Morris, Benny. *The Birth of the Palestinian Refugee Problem, 1947–1949*. Cambridge: Cambridge University Press, 1987.

———. *Israel's Border Wars, 1949–1956: Arab Infiltration, Israeli Retaliation, and the Countdown to the Suez War*. Oxford: Clarendon, 1993.

———. *1948: A History of the First Arab-Israeli War*. New Haven, CT: Yale University Press, 2008.

———. *1948 and After: Israel and the Palestinians*. Oxford: Clarendon, 2003.

Muhsam, Helmut V. *Beduin of the Negev: Eight Demographic Studies*. Jerusalem: Jerusalem Academic Press, 1966.

Musil, Alois. *Arabia Petrea Edom*. Vol. 2. Vienna: Holder, 1907. Reprint, Hildesheim, NY: G. Olms, 1989 [German].

———. *The Manners and Customs of the Rwala Bedouins*. New York: American Geographical Society, 1928.

Nasasra, Mansour. "Two Decades of Bedouin Resistance and Survival under Israeli Military Rule, 1948–1967." *Middle Eastern Studies* 56, no. 1 (2020): 64–83.

Noah, Haya. *HaKfarim SheHayu VeEinam: HaKfarim HaLo Mukarim BaNegev* (The Villages That Existed and Do Not Exist: The Unrecognized Bedouin Villages in the Negev). Haifa: Pardes, 2009 [Hebrew].

Ofer, Zeev, and Tehila Ofer. *HaGedud HaRishon* (The First Battalion). Self-Published: Tel Aviv, 2008 [Hebrew].

Oren, Elhanan. "Be'er Sheva BeMa'arakhot HaNegev, 1939–1949" ("Be'er-Sheva in the Battles of the Negev, 1939–1949"). In *Sefer Be'er Sheva* (The Book of Be'er Sheva), edited by Yehuda Gradus and Yair Stern, 119–61. Jerusalem: Keter, 1979 [Hebrew].

———. "MeHatsa'at HaTransfer, 1937–1938, El 'Transfer BeDia'vad' 1947–1948" ("From the Transfer Proposal of 1937–1938, to the 'Transfer de Facto' of 1947–1948"). *Iyunim Bitkumat Israel* 7 (1997): 75–85 [Hebrew].

Oz, Shimon, Hagai Katz, and Relli Shechter. "Between two Hegemonies: Fellahin, Bedouins and the State in the Negev during the Military Administration." In *Bedouin of the Negev: Tribalism, Politics and Criticism*, edited by Havatzelet Yahel and Emir Galilee, 105–31. Tel Aviv: Herzl Institute and the Chaikin Cahir for Geostrategy Haifa University, 2023.

Ozacky-Lazar, Sarah. "HaMimshal HaTseva'i KeManganon Shlita BaEzrahim Ha'Aravim" ("The Military Government as a Mechanism of Control over Arab Citizens"). *HaMizrah HaHadash* 43 (2002): 104–32 [Hebrew].

———. "Hitgabshut Yahasey HaGomlin Bayn Yehudim Le'Aravim BeMedinat Israel: Ha-'Asor HaRishon 1948–1958" ("The Formation of the Relationship between Jews and Arabs in the State of Israel: The First Decade 1948–1958"). PhD diss., Haifa University, 1996 [Hebrew].

———. "Security and Israel's Arab Minority." In *Security Concerns: Insights from the Israeli Experience*, edited by Daniel Bar-Tal, Dan Jacobson, and Aaron S. Klieman, 347–69. Stanford: JAI, 1998.

Parizot, Cedric. "Counting Votes That Do Not Count: Negev Bedouin and the Knesset Elections of May 17th, 1999, Rahat, Israel." In *Nomadic Societies in the Middle East and North Africa: Entering the 21st Century*, edited by Dawn Chatty, 176–203. Leiden: Brill, 2006.

Peled, Kobi. "Palestinian Oral History as a Source for Understanding the Past: Insights and Lessons from an Oral History Project among Palestinians in Israel." *Middle Eastern Studies* 50, no. 3 (2014): 412–25.

———. *Words Like Daggers: The Political Poetry of the Negev Bedouin*. Leiden: Brill, 2022.

Peterson, John E. "Tribe and State in the Arabian Peninsula." *Middle East Journal* 74, no. 4 (2020): 501–20.

Popper, Karl R. *The Open Society and Its Enemies: The Spell of Plato*. Vol. 1. London: George Routledge, 1945.

Porat, Hanina. *HaBedu'im BaNegev Beyn Navadut Le'Iyur 1948–1973* (The Bedouin in the Negev: Between Nomadism and Urbanization 1948–1973). Be'er Sheva: Ben-Gurion University, 2009 [Hebrew].

———. *HaMukhtarin HaIvriyim BaNegev: Sipuram Shel MuKhtarey HaYishuvim HaIvrim VeKshareihem Im HaShilton HaBriti VeHaShkhenim HaBedu'im, 1908–1948* (The Jewish Mukhtars in the Negev: The Story of the Mukhtar of the Jewish Settlements and their Relations with the British Government and the Bedouin Neighbors 1908–1948). Mikve Israel: Yehuda Dekel Library and Council for the Preservation of Heritage Sites in Israel, 2015 [Hebrew].

———. "Mediniyut Hapituah VeShe'elat HaBedu'im BaNegev BiShenoteha HaRishonot Shel HaMedinah, 1948–1953" ("Settlement and Development Policy and the Negev Bedouins in the First Years of the State"). *Iyunim Bitkumat Israel* 7 (1998): 386–438 [Hebrew].

———. "Trumat HaTfisa HaGeografit-Yeshuvit Shel Ben-Gurion LaHityashvut BaNegev VeLePituho BeShnot HaMedina HaRishonot Sheleahar HaMilhama" ("The Contribution of Ben-Gurion's Local-Geographical Concept to the Settlement and Development of the Negev in the First Post-War Years of the State"). *Iyunim Bitkumat Israel* 3 (1993): 114–43 [Hebrew].

Rabi, Uzi. *Tribes and States in a Changing Middle East*. New York: Oxford University Press, 2016.

Reches, Eli. "Yesodot HaMediniyut Klapey HaHukhlusiya HaArvit BeIsrael" ("Fundamentals of Policy toward the Arab Population in Israel"). In *HaMa'avar MeYishuv Lemedina—Retzifut VeTmurot: 1947–1949* (The Transition from Locality to State—Continuation and Transformation: 1947–1949), edited by Varda Pilowsky. Lectures given at a conference at the University of Haifa on June 5–8, 1988. Haifa: University of Haifa, 1990 [Hebrew].

Rickenbacher, Daniel. "Arab States, Arab Interest Groups and Anti-Zionist Movements in Western Europe and the US." PhD diss., University of Zurich, 2017.

Riftin, Ya'akov. *BaMishmeret* (On Guard). Tel Aviv: Sifriyat Poalim and Kibbutz Ein-Shemer, 1978 [Hebrew].

Robinson, Shira. *Citizen Strangers: Palestinians and the Birth of Israel's Liberal Settler State*. Stanford, CA: Stanford University Press, 2013.

Rubin, Rehav. "Geografia Historit BeIsrael: Kivuney Mehkar VeMegamot Metodologiyot" ("Historical Geography in Israel: Research Directions and Methodological Trends"). *Cathedra* 100 (2001): 339–60 [Hebrew].

Rubinstein, Amnon, and Barak Medina. *HaMishpat HaHukati Shel Medinat Israel* (The Constitutional Law of the State of Israel). Tel Aviv: Shoken, 2005 [Hebrew].

Rudnizky, Arik, and Thabeth Abu Ras. *The Bedouin Population in the Negev*. Neve Ilan: Abraham Fund Initiative, 2012.

Salomon, Yaakov. *BeDarki Sheli* (In My Way). Jerusalem: Idanim, 1980 [Hebrew].

Salzman, Philip C. *Culture and Conflict in the Middle East*. Amherst, NY: Humanity Books, 2008.

———. *Pastoralists: Equality, Hierarchy, and the State*. Boulder, CO: Westview Press, 2004.

———. *When Nomads Settle: The Process of Sedentarization as Adaption and Response*. New York: Praeger, 1980.

Sandberg, Haim. *Hesder Zkhuyot BeMekarke'in BeEretz Israel VeBimedinat Israel* (Land Title Settlement in Eretz-Israel and the State of Israel). Jerusalem: Land Use Research Institute KKL and Sachar Institute, 2000. [Hebrew].

———. *Land Law and Policy in Israel: A Prism of Identity*. Bloomington: Indiana University Press, 2022.

Sarig, Nahum. "Hativat HaPalmah BaNegev" ("Palmah Brigade in the Negev"). In *Hativat HaNegev BaMa'rakha* (The Negev Brigade in the Battle). Tel Aviv: Ma'arakhot, 1949 [Hebrew].

Shadar, Hadas. *Arad: Ir Nisyonit (Arad: an experimental town)*. Tel Aviv: Yehuda Dekel publication—The Council for Conservation of Heritage Sites in Israel, 2022 [Hebrew].

Shamir, Ronen. "Suspended in Space: Bedouins under the Law of Israel." *Law and Society Review* 30, no. 2 (1996): 231–57.

Shamir, Shimon. "The Collapse of Project Alpha." In *Suez 1956: The Crises and Consequences*, edited by William Roger Louis and Roger Owen, 73–100. Oxford: Oxford University Press, 1989.

Sharon, Moshe. "HaBedu'im BeEretz Israel BeMeot HaShmone Esre VeHaTsha Esre" ("The Bedouin in Palestine during the Eighteenth and Nineteenth Centuries"). MA thesis, Hebrew University of Jerusalem, 1964 [Hebrew].

Shemesh, Moshe. "Mashber HaManhigut HaPalestinit" ("The Palestinian Leadership Crisis"). *Iyunim Bitkumat Israel* 14 (2004): 285–335 [Hebrew].

Shimoni, Yaacov. *Araviye Eretz Israel* (Arabs in the Land of Israel). Tel Aviv: Am-Oved, 1947 [Hebrew].

Shmueli, Avshalom. "The Bedouin of the Land of Israel—Settlement and Changes." *Urban Ecology* 4 (1980): 253–86.

———. *Ketz HaNavadut: Hevrat Bedu'im BeTahalikhey Hityashvut* (The End of Nomadism—Bedouin Society during the Settlement Process). Tel Aviv: Dvir, 1980 [Hebrew].

Shmueli, Avshalom, and Yehuda Gardus, eds. *Eretz HaNegev: Adam VeMidbar* (The Land of the Negev: Man and Desert). Tel Aviv: Ministry of Defense, 1979 [Hebrew].

Shmueli, Deborah, and Rassem Khamaisi. *Israel's Invisible Negev Bedouin: Issues of Land and Spatial Planning*. Cham: Springer, 2015.

Shoked, Noam. "Housing Others: Design and Identity in a Bedouin Village." *International Journal of Islamic Architecture* 8, no. 2 (2019): 307–35.

Sicron, Meshoulam. "HaEzor HaMeforaz BeSvivat Nitzana Bashanim 1949–1956" ("The Demilitarized Zone in the Vicinity of Nitzana"). MA thesis, Ben-Gurion University of the Negev, 2002 [Hebrew].
Sinanoglou, Penny. *Partitioning Palestine: British Policymaking at the End of Empire*. Chicago: University of Chicago Press, 2019.
Stendel, Uri. *Arviye Israel Beyn HaPatish LaSadan* (The Arabs in Israel between the Hammer and the Anvil). Jerusalem: Akademon, 1992 [Hebrew].
Stewart, Frank H. "Boundaries in Central Sinai and the Southern Negev: A Document from the Ahaywat Tribe." *Mediterranean Language and Culture Monographs* 2 (1986): 11–62.
———. "Customary Law among the Bedouin of the Middle East and North Africa." In *Nomadic Societies in the Middle East and North Africa: Entering the 21st Century*, edited by Dawn Chatty, 239–79. Leiden: Brill, 2006.
———. "Notes on the Arrival of the Bedouin Tribes in Sinai." *Journal of Economic and Social History of the Orient* 34 (1991): 97–110.
———. "The Structure of Bedouin Society in the Negev: Emanuel Marx's *Bedouin of the Negev* Revisited." In *Serendipity in Anthropological Research: The Nomadic Turn*, edited by Haim Hazan and Ester Herzog, 257–89. Farnham: Ashgate, 2012.
———. "What Is Honor." *Acta Historiae* 8 (2000): 13–28.
Sussar, Asher, and Atlas Duygo. *The Emergence of the Modern Middle East*. Tel Aviv: Moshe Dayan Center for Middle Eastern and African Studies, 2017.
Suwaed, Muhammad Y. "HaBedu'im BeEretz Israel Beyn Hashanim 1804–1904" ("The Bedouin in the land of Israel between 1804–1904"). MA thesis, Bar-Ilan University, 1992 [Hebrew].
———. "HaBedu'im BeMilḥemet Ha'Atsma'ut: Ben Tsiyonut LePalesṭiniut" ("The Bedouin in the War of Independence: Between Zionism and Palistinization"). *Aley Zayit VeHerev* 16 (2016): 244–80 [Hebrew].
———. *Historical Dictionary of the Bedouins*. Lanham, MD: Rowman & Littlefield, 2015.
———. "Yahasey Bedu'im-Yehudim BeEretz Israel HaMandaṭorit: 1918–1948" ("Bedouin-Jewish Relations in Mandatory Palestine"). PhD diss., Bar-Ilan University, 1998 [Hebrew].
Talmon, Micah. "HaHityashvut HaHakla'it BaNegev: 1949–1959" ("The Agriculture Settlement in the Negev"). *Idan* 6 (1985): 146–56 [Hebrew].
Teveth, Shabtai. *Moshe Dayan: The Soldier, the Man, the Legend*. Boston: Houghton Mifflin, 1973.
Troen, Ilan S., and Moshe Shemesh. *The Suez-Sinai Crisis: A Retrospective and Reappraisal*. New York: Columbia University Press, 1990.
Tubi, Amit, and Eran Feitelson. "Changing Drought Vulnerabilities of Marginalized Resource-Dependent Groups: A Long-Term Perspective of Israel's Negev Bedouin." *Regional Environmental Change* 19, no. 2 (2019): 477–87.
———. "Drought and Cooperation in a Conflict Prone Area: Bedouin Herders and Jewish Farmers in Israel's Northern Negev, 1957–1963." *Political Geography* 51 (2016): 30–42.
Tzfadia, Erez, and Batya Roded. *Mabat Hashva'ati Al Hitpathut HaHakara BeZkhuyot Karka Shel Amim Yelidim: HaMikre Shel Bedu'im BaNegev* (A Comparative Perspective on the Development of the Recognition of Land Rights of Indigenous Peoples: A Case of the Bedouin in the Negev). Be'er Sheva: Center for the Study of Bedouin Society and Its Development, 2011 [Hebrew].
Tzur, Yosi. "HaKooperativ HaBedu'i HaRishon BeTsfon HaNegev" ("The First Bedouin Cooperative in the Northern Negev"). Research report. Shoval, 2006 [Hebrew].

Ueno, Masayuki. "In Pursuit of Laicized Urban Administration: The Muhtar System in Istanbul and Ottoman Attitudes toward Non-Muslim Religious Authorities in the Nineteenth Century." *International Journal of Middle East Studies* 54, no. 2 (2022): 302–18.

Vilnay, Zeev. "Arad." *Ariel Encyclopedia* 7. Tel Aviv: Am-Oved, 1979 [Hebrew].

Wallach, Jehuda. *Atlas Karta LeToldot Eretz Israel MeReshit HaHityashvut Ve Ad Kum HaMedina* (The Carta Atlas of Eretz Israel from Early Settlement to Statehood). Jerusalem: Carta, 1974 [Hebrew].

Wallach, Jehuda, and Moshe Lissak. *Aṭlas Karṭa LeToldot Medinat Israel: Shanim Rishonot: 1948–1960* (The Carta Atlas of the State of Israel in the Early Years). Jerusalem: Carta, 1978 [Hebrew].

Weber, Max. *Politics as Vocation*. Philadelphia: Fortress, 1965.

Weiner, Mark. *The Rule of the Clan: What an Ancient Form of Social Organization Reveals about the Future of Individual Freedom*. New York: Farrar, Straus and Giroux, 2013.

Weitz, Yosef. *Yomani VeIgrotay LaBanim* (My Diary and Letters to My Sons). Ramat-Gan: Masada, 1973 [Hebrew].

Winkler, Onn. *Meahorey HaMisparim—Politika Demographit BeIsrael* (Behind the Numbers—Political Demography in Israel). Haifa: University of Haifa Chaikin Chair in Geo-Strategy, 2015.

Yahel, Havatzelet. "The Conflict over Land Ownership and Unauthorized Construction in the Negev." *Contemporary Review of the Middle East* 6, nos. 3–4 (2019): 352–69.

———. "Hatsa'ot LeYishuv Bedui'ey HaNegev Bimey Trom VeReshit Medinat Israel: 1948–1949" ("Proposals for Bedouin Settlement in the Negev in the Pre- and Early Days of the State of Israel: 1948–1949"). *Israel* 25 (2018): 1–29 [Hebrew].

———. "Land Disputes between the Negev Bedouin and Israel." *Israel Studies* 11, no. 2 (2006): 1–22.

———. "'Lifnim MeShurat HaDin': HaMa'alakhim LeGibush Hatza'ot Pshara BeTvi'ot HaBa'alut Shel HaBedu'im BeShnot HaShiv'im" ("Beyond the Letter of the Law: Process to Formulate a Compromise in the Negev Bedouin Ownership Claims in the 1970s"). *Iyunim Bitkumat Israel* 38 (2017): 84–127 [Hebrew].

———. "Lo Huki Akh Mishtalem: Haktsa'at Migrashim BaNegev LeMishpahot Poligamiyot" ("Illegal but It Pays Off: The Allocation of Plots of Land in the Negev to Polygamous Families"). *Tikhnun* 14, no. 1 (2017): 204–11 [Hebrew].

———. "Mediniyut Hanhagat HaYishuv HaYehudi VeMedinat Israel BeNogea LaBedu'im, LeHityashvutam VeLaba'alut Al Karka'ot HaNegev BeMilhemet Ha'Atsma'ut: 1947–1949" ("Policy of the Leadership of the Jewish Yishuv and the State of Israel Regarding the Bedouin Settlement and Ownership of Negev Lands during the War of Independence: 1947–1949"). PhD diss., Hebrew University of Jerusalem, 2009 [Hebrew].

———. "Rural or Urban? Planning Bedouin Settlements." *Middle Eastern Studies* 57, no. 4 (2021): 606–24.

Yahel, Havatzelet, and Atef Abu-Ajaj. "Tribalism, Religion, and the State in Bedouin Society: Between Conservation and Change." *Strategic Assessment* 24, no. 2 (2021): 54–71.

Yahel, Havatzelet, and Ruth Kark. "Israel's Negev Bedouin during the 1948 War: Departure and Return." *Israel Affairs* 21, no. 1 (2015): 48–97.

———. "Land and Settlement of Israel's Negev Bedouin: Official (Ad-Hoc) Steering Committees, 1948–1980." *British Journal of Middle Eastern Studies* 45, no. 5 (2018): 716–41.

———. "Reasoning from History: Israel's 'Peace Law' and the Resettlement of Tel Malhata Bedouin." *Israel Studies* 21, no. 2 (2016): 102–32.

Yiftachel, Oren. "Ethnocracy: The Politics of Judaizing Israel/Palestine." *Constellations* 6, no. 3 (1999): 364–90.

Zarhi, Shaul, and Avraham Achiezra. *The Economic Conditions of the Arab Minority in Israel* (No. 1). Givat Haviva: Center for Arab and Afro-Asian Studies, 1966.

Zivan, Zeev. *Yaḥasey Yehudim VeBedu'im BiShnot Ha'Arba'im VeHaHamishim BaNegev* (Jewish-Bedouin Relations in the Forties and Fifties in the Negev). Be'er Sheva: Negev Regional Development Center, 2017 [Hebrew].

INDEX

NAMES

Abu 'Abdallah, Hasan, 171n127
Abu 'Abdun, Hasan 'Id, 171n125
Abu 'Abdun, Ibrahim, 168n60
Abu Blal, Salman a-Shteywi, 74
Abu Ghalyun, Gharem, 170n107
Abu Ghalyun, Salamah, 171n125
Abu Ghanem, 'Ali, 165n8
Abu Grenat, 'Ali Salman, 75, 180n8
Abu Jaber, Hasan, 34, 116n29
Abu Jwe'ed, Muhammad Mheisen, 180n8
Abu Madun, 'Ali, 166n29
Abu Midyan, Mustafa, 37
Abu Mu'ammar, 'Awdah Mansur, 38, 39, 47, 88, 131, 139–143, 141, 146, 147, 168n68, 188n96, 193n83
Abu 'Omrah, Hlayyel 'Asi, 171n125
Abu Rabi'ah, Hammad Khalil, 180n8, 186n55–56
Abu Rabi'ah, Hasan, 180n8, 188n96
Abu Rabi'ah, 'Id, 168n60
Abu Rashid, Musa, 37
Abu Rgayyig, 'Abd, 170n107
Abu Rgayyig, 'Awwad, 29, 171n125, 180n8
Abu Rgayyig, Harb, 171n125
Abu Rgayyig, Hasan, 190n26
Abu Rgayyig, Ibrahim, 129, 190n24, 190n26
Abu Rgayyig, Nayif, 191n58
Abu Shade, Sami, 3
Abu Sittah, 'Abadallah, 36
Abu Sittah, Ibrahim, 37
Abu Taha, Ahmad, 192n64
Abu Taha, Hadi Hamid, 135, 136
Abu Taha, Ibrahim, 192n64
Abu Taha, Muhammad, 191n58, 192n64

Abu Taha, Razi, 192n64
Abu Yihya, Farhan, 170n107, 171n125
Allon, Yigal, 47–50, 60–61, 103–105, 135, 136, 137
Aloni, Reuven, 71–72, 81, 93–96, 101, 105, 109, 192n66
Amir, Pinhas, 38, 74, 82–83, 85, 90, 95–96, 99, 101–102, 104, 109–110, 175n11
Amit, Meir, 73
al-'Aref, 'Aref, 5, 13, 14, 17, 20, 37, 53, 163n64
al-A'sam, Salman Muhammad, 171n125
al-'Atawnah, Musa Hasan, 92, 96, 99, 102–103, 106, 109, 113, 142, 180n8
al-Atrash, Sliman, 3
Avigur, Shaul, 47
Avner, Elimelech, 47, 50–51

Bar-Lev, Omer, 3
Bar-Zvi, Sasson, 5, 75, 96, 101–102, 110, 113, 117–119, 175n6, 190n24
al-Baz, Farhan, 191n58
Begin, Benny, 153
Ben-Gurion, David, 29, 34–35, 41–43, 46–51, 54, 60, 65, 73, 84, 88, 93, 103, 108, 174n182, 188n89
Bentov, Mordechai, 96, 132, 134, 145
Berdichevsky, Ya'akov, 43–44, 50
Berger, Meir, 83, 97
Bernadotte, Folke, 40–41
al-Breiqi, Salam, 168n60
Bunche, Ralph, 50

Danin, Ezra, 47, 49, 60
Dayan, Moshe, 24, 67, 68, 81, 92–99, 101–103, 108, 111, 114

al-Efranji, Hasan, 166n29, 168n60
Efrat, Aryeh, 85, 91, 97
Eliav, Aryeh (Lova), 105, 185n27
Epstein (Elath), Eliahu, 5
Eshkol, Levi, 108, 111, 113–114, 118, 147

Falah, Ghazi, 6

Ginat, Joseph, 126–127, 128, 129, 132, 189n10, 190n31
Gluzman, Zvi, 132
Goldberg, Eliezer, 153

Hanegbi, Michael, 19, 43–45, 47, 50, 53–54, 55, 60–63, 65–66, 69, 76, 146, 175n6, 175n22, 176n45
Harel, Issar, 118, 188n89
Harsina, Aaron, 85, 97, 101, 104–105, 119, 121, 125
Hashemite family, 31
al-Husseini, Hajj Amin, 17, 31, 36
al-Huzayyil, Salman, 34–35, 37–39, 43, 51, 67, 68, 74, 111, 131, 147, 163, 168n67, 170n110, 171n125, 177n68

Ibn Bari, 'Abdul Qader, 135
Ibn Hdheirah, 'Id, 170n107
Ibn Sa'id, Salamah, 35, 37–38

Kazzaz, Nissim, 131, 191n42
Khamis, Yusef, 85, 93, 114
King Abdullah, 31, 34, 37
Kron, David, 43, 170n110
Kukia, Yosef, 85

Layish, Aharon, 99, 105, 115, 149
Levi, Shulamit, 125
Lif (Lifshitz), Zalman, 49, 60, 62–63, 172n152
Lubotkin, Binyamin, 85, 101, 105, 175n11
Lubrani, Uri, 101
Luz, Kadish, 85, 93, 180n4

Marx, Emanuel, 5–6, 16, 66–67, 75, 83, 97, 179n103, 179n3
Meir, Golda, 23
Molcho, Haim, 109
Mor, Uri, 126, 140, 189n10
Muhsam, Helmut, 14, 16
al-Musaddar, Freih, 166n29

a-Nasasrah, Hasan Salem, 188n84
a-Nasasrah, Sliman Mustafa, 117
Nashashibi clan, 31

Peled, Arieh, 132
Peres, Shimon, 96, 184n101
Pressman, Yosef, 101

Ratner, Yohanan, 73
Rosen, Pinhas, 88, 97

Sager al-Huzayyil, Salamah, 74
a-Sane', Ibrahim, 32, 35, 66, 168n60, 170n108, 171n125, 171n127, 176n45
a-Sane', Sliman 'Id, 171n125, 180n13
Sarig, Nahum, 47
Shacham, Mishael, 84, 86
Sharon, Ariel, 74, 153
Shatner, Mordechai, 71–72, 177n73
Shayek, Elyahu, 82, 97, 140
Shiloah, Reuven, 47
Shimoni, Ya'akov, 5, 46–48, 53
Sokolovsky, Yitzhak, 43
a-Sufi, Shawkat, 32
a-Surani, Musa, 37
Svardalov, Shalom, 71, 82, 97

Tartakover, Ya'akov, 84, 86–88, 97
Toledano, Shmuel, 126–127, 137, 139, 141–142, 189n11
Toubi, Tawfik, 115
Truman, Harry, 37

al-'Ugbi, Ibrahim, 168n60
al-'Ugbi, Sliman Muhammad, 169n79, 176n53

Vardimon, Yitzhak, 102–103, 105
Verbin, Joshua, 71–74, 175n6

Weitz, Yosef, 34, 45, 47–50, 53, 60–61, 63, 65, 76, 84, 101–102, 104–105, 108, 114–115, 165n9
Wigard, Gideon, 116

Yadin, Yigael, 47, 49–50, 67, 68
Yarkoni, Amos, 139–140, 193

a-Zabargah, Muhammad Salman, 117
Zuckerman, Asa'el, 60
Zuckerman, Yoav, 71–72, 109

Subjects

Ahdut Haavodah–Poalei Zion (political party), 103
Al Hamishmar (newspaper), 102, 116
Arab Higher Committee, 20, 31–32, 37
Arab Legion, 165n9
Arab Spring, 7

Bedouin
  Afro-Bedouin, 12, 150
  Bedouin-Jewish relationship, 6, 17, 29, 72, 81, 97, 179n3; Fellahin-Bedouin, 11–12, 14, 23, 31, 40, 43, 61–62, 71, 75–77, 117, 129, 134, 146, 148, 150, 165n8
  Immigration from Israel, 66
  Kazzaz's army, 131
  Pastoral nomads, 9–10, 61
  Population, 3, 9–10, 14, 16, 45, 65, 93, 97, 102, 104, 107, 116, 120, 148, 150
  Sheikh's role, 12–13, 67, 91, 97, 125, 131, 152
  Tribal affiliation, 4, 9, 11, 66, 92, 116, 125, 129, 141, 148, 184n100, 188n83
  Tribal courts, 14, 24, 63, 69–70, 76, 145, 177n62
  Tribes and confederations
    Abu 'Abdun, 103
    Abu 'Abed, 117
    Abu 'Ammar, 117
    Abu Blal, 74, 101, 106
    Abu Grenat, 106
    Abu Gweder, 117
    Abu Jwe'ed, 106
    Abu 'Omrah, 102
    Abu Rabi'ah, 102, 106, 117, 129, 170n107
    Abu Rgayyig, 50, 63, 102–103, 106, 129, 136–137, 141, 192n69
    Abu Sitta, 31
    Abu Srihan, 103, 106
    Abu Sukut, 40
    al-Afinish, 103, 106
    Ahaywat, 15, 16
    'Alamat, 39
    al-Asad, 50, 106
    al-A'sam, 50, 103, 106
    al-'Atawnah, 86, 96
    'Azazmah, 14, 15, 16, 34–35, 37–39, 47, 50–51, 53, 60, 63, 65, 70, 88, 103, 106, 140, 142, 190n17
    Dhullam, 44, 47, 50, 63, 67, 101, 175n22
    al-Gawa'in, 103, 106, 184n100
    Hanajrah, 15, 16, 31, 35, 37, 39
    al-Hawashlah, 137, 192n69–70
    Jarawin, 44, 170n107
    Jubarat, 15, 16, 35, 37, 39, 41, 47, 168n55, 168n74
    Sager al-Huzayyil, 184n100
    Saidiyin, 15
    a-Sane', 101–103, 106, 184n3
    Sarahin, 178n94
    a-Sufi, 35
    Tarabin, 14, 15, 16, 31–32, 34–37, 39–40, 47, 50–51, 53, 60, 63, 65, 70, 103, 106, 136
    Tiyaha, 14, 15, 16, 31–32, 35, 39, 43–45, 47, 50–51, 60, 67, 175n22, 176n31
    al-'Ugbi, 39–40, 67, 106
British Mandate, 5, 14, 16–18, 32, 39, 42, 62, 67, 69, 163n54, 177n55, 189n7

Central Committee for Security Issues, 84–85, 119, 126–127, 190n31
Circassians, 49
Climate change, *see*: Drought
Colonialism, 6–7
Committee Appended to the Military Government, 50–51
Committee for Bedouin Affairs, 49–51
Committee for Refugee Affairs, 55, 60
Custodian of Absentee Property, 62, 71

Davar (newspaper), 70, 177n67
Dayan Plan (1960), 92–96, 98, 101
Democracy, 4, 9–10, 20–22, 55, 70, 73, 76–77, 82, 137, 140, 143–145, 147–150, 154, 164n94
Development Authority, 59–60, 71, 74, 82, 84–85, 184n6
Drought, 24, 67, 77, 81, 88–91, 93–94, 97–99, 108–110, 113, 118, 120, 127, 142, 148, 177n68, 180n3, 182n58, 182n60; Compensation policy, 90, 97–98, 108–109, 186n53
Druze, 49

Fedayeen, 56, 59–60, 74, 82

Gaza National Committee, 36
Great Arab Revolt (1936-1939), 17, 172n153

Haaretz (newspaper), 111
Hagana, 5, 19, 31, 36, 73, 93, 172n153
Harsina Proposal, 85, 101, 104–105, 181n29
High Bedouin Committee, 132, 139–140
Histadrut, 81, 85, 91, 97, 179n2

Index 213

Holocaust, 56
Human rights, 21, 55, 77, 109, 141, 148–150
Industrial Revolution (1760–1840), 20
Infiltration, *see also: Fedayeen*, 56, 59, 73, 75
Interministerial Committee, 104–105, 108, 111, 114–115, 119
Interministerial Directors General Committee, 114
Islam, 10, 18, 105, 144, 149, 163n47
Israel Defense Force (IDF), 14, 40–41, 42, 42, 44, 49–51, 57, 60, 73, 85, 93, 95–96, 101–102, 104, 110, 118, 130–131
   Bedouin Tracker Unit, 146
   Division for Settlement and Territorial Defense, 84–85, *100*
   Intelligence Division, 40, 51, 71
   Southern Command, 57, 60, 67, 93, 126, 189n12
   Unit, 101 74
Israel Land Administration, 101, 106, 114, 116, 118, 120, 184n6
Israeli Security Agency, 59, 189n3, 189n12
al-Ittihad (newspaper), 117

Jabhat al-Shabab (organization), 36
Jewish Agency, 5
Jewish-Arab conflict, 6–7, 9, 53, 55, 144, 149
Jewish Immigration, 11, 56, 60
Jewish National Fund (JNF), 17, 34, 63, 71, 86
Joint List party, 3

K*hams*, 11
Knesset, 65, 70–71, 73–74, 85, 93, 97, 109, 111, 115, 149, 177n68

Lamerhav (newspaper), 134
Land settlement, 3, 7, 16–17, 24, 43, 45, 49–51, 53, 60–63, 70–72, 74, 81–88, 94–99, 101–102, 106, 109, 113–115, 119–120, 131, 137, *138*, 139, 142–143, 146, 150–154, 178n81, 184n3, 188n100, 191n54, *see also*: Subcommittee for Land Settlement, Supreme Committee for Land Settlement
Lease Committee, 127

Mafdal (political party), 105
Maki (political party), 115, 117
Mapai (political party), 56, 70, 81, 88, 93, 96, 117, 179n2
Mapam (political party), 56, 65–66, 81, 85, 96, 102–103, 126, 132, 135, 145
Matruka lands, 16

Mewat lands, 16–17, 186fn35
Ministerial Committee Examines the Military Administration, *see*: Rosen Committee
Ministerial Committee for Economic Affairs, 95–96, 113–115, 120
Ministry of Agriculture, 59, 62, 71, 74, 81–82, 90–91, 92, 94, 96–98, 108–109, 111, 118
Ministry of Commerce and Industry, 182n54
Ministry of Defense, 49, 105, 114
Ministry of Finance, 96, 113
Ministry of Housing, 115, 132, 139–141
Ministry of Interior, 131
Ministry of Justice, 4, 69, 84–85, 104, 137
Ministry of Labor, 91, 95, 114
Ministry of Minorities, 45, 53, 175n15
Ministry of Social Affairs, 104
Miri lands, 61
Morrison Grady Plan (July 1946), 18
Mulk lands, 16
Muslim Brotherhood, 31, 40

Negev Committee, 34
Negev Military Administration, 19, 23, 43, 56–57, 60, 62–63, 64, 65–67, 69–77, 82–84, 91–92, 96–99, 101, 108, 110, 113, 116, 118–120, 127, 145–146, 175n6, 176n37, 188n89
Negev Regional Committee, 127, 129, 139–140
The New Negev Cooperative (Abu Siyam Cooperative), 92

O*lim*, *see*: Jewish Immigration
Ottoman regime (1517–1917), 12–14, 16–18, 62

Peace Treaty with Egypt (1979), 152
Polygamy, 11, 130, 162n18
Population Committee, *see also*: Urbanization, 131, 140–141

Ratner Committee, 73–74
Rosen Committee, 88, 179n2

al-Salam (cooperative), 92, 182n68
Sinai Campaign (1956), 73, 75, 81–82, 93, 146
Six-Day War (1967), 129–130, 142
State Comptroller, 125
Subcommittee for Land Settlement in the Negev, 86
Supreme Bedouin Committee, 115, 127
Supreme Committee for Land Settlement, 84, 88
Supreme Muslim Council, 37

Tribalism, 7–11, 22–24, 54, 66, 70, 76–77, 82, 91, 117, 120–121, 125, 129, 139, 144–150, 152, 154
Trusteeship Plan, 37

UN, 32, 44, 50, 66, 70, 101, 119, 184n3
  Partition Plan (1947), 29, 32, 33, 34, 36–37, 41, 47, 51, 59, 172n152, 173n159
  Peace Keeping Force, 129
  Security Council, 40, 44, 51
  Special Committee on Palestine (UNSCOP), 32, 34
Urbanization, *see also*: Tel Sheva, 5, 18, 24, 53, 99, 108, 111, 114, 116, 127, 129, 131–132, 134, 136, 136–137, 139–143, 148, 151–154, 183n95

W*aqf* lands, 16
War of Independence (1948), 23, 29, 36, 41, 42, 131, 145, 164, 192–193
  Operation Assaf, 50
  Operation Horev, 51
  Operation Lot, 44
  Operation Uvda, 53, 174n186
  Operation Yoav, 42, 44, 51, 170n99
  Plan D, 36–37

Y*edioth Ahronoth* (newspaper), 103
Yishuv, 23, 31, 34

Zionism, 5–6, 17, 19–20, 31, 162n18, 172n152, 193n1

Places

Alumim (Hazale), 35, 59–60, 164n84
Arad, 66, 99, 101–105, 111, 120, 126, 132, 184n1, 184n3, 187n56, 189n4
Arara BaNegev, 152, 173n161
Arava, 16, 131
Ashdod, 127

Bahrain, 8
Be'er Sheva, 3–5, 13, 14, 15, 16–18, 30, 32, 34–35, 37, 39, 41, 42, 43–47, 50–51, 53, 57, 60–61, 65, 70, 87–88, 89, 93–94, 96, 99, 101, 104, 106, 113–115, 129, 137, 147, 154
Be'eri, 40
Beit Eshel, 18, 41, 41, 59, 87
Beit Kama, 127, 174n184
Bnei Brak, 127
Bnei Shimon, 81, 83, 97

Dead Sea, 18, 44, 99
Dhahiriyya, 43, 47, 174n184
Dimona, 132, 137
Dorot, 35, 37, 43, 85, 169
Drijat, 53

Egypt, 13, 29, 37–45, 47–48, 50–51, 53–54, 59–60, 70, 73–74, 82, 85, 129–130, 152, 169n82, 178n94, 179n108

al-Fahr (Khirbat), 35
al-Fallujah, 34, 43

Galilee region, 6, 22, 29, 56, 61, 84, 93, 115, 139, 164n81, 179n3

Gaser a-Sirr, 137
Gaza, 16, *30*, 34, 36–37, 39, 51, 60, 65, 130
Gedera, 127
Gvulot, 18, 31

Haifa, 127, 164n81
Halutza, 39, 60, 164n84, 169n75
Hatzerim, 35, 37, 40, 44–45, 60
Hebron, 20, 32, 39, 51, 53, 65, 87–88, 96, 101
Herzliya, 127
Hulon, 127
Hurah, 53, 96, 102, 183n95

al-ʿImarah, 35–36, 40
Iraq, 8, 31, 99, 115

Jaffa, 95
Jawarish neighbourhood, 184n99
Jerusalem, 31–32, 36, 39, 127, 130, 164n81, 190n28
Jordan, 8, 13, 29, 31, 66, 70, 85, 101, 103, 109, 130, 165n9, 184n3

Kfar-Darom, 37, 39
Khuweilfah, 47, 60, 168n74
Kiryat Gat, 39
Kohlah, 168n74
Kseyfah, 106, 125, 129, 152

Lagiyyah, 53, 101, 106, 184n3
Lod, 93–94, *110*, 127, 183n85

Magen, 109
Mahazz (Khirbat Mahazz), 39, 41

Makhul, 53
Migdal Gad (Ashkelon, Majdal), 60, 175n19
Mishmar HaNegev, 35, 109
Mitzpe Ramon, 131
Mivtahim, 45, 164n84

Nahalal, 93
Nazareth, 6
Negba, 19, 43, 170n99
Ness Ziona, 93
Nevatim, 18, 34, 45, 51, 60, 87, 169n80
Nir Am, 19, 35
Nirim, 45
Nitzana, 15, 178n94

Oman, 8

Palmahim, 127
Patish, 109

Qatar, 8

Rahat, 106, 114, 130, 191
Ramat Negev, 59
Ramleh, 24, 93–96, 127, 183n85
Rehovot, 93, 127, 183n85
Revivim, 18, 38–39, 168n75
Rishon LeZion, 93, 127

Rosh Ha'Ayin, 127
Ruhama, 35, 43, 169n84
Saudi Arabia, 8, 13, 39
Sayig region, 70, 76, 82, 84, 89–91, 92, 95–96, 113, 120, 126–127, 130, 150
    B1 and B2 zones, 65–66, 85, 87, 89n101, 93, 101–102, 104, 184n3
Sdom, 18
Shari'ah (Wadi, Tel), 17, 32, 48, 170n110
Shoval, 19, 34–35, 60, 63, 66, 106, 114–115, 125, 130, 175n22
Sinai (Peninsula), 6, 13, 15, 51, 76, 93, 130, 152
Syria, 8, 37, 99, 115, 130

Tel Aviv, 4, 127
Tel HaShomer, 127
Tel Malhata (Tall al-Malih), 63, 101, 114–116, 152, 173n161
Tel Sheva, 106, 113–114, 125, 129, 131–132, 133, 134, 134, 135, 135, 136, 136, 139–142, 145, 192n66
Tze'elim, 35, 40, 60, 164n84

Umm Batin, 63, 69
United Arab Emirates, 8

Yad Mordechai, 39
Yemen, 8
Yeruham, 132

LAWS AND ORDINANCE

Basic Law: Israel Lands, 184n6
Bedouin Control (Application of Ordinance) Order (1942), 14, 163n58
Collective Punishment Ordinance (1926), 14
Israel Land Administration Law, 184n6
Land (Settlement of Title) Ordinance (1928), 16, 192n68
Land (Settlement of Title) Ordinance (New Version) (1969), 192n68
Land Acquisition Law (Validation of Acts and Compensation) (1953), 71–73, 87, 177n72, 178n82, 178n84
Land Ordinance (Acquisition for Public Purposes) (1943), 87
Mewat Land Ordinance (1921), 17, 163n70
Ottoman Land Law (1858), 16–17
Prevention of Crime (Tribal and Village Areas) Ordinance (1924–1925), 177n55

HAVATZELET YAHEL is Professor at the Ben-Gurion Research Institute for the Study of Israel and Zionism, Ben-Gurion University of the Negev. She is Head of the Israel Studies Program and holds the Michael Feige Career Development Chair in Israeli Society. Yahel is a member of the Israeli Bar and advises governmental entities and others in land policy and legal issues. She has published numerous academic articles on Bedouin issues, governance, land, and settlement policies, and she is author with Emir Galilee of *Bedouin of the Negev: Tribalism, Criticism and Politics*, which was recently published in Hebrew.

For Indiana University Press

Dan Crissman, *Acquisitions Editor and Editorial Director*
Anna Francis, *Assistant Acquisitions Editor*
Anna Garnai, *Editorial Assistant*
Brenna Hosman, *Production Coordinator*
Katie Huggins, *Production Manager*
Darja Malcolm-Clarke, *Project Manager/Editor*
Dan Pyle, *Online Publishing Manager*
Michael Regoli, *Director of Publishing Operations*
Leyla Salamova, *Artist and Book Designer*
Stephen Williams, *Rights Manager and Assistant Marketing Director*

www.ingramcontent.com/pod-product-compliance
Lightning Source LLC
Chambersburg PA
CBHW030649230426
43665CB00011B/1014